ACTIVATING
the
VISION

The Four Keys of Mathematics Leadership

Bill Barnes & Mona Toncheff
Foreword by Timothy D. Kanold

Solution Tree | Press

a division of
Solution Tree

NATIONAL COUNCIL OF
TEACHERS OF MATHEMATICS

555 North Morton Street
Bloomington, IN 47404
800.733.6786 (toll free) / 812.336.7700
FAX: 812.336.7790

email: info@SolutionTree.com
SolutionTree.com

Visit **go.SolutionTree.com/leadership** to download the free reproducibles in this book.

Printed in the United States of America

20 19 18 17 16   1 2 3 4 5

Library of Congress Cataloging-in-Publication Data

Names: Barnes, Bill (Mathematics teacher) | Toncheff, Mona.

Title: Activating the vision : the four keys of mathematics leadership / Bill

    Barnes and Mona Toncheff.

Description: Bloomington, IN : Solution Tree Press, [2016] | Includes

    bibliographical references and index.

Identifiers: LCCN 2016020850 | ISBN 9781942496946 (perfect bound)

Subjects: LCSH: Mathematics--Study and teaching. | Educational leadership. |

    Mathematics teachers--Training of. | Effective teaching.

Classification: LCC QA11.2 .B3534 2016 | DDC 510.71--dc23 LC record available at https://lccn.loc.gov/2016020850

Solution Tree
Jeffrey C. Jones, CEO
Edmund M. Ackerman, President

Solution Tree Press
President: Douglas M. Rife
Editorial Director: Tonya Maddox Cupp
Managing Production Editor: Caroline Weiss
Senior Production Editor: Kari Gillesse
Senior Editor: Amy Rubenstein
Copy Editor: Miranda Addonizio
Proofreader: Jessi Finn
Text and Cover Designer: Abigail Bowen

This book is dedicated to Jerry Cummins, one of my most influential mentors as a new mathematics leader. He had a divine gift for spreading the joy of mathematics and was a true servant leader.

—Mona Toncheff

ACKNOWLEDGMENTS

My wife and daughter, Page and Abby, fill my life with love and laughter. I am so grateful to both of you for supporting me as a father and as a professional. I love you both so much! My friends and colleagues from the Howard County Public School System and my extended Maryland mathematics leadership family provide me with inspiration and support and serve as valued critical friends. Thank you for the honor of working with and learning from you each and every day. Finally, Mona, thank you for encouraging me to express my ideas in this book. Your friendship and patience have helped me grow through this process.

—Bill Barnes

I was privileged during my first twenty-four years as an educator to work with colleagues who pushed me to become a better teacher and leaders who encouraged my own leadership growth. Thank you to Phoenix Union High School District for the opportunities to cultivate my mathematics leadership skills. As always, I cannot adequately express my love and gratitude to "Team Toncheff," which always supports my professional endeavors. Finally, thank you Bill for your collaboration and support to bring this book to fruition. I enjoy learning with you.

—Mona Toncheff

We also want to thank our peers in the National Council of Supervisors of Mathematics for constantly fueling our passion for mathematics leadership. We want to especially thank Tim Kanold for his mentorship and guidance. Through his visionary leadership, we have been able to impact the lives of teachers and students across the United States.

Personal thanks to Solution Tree—Jeff, Douglas, Kari, Tonya, and Kendra—for their dedication, time, and energy to support mathematics teaching and learning.

Sincere thanks to the National Council of Teachers of Mathematics and the Educational Materials Committee for their support of this book and their leadership in the mathematics education of teachers and students.

—Bill Barnes and Mona Toncheff

Solution Tree Press would like to thank the following reviewers:

Julia Haun
Elementary Mathematics Coordinator
Plano Independent School District
Plano, Texas

Timothy D. Kanold
Education Consultant
Chicago, Illinois

Nita Keesee
Director of Mathematics
Abilene Independent School District
Abilene, Texas

Mary Kemper
Director of Mathematics
Coppell Independent School District
Coppell, Texas

Matthew Larson
K–12 Mathematics Curriculum Specialist
Lincoln Public Schools
Lincoln, Nebraska

Donna Simpson Leak
Superintendent
Community Consolidated Schools District 168
Sauk Village, Illinois

Michele Ogden
Coordinator of K–12 Mathematics
Irvine Unified School District
Irvine, California

Derek Pipkorn
Mathematics Specialist
Mequon-Thiensville School District
Mequon, Wisconsin

Kathleen M. Sapanski
Director of Mathematics K–12 and Business
   Education
West Islip School District
West Islip, New York

Sarah Schuhl
Senior Associate, Mathematics at Work™
Solution Tree PLC and Common Assessment
   Associate
Education and Mathematics Consultant
Gresham, Oregon

Mindy Shacklett
Mathematics Coordinator
San Diego County Office of Education
San Diego, California

David A. Smith
STEM Coordinator and Elementary Mathematics
   Specialist
Utah State Office of Education
Salt Lake City, Utah

John Staley
Director of Mathematics, PreK–12
Baltimore County Public Schools
Baltimore, Maryland

Visit **go.SolutionTree.com/leadership** to download the free reproducibles in this book.

TABLE OF CONTENTS

Reproducible pages are in italics.

PART III — Key 3 Overview: Develop Systems for
Activating the Vision 81

ABOUT THE AUTHORS

Bill Barnes is director of secondary and preK–12 curricular programs for the Howard County Public School System in Maryland. He is also the director of Eastern Region 2 for the National Council of Supervisors of Mathematics and has served as an adjunct professor for Johns Hopkins University, the University of Maryland–Baltimore County, McDaniel College, and Towson University.

Bill is passionate about ensuring equity and access in mathematics for students, families, and staff. His experiences drive his advocacy efforts as he works to ensure opportunity and access to underserved and underperforming populations. He fosters partnership among schools, families, and community resources in an effort to eliminate traditional educational barriers.

A past president of the Maryland Council of Teachers of Mathematics, Bill has served as the Affiliate Service Committee Eastern Region 2 representative for the National Council of Teachers of Mathematics and regional team leader for the National Council of Supervisors of Mathematics.

Bill is the recipient of the 2003 Maryland Presidential Award for Excellence in Mathematics and Science Teaching. He was named Outstanding Middle School Math Teacher by the Maryland Council of Teachers of Mathematics and Maryland Public Television and Master Teacher of the Year by the National Teacher Training Institute.

Bill earned a bachelor of science degree in mathematics from Towson University and a master of science degree in mathematics and science education from Johns Hopkins University.

Mona Toncheff, an education consultant and author, is project manager for the Arizona Mathematics Partnership, a National Science Foundation–funded grant. As a writer and consultant, Mona works with educators across the United States to build collaborative teams, empowering them with effective strategies for aligning curriculum, instruction, and assessment to ensure all students receive high-quality mathematics instruction. She is a former mathematics content specialist for Phoenix Union High School District in Arizona, where she provided professional development and curriculum development to high school teachers and administrators.

Mona supervised the cultural shift from teacher isolation to professional learning communities when she worked in the curriculum division in Phoenix Union High School District. This change was instrumental in creating articulated standards and relevant district common assessments, as well as in providing ongoing professional development on best practices, equity and access, technology, response to intervention, high-quality grading practices, and assessment *for* learning.

Mona is first vice president of the National Council of Supervisors of Mathematics. She also served as secretary (2007–2008), director of Western Region 1 (2012–2015), and second vice president (2015–2016). Mona is president-elect of Arizona Mathematics Leaders. She was named 2009 Phoenix Union High School District Teacher of the Year, and in 2014 she received the Copper Apple Award for leadership in mathematics from the Arizona Association of Teachers of Mathematics.

Mona earned a bachelor of science degree from Arizona State University and a master of education degree in educational leadership from Northern Arizona University.

To book Mona Toncheff or Bill Barnes for professional development, contact pd@SolutionTree.com.

FOREWORD

By Timothy D. Kanold

I have spent my entire professional life engaged in the same elements that form the foundation of this book. As I read the early drafts of the manuscript, I kept thinking, "If only I had this book when I was doing all my front-line mathematics leadership work at Stevenson High School District 125!" It would have saved me and those around me from some of the bumps and bruises we endured along the way. Maybe it would have helped us achieve greater levels of student learning, equity, and access at a much brisker pace.

As Bill and Mona wrote this book, I happened to be working simultaneously with a remarkable group of school leaders from ten California school districts participating in the Math in Common (MiC) project with the California Education Partners initiative. Multiple stakeholders from each school district met four times per year to develop and implement a comprehensive mathematics program vision. The work was both daunting and exciting as participants revealed realities, developed visions, took focused action, and closely examined results.

Why mention this to you?

I mention it because the districtwide teams participating in the ongoing mathematics improvement work of the MiC exemplify the mathematics leadership team (MLT) Bill and Mona describe in chapter 1. Those stakeholders represent all those who need to read this book and use it as a tool in their daily work lives. Moreover, in my personal experiences with deep and sustained school improvement, the most successful districtwide initiatives require the guidance and vision of an MLT. All stakeholders must join their voices in the mission, vision, values, and goals of their community's K–12 mathematics program. The MLT must provide teachers—those closest to the action—the confidence and skills to carry out the MLT's declared vision.

This book provides you with the practical skills and tools to sustain systemic change over time. It will help all adults garner the wisdom and confidence they need to help students access their college and career dreams and overcome the barriers they often face in their mathematics learning experiences.

As you will discover, Bill and Mona are U.S. thought leaders on the serious issues of K–12 mathematics education, and they are practitioners like you and me, working hard to make district and school site mathematics leadership efficient, focused, and effective. They have produced a road map for diagnosing the current state of mathematics affairs in your district and responding in ways that work. Supported by research, built on experience, and written with a level of complexity and clarity we can all embrace, this book takes school leaders to a place we are wise to go to.

Bill and Mona build upon the critical belief that all students deserve rigorous mathematics curriculum via adults' effective collaboration and work in teaching and leading them. This is, above all, a book about the pursuit of equity and access.

Furthermore, Bill and Mona based the book on four keys of effective mathematics leaders and twelve actions of all community stakeholders, and designed it to enhance the capacity of every adult responsible for implementing a great mathematics program in your school or district. The four keys provide a clear yet comprehensive pathway for you to evaluate your current mathematics program, diagnose the reality of current strengths and weaknesses, and examine areas with gaps on which to focus your actions moving forward. The four keys give you and your program a purpose.

The four keys are as follows.

1. Establish a clear vision for mathematics teaching and learning.

2. Support visionary professional learning for teachers and teacher leaders.

3. Develop systems for activating the vision.

4. Empower the vision of family and community engagement.

As you read and use the tools in this book, you may examine these keys to your leadership development and practice and think each one deserves 25 percent of your time, and you would be correct!

But in practice, that is rarely true. My experience in hundreds of school districts across the United States is that Key 2 receives the majority of mathematics leaders' time and attention. It is the nature of how we traditionally define our mathematics leadership jobs. Most likely Key 2 garners nearly 80 percent of your time. Most of us view our primary job as providing the professional development necessary to empower teachers.

And yet, professional learning does not stick without Keys 1, 3, and 4.

Thus, we would be wise to heed Bill and Mona's advice to take the time to create a clear and *shared* vision of mathematics teaching and learning (Key 1) with all stakeholders in our education communities. I suspect Bill and Mona chose *shared vision* as the first key for a reason. All types of school mathematics leaders, from teachers to principals to district office leaders, often forget it. It is not flashy. It is labor intensive. Yet it is your first order of business. Without it, your mathematics leadership life will have mild impact. Bill and Mona help you learn how to engage all members of the MLT in creating or reviewing your mathematics vision and connecting every schoolwide decision, by every stakeholder, to that vision time and time again.

Perhaps the most powerful aspect of this book is Key 3, an often misunderstood and very difficult leadership area. Bill and Mona help every one of us become great at turning the vision we developed in Key 1 and the professional development work we did in Key 2 into realized action in *every* classroom. Key 3 becomes your bridge from isolated pockets of excellence in your district to widespread excellence in every school and classroom.

Bill and Mona save the best key for last. Key 4 connects your work at school to the wider community of stakeholders. They challenge you to activate the student voice in your classrooms, your schools, and your families by connecting that voice to your district vision for mathematics. With Key 4, they address the world of an often underused resource in our work: our families. However *family* is defined, they make it clear we cannot operate as if *we* (the inner school community of stakeholders) does not include the broader *we* of all education stakeholders.

This is a deeply reflective book. I would encourage you to take advantage of the audit Bill and Mona provide in figure 1.4 (page 12) to assess your current reality, and then plow into the tools and actions of greatest need for your district. They give you plenty of groundwork for your leadership and multiple entry points into the fray of focused improvement. The tools in this book provide incredible support no matter where you begin. Regardless of your current progress in the mathematics teaching and learning cycle, this book is a resource you will be able to use for a lifetime of improved student learning in K–12 mathematics.

My thanks to Bill and Mona for writing such a comprehensive work. We are all the better for it. My thanks to readers for taking on the challenge of committing to the four keys of mathematics leadership outlined in this book. Your students will be all the better for it, as well.

Introduction

A leader takes people where they want to go. A great leader takes people where they don't necessarily want to go, but ought to be.
—Rosalynn Carter

It has never been a more exciting time to be a mathematics leader. A convergence of educational reform initiatives has brought recommendations and findings from decades of meaningful research on mathematics teaching and learning to the forefront of action. Emerging technologies, such as social media and social networking, coupled with a movement focused on increasing expectations for student mathematics learning, provide mathematics leaders with the tools and leverage to engage stakeholders in cycles of continuous improvement. As a mathematics leader, your challenge is to seize opportunities made available by this convergence of research, resources, and reform.

To meet curricular, instructional, and assessment expectations, mathematics teachers must shift away from traditional mathematics instruction that focuses significantly on the development of procedures and algorithms. Instead, they must design engaging learning experiences that feature a balance of student-centered exploration and teacher-facilitated sense making to engage students in rigorous instruction. This shift results in instruction that "builds fluency with procedures on a foundation of conceptual understanding so that students, over time, become skillful in using procedures flexibly as they solve contextual and mathematical problems" (National Council of Teachers of Mathematics [NCTM], 2014, p. 10). Students must adopt new roles in the mathematics classroom. Rather than sit as passive consumers, they must work collaboratively as they engage in worthwhile tasks that deepen understanding through productive struggle that is supported by student-to-student discourse. Redefining the mathematics classroom learning experience in this way has created a sense of anxiety for staff and families alike. Teachers, familiar with the strategies for developing procedural fluency, are busy learning new teaching strategies. Families, dependent on the traditional mathematics textbook to guide support at home, find themselves unsure how to support multiple algorithms, mathematics investigation, and multiple representations. For district leaders, the challenges associated with stakeholder shifts are compounded with issues of equity and access, increased political attention through the media, greater emphasis on college preparedness, and evolving high-stakes assessment systems that bring the sobering truths about mathematics education into focus.

Here is some good news. Throughout the history of the United States, we have faced complex challenges that tested the very foundation of our democracy. The United States has overcome civil war, economic depression, and civil rights issues. In each of these cases, we have been fortunate to have citizens who possessed the passion, skills, and knowledge to solve these complex problems. At a time when it seems that fewer and fewer of our students graduate with access to their dreams intact, we, as a mathematics community, are so very fortunate to have *you*! You have joined this profession at just the right time. Your passion, skills, and knowledge, when applied with focus and resolve, will lead to better futures for our students. Through your leadership, teachers will work collaboratively to develop the skills and knowledge to transform mathematics classrooms into vibrant centers of thinking and reasoning. Students will graduate ready to thrive in an ever-evolving world. Families will engage as partners in mathematics education. All of these things will happen because of *you*.

Mathematics leaders come in many forms. You could be a director of mathematics at the district level or a principal who oversees mathematics in a rural district. You could be a curriculum director or assistant superintendent who oversees mathematics or a mathematics coach who serves one school or more than thirty schools. You could be a department chair or a course- or grade-level team leader. All of these roles have one thing in common: those who hold them must possess the leadership skills and knowledge to move the vision of teaching and learning mathematics forward to promote student achievement.

So how do we accomplish that great work? The task of developing systems to substantively improve mathematics teaching and learning is daunting. Regardless of your role in mathematics leadership, you will strengthen your own knowledge and the knowledge of those serving on your team. You will develop tools and resources to activate the vision for teaching and learning mathematics. You will rely on effective communication to support data collection that feeds reflective practices. You will build a strong cadre of empowered leaders committed to equity, access, and excellence for each and every student. Each of these actions requires careful attention.

We designed this book to guide you along your journey. We provide mathematics leaders with insight, taken from many years of experience with this work, and a road map for developing a culture focused on collaboration and continuous improvement. We build on the following set of beliefs.

- ◆ Issues of equity, opportunity, and access drive leadership decisions and actions.
- ◆ All teachers deliver high-quality, rigorous mathematics instruction to all students. All teachers strive to ensure that every student will develop an understanding of rich and meaningful mathematics.
- ◆ Effective collaborative teams work to accelerate adult learning and result in substantive improvements in mathematics teaching and student learning.
- ◆ Students, families, and community stakeholders have the potential to transform the work of mathematics leaders by serving as significant catalysts for change.

We structured this book to build your capacity as a mathematics leader by focusing on the following four keys of effective mathematics leadership.

1. Establishing a clear vision for mathematics teaching and learning
2. Supporting visionary professional learning for teachers and teacher leaders

3. Developing systems for activating the vision

4. Empowering the vision of family and community engagement

Each of these keys unlocks the purposeful actions of mathematics leaders to support a highly effective mathematics program. As each of the keys is developed, you will notice connections among the leadership actions aligned to a specific key and the skills needed to build other keys. These leadership actions are highlighted with a picture of a key to emphasize the potential use to build a different key's skillset. These connections are vital as we explore and create substantive action steps for developing all four keys.

These chapters will guide your visionary leadership actions across every level of mathematics leadership based on the differentiated needs of your mathematics program. While you can certainly use the book as a cover-to-cover resource, you may find that, based on the results of the mathematics program audit in chapter 1, your focus rests on the content of just two or three chapters. Mathematics leadership is daunting and the breadth of work is significant, so use the book as a resource that best meets your needs as a leader. We organized the chapters to support your leadership by helping you:

◆ Take stock of current realities

◆ Reconcile current beliefs and actions with relevant research and effective practices

◆ Engage in activities to strengthen the community's collective skills and knowledge

◆ Design mechanisms for managing, monitoring, and celebrating desired growth

In part I, we address Key 1 and outline how to establish a clear vision for mathematics teaching and learning. We challenge you to survey mathematics teachers and other key stakeholders to determine if there is a clear and consistent understanding of the expectations for mathematics teaching and learning in your school or district. We share strategies for collaboratively developing and teaching a common vision, and we provide strategic action steps to create supportive conditions for improved teaching and learning.

Chapter 1 focuses on the development of a mathematics leadership team (MLT) that is trained and empowered to lead a mathematics program audit. In chapter 2, leaders will explore strategies for synthesizing the data collected from the program audit to create a clearly articulated vision for exemplary mathematics teaching and learning. MLT members leverage current research and best practices to develop SMART (strategic, measurable, attainable, results oriented, and time bound) goals that will guide vision communication and teaching. In chapter 3, MLT members establish clear measures of success with a timeline for continuous monitoring of the vision.

In part II, we address Key 2 and explore how to support visionary methods for building the capacity of those you lead. Change is complex. Teachers and teacher leaders require supportive conditions to embrace it. Mathematics leaders can create opportunities to engage new learning, application, and action research to evaluate the impact of the new learning.

Chapter 4 focuses on effective strategies for developing collective capacity across the mathematics program by designing meaningful professional learning experiences and developing a culture of continual growth and learning. In chapter 5, leaders will explore strategies for building capacity with existing and emerging mathematics leaders and explore the importance of communication across the community of leaders. In chapter 6, leaders will learn how to effect positive instructional change by becoming experts at developing mathematics leadership in the places that matter most: the school and the boardroom.

In part III, we address Key 3 and share strategies for developing systems to activate the collaboratively developed vision for mathematics teaching and learning. You will be able to put systems in place to monitor, evaluate, and revise districtwide and site-based goals and action steps. The chapters in part III guide you through the design of reflective practices and processes to ensure stakeholder actions align with the teaching and learning vision.

Chapter 7 focuses on structures that support teachers and leaders working in a PLC culture and utilizing research-affirmed collaborative team actions. These structures ensure consistent implementation of instructional strategies that support the vision for exemplary mathematics teaching and learning developed in chapter 2. In chapter 8, leaders will learn how to coach teams to move beyond textbooks to design a guaranteed and viable curriculum (Marzano, 2003) focused on the Standards for Mathematical Practice, determine assessments for curriculum, engage students in the assessment cycle, and challenge grading practices by providing appropriate feedback. Chapter 9 focuses on developing and monitoring clear expectations for desired teacher actions and student learning behaviors in mathematics classrooms. Further, leaders will explore how effective feedback, when provided to teachers and students, improves the quality of teaching and learning in the mathematics classroom.

In part IV, we address Key 4 and explain how to empower students, families, and community members as engaged advocates for mathematics education in your school or district.

Chapter 10 focuses on strategies for engaging students as advocates and partner-leaders for the improvement of mathematics teaching and learning. Leaders will explore a variety of strategies along a continuum of engagement to support an increased student voice. In chapter 11, you will explore strategies for engaging parents and families as partners in mathematics education. You will learn how to engage parents as advocates and champions for your mathematics vision. Chapter 12 focuses on engaging business and community partners in your district. These local resources have the potential of bringing the real world into the mathematics classroom so that students graduate with a network of support already in place.

Your roles and responsibilities as a mathematics leader present you with a robust and diverse set of opportunities. As mathematics leaders ourselves, we understand these challenges because we live them every day. Our goal is to not only strengthen your leadership with our ideas and resources, but also compel you to actively participate in a community of leaders across North America and beyond that engage in the same critically important work. We understand the complexities associated with ensuring equitable access to meaningful mathematics for all, with developing curricular resources to support the wide range of student strengths in the classroom, and of supporting staff through comprehensive reform efforts. We believe that the answers to our shared, complex problems rest within the larger mathematics community. Our challenge is to harness our collective skills, knowledge, and experiences to engage in truly innovative leadership actions. It is important that we work together to meet this challenge because our students' hopes and dreams depend on it!

Key 1 Overview:
Establish a Clear Vision for Mathematics Teaching and Learning

The best educational leaders are in love—in love with the work they do, with the purpose their work serves, and with the people they lead and serve.

—Richard DuFour and
Robert J. Marzano

A collaboratively written and clearly articulated vision for exemplary mathematics teaching and learning provides the fuel and direction for a district mathematics program. In Key 1, we will explore the collaborative systems that you will establish, nurture, and leverage to develop a vision that will guide your decision making going forward. Further, we will describe how to form a strategic plan to make your vision a reality.

The big ideas and essential understandings of Key 1 will prepare mathematics leaders to engage in the following leadership actions.

- Develop a plan for creating a culture of transparency, trust, and creative problem solving.

- Recruit and empower a mathematics leadership team (MLT) committed to equity and excellence for all students.

- Engage the MLT in a data collection process using the mathematics program audit to inform strategic planning.

- Collaboratively design a vision for exemplary mathematics teaching and learning.

- Develop SMART goals (strategic, measurable, attainable, results oriented, and time bound) with clearly defined measures for improvement and success.

- Create and nurture a culture of accountability and celebration.

Take Stock of Your Mathematics Program's Health

Destiny is not a matter of chance, it is a matter of choice; it is not something to be waited for, it is a thing to be achieved.

—William Jennings Bryan

The office phone rings and the voice on the line is a reporter from the *Washington Post*. She is gathering information for a story showcasing the nation's top mathematics programs. She begins by asking for your name and official job title. Then, in rapid-fire succession, she asks these two questions: "Would you describe your mathematics program as healthy?" and "What evidence can you provide to back up your claim?" After a long pause, you take a deep breath and begin to speak.

Effective mathematics leaders know exactly what to say in such situations. They know exactly which words to use to describe exemplary mathematics teaching and learning for students, effective professional learning programs for staff, and engaging partnerships with families and community stakeholders. Effective leaders know exactly which measure of progress to reference when describing growth for each part of their program. So, what exactly will you say to the reporter? If the reporter were to interview fifty members of your mathematics community, would they say the same thing? In this chapter, you will explore strategies for critically analyzing your mathematics program. You will learn how to recruit and train a representative team of stakeholders who will gather data using a mathematics program audit. Finally, you will explore strategies for empowering your team to engage the entire mathematics community of teachers, leaders, and community members in a transparent and continuous process of program improvement.

Highly effective mathematics leaders routinely engage in self-reflection and thorough analysis of feedback that they collect regularly from representative stakeholders. Self-reflection begins with this simple exercise adapted from Mona Toncheff and Timothy Kanold (2015): in thirty seconds or less, write down your vision for exemplary mathematics teaching and learning. After writing down your thoughts, ask at least twenty stakeholders from your district, "What is our vision for exemplary mathematics programming?"

Be sure to include teachers, students, parents, community leaders, central office leaders, special educators, English learners staff, and school-based administrators. Each time that a stakeholder provides a response that very closely aligns to what you wrote, give yourself a point. Each time a stakeholder provides a response that does not, take one point away. Each time a stakeholder responds, "I don't know," or provides an answer diametrically opposed to your vision, take away two points. At the end of the exercise, consider your total and how it reflects your leadership. Of course, developing, communicating, and living a common vision for mathematics programming is just one of several checkpoints for effective mathematics leaders. Figure 1.1 contains a few other checkpoints to consider.

Answer the following questions and list the evidence to support the answer choices.

- ◆ Do students, teachers, and families have access to high-quality curricular resources that align directly to clearly developed student learning targets? Are other stakeholders invited, regularly, to scrutinize the curriculum to stimulate growth?
- ◆ Are collaborative teams of mathematics teachers developing common assessments with common scoring practices and providing students with high-quality feedback to guide their goal setting?
- ◆ Are teachers receiving high-quality professional learning so that they have the resources, skills, and knowledge to teach students effectively?
- ◆ Are school-based administrators providing meaningful formative feedback to teachers during formal and informal observations? How variant are those conversations from school to school?
- ◆ Are the powerful voices of students, families, and community partners leveraged to improve mathematics classroom instruction?

Figure 1.1: Taking stock of the district mathematics program (self-reflection).

*Visit **go.SolutionTree.com/leadership** for a free reproducible version of this figure.*

A leader's self-reflection coupled with the examination of stakeholder feedback is an excellent gauge of the health of the mathematics program. However, to become an elite mathematics leader, you will need to engage a collaborative team of stakeholders in a comprehensive program audit of your mathematics program.

Securing Representation

Caveat: It may be difficult to secure representation from all of the listed stakeholders. If this is the case, be sure that members of the team consider the perspectives of each stakeholder group listed. Further, members should take responsibility for gathering data from these groups.

Engage Stakeholders as Members of a Mathematics Leadership Team

Undoubtedly, every mathematics program has components that function at high levels. But, it is also likely that programs contain components that remain underdeveloped, require a slight tune-up, or need a complete overhaul. How do effective leaders know which segments of the mathematics program are high functioning?

The first and most important step in closely analyzing your mathematics program is to assemble representative stakeholders, critical friends, and field experts to serve on your MLT. Creating this team ensures that your finger is on the pulse and that you are fully aware of the needs of those you serve. Stakeholders are much more likely to fully engage in district initiatives when leaders they trust fully represent and support them. MLTs should include students, parents, community partners, mathematics teachers (all levels), special education teachers, English learners teachers, representatives from institutions of higher education, curriculum directors, mathematics coaches, and other interested stakeholders. As you consider which stakeholders to recruit, take a moment to think about the following three questions.

1. Who are the trusted members of the mathematics community whom leaders count on for advice and guidance?

2. Do these trusted community members represent all student and stakeholder groups or do we need to find additional candidates?

3. Do these trusted community members believe that each and every student can learn rigorous mathematics? Further, do they believe that all students should have access to the full mathematics program by the time they graduate?

The responses to these questions will provide leaders with a great list of candidates to begin recruiting for the MLT. But before reaching out to each candidate, take a moment to consider question 3 at greater depth. There is one important characteristic that each member of the leadership team must share; each member must believe, in the deepest part of his or her heart, that all students deserve access to rigorous mathematics instruction. Issues of equity and access in the mathematics program will be part of each and every MLT discussion and decision. There is simply no place on the MLT for stakeholders who believe that mathematics is for an elite few, those born with the capacity, or that some students, given their limited supports at home, just won't be able to understand calculus. These attitudes permeate every school district and we cannot ignore them, but neither can we allow them to bog down the important work of the MLT. One of the critical roles of an MLT leader is to bring a common understanding of issues of equity and access to light. Timothy Kanold and Matthew Larson (2012) describe the challenge like this: "To pursue equity, you, your teams, and other mathematics leaders [and members of your MLT] need to break through the social issues and disparities to engage each student in rich mathematics experiences" (p. 113).

It is unlikely that all members of the team will initially possess a deep understanding of the complex issues of institutional inequity, but leaders can nurture and strengthen it over time. If you doubt a potential team member's beliefs about issues of equity and access, ask the following questions and pay careful attention to the team member's response and his or her tone and body language.

◆ Do you believe that every student can successfully complete algebra 1 prior to entering high school? Why or why not?

◆ What do you believe are the root causes of our gap in achievement among student groups?

Pay attention to who takes ownership of the issues of equity that persist in our profession. Look to recruit those who believe that there are adult actions that will reduce or eliminate student opportunity gaps. On the other hand, if prospective candidates begin by placing blame on society, families, lifestyles, or family income, thank them politely and cross them off the list of MLT candidates. Once you finalize the prospective list, place a personal phone call to invite each potential candidate to join the team. Figure 1.2 (page 10) provides some key talking points for reaching out to recruit MLT candidates.

- Explain *why* you are forming an MLT.
  - ◇ Create systematic and sustained program improvement.
  - ◇ Ensure students receive the highest quality mathematics instruction.
  - ◇ Ensure teachers who support mathematics instruction receive the support, resources, and training they deserve.
  - ◇ Empower students, families, and community stakeholders as equal partners in the mathematics instructional improvement process.
- Clearly explain the intended work of the MLT.
  - ◇ Conduct and analyze results from a mathematics program audit (figure 1.4, page 12).
  - ◇ Develop a vision for exemplary mathematics programming.
  - ◇ Develop SMART goals with clear performance measures.
- Clarify time commitments and describe how long members will be involved with the MLT.
  - ◇ Initially, the time commitment will be high (biweekly).
  - ◇ After the work associated with the audit, the time commitment will be moderate (monthly).
  - ◇ After the team sets goals, establishes supporting systems, and clearly defines measures of performance, the time commitment will be light (quarterly).
- Explain exactly *why* you have identified someone as an excellent MLT candidate.

Figure 1.2: Talking points for MLT recruitment.

Once you form the MLT, it is time to bring the team together to engage in a mathematics program improvement process. During the first meeting, focus on the two objectives of (1) establishing a collaborative and inclusive team culture and (2) analyzing and, if necessary, revising the mathematics program audit. Figure 1.3 is an agenda example for the first meeting of the MLT.

MLT Preliminary Meeting
Agenda
   I. Introductions and icebreaker
   II. Collaborative establishment of norms and protocols
   III. Review of anticipated goals and outcomes
      a. Build a strong MLT. *How will we work together?*
      b. Examine and propose edits to the mathematics program audit.
      c. Take stock. Discuss data and review student performance data.
   IV. Action items

Figure 1.3: Agenda example for the first MLT meeting.

During the first meeting, ensure that team members get to know one another and begin to develop an understanding of the team's strengths. To accomplish this, schedule time for team-building activities. Also, be sure to establish meeting norms and discussion protocols. One of the strongest messages mathematics leaders send is to value each and every team member's ideas and perspectives. At subsequent meetings, display meeting norms on the agendas and on presentation slides as a reminder of the team commitment to foster a fully inclusive and collaborative team environment. (Visit www.allthingsplc .info/tools-resources for additional ideas.)

Nurturing positive group dynamics will pay dividends during the tough work ahead. Consider investing a little time during each meeting to bring the group closer together. At the beginning of each meeting, invite MLT members to share personal or professional moments of joy or inspiration. Build on personal celebrations by celebrating the team's work. Select stories that highlight the team's accomplishments since the last meeting. These actions will nurture a community that operates in the spirit of collaboration, trust, and transparency.

Mathematics Program Audit

After the introductory portion of the meeting, provide the MLT with a copy of the mathematics program audit (figure 1.4, page 12).

As an exercise, give individual team members time to carefully preview the audit. After five to ten minutes, the facilitator of the MLT asks small groups of two or three team members to relate their observations and to make a list of questions or concerns they would like to share with the whole group. This is an important moment in the group's early development, since the whole-team debriefing serves as another opportunity to build buy-in and consensus. The facilitator of the MLT should ask the following four questions to drive the whole-group discussion.

1. What meaningful observations did you make about the mathematics program audit?

2. What did you like about the audit and why?

3. What changes in the audit would you recommend and why?

4. As representatives of stakeholder groups, how might we collect data to inform each statement in the audit? What specific processes might we use?

We designed the first three questions to invite revision of the audit process. Mathematics leaders understand that each of the four keys to effective mathematics leadership represents a vital component of the mathematics program. One responsibility of mathematics leaders is to invite revision while maintaining the integrity of the audit review process. Inevitably, some members of the MLT may be less comfortable collecting data for one or more statements in the audit. It is the MLT facilitator's job to determine whether the proposed revision strengthens or weakens the audit process. If a proposed change weakens the audit process, the facilitator must have the courage to say so and take care to confront important issues such as this to maintain the integrity of the audit review process. Then, the facilitator must challenge the group to strengthen the proposed change.

> ### Effective Leadership Tip
>
> *As the leader, you may want to digitize the process using an application such as Google Forms. Google Forms is an easy-to-use survey tool that records participant responses in a spreadsheet. Leaders can archive and evaluate responses over time as a strategy for monitoring the mathematics program's health.*

We designed the fourth question of the list to invite suggestions for the data collection process. The audit will be most meaningful if the facilitator empowers each member of the MLT to collect data from the stakeholders they represent. This action reinforces each MLT member's role as a representative of specific stakeholder groups. The data collected from the audit will serve to drive the vision setting, SMART goal setting, and decision making for the mathematics program, so it is best to be as inclusive as possible.

	4—Strong Evidence	3—Some Evidence	2—Little Evidence	1—No Evidence
	This statement consistently aligns with site-based collaborative teams and district leaders.	This statement somewhat represents the actions of site-based collaborative teams and district leaders.	This statement occasionally represents the actions of site-based collaborative teams and is not a consistent action from district leaders.	This statement does not reflect the actions of site-based collaborative teams and district leaders.

Key of Mathematics Leadership	Mathematics Leadership Actions	Statements	Self-Rating	Comments
Establish a clear vision for mathematics teaching and learning.	Develop a collaborative vision for an exemplary mathematics program.	All stakeholders collaboratively develop, clearly articulate, and understand the vision for exemplary mathematics teaching and learning.	4 3 2 1	
		The vision for exemplary mathematics teaching and learning drives strategic planning, SMART goal setting, budgetary expenditures, and professional learning, and includes measures of success.	4 3 2 1	
		All mathematics teachers and leaders believe in high expectations for all students.	4 3 2 1	
	Establish measures of success.	The mathematics program's vision promotes equity and access to rich, meaningful mathematics for all students.	4 3 2 1	
		Mathematics leaders continually monitor the vision of teaching and learning and consistently provide feedback to teachers, administrators, students, and parents.	4 3 2 1	
		Mathematics leaders clearly define, monitor, and celebrate measures of success with stakeholders during the school year.	4 3 2 1	
		Collaborative teams set SMART goals aligned to the district mathematics vision.	4 3 2 1	
		Student enrollment in advanced coursework (such as AP and college-level courses) proportionally represents district demographics.	4 3 2 1	
		The entire system utilizes evidence of data-driven processes. Collaborative teams adapt instruction based on student thinking, use trends in benchmark assessments to modify curriculum, use trends in student performance to create or modify interventions, and use data to drive decision-making processes.	4 3 2 1	
		Mathematics leaders provide meaningful, action-oriented feedback on student performance and clearly communicate it to all stakeholders.	4 3 2 1	

Key of Mathematics Leadership	Mathematics Leadership Actions	Statements	Self-Rating	Comments
Support visionary professional learning for teachers and teacher leaders.	Engage teachers in worthwhile and differentiated professional learning.	Collaboration is a vital element of continuous professional learning. Every part of the mathematics program (such as curriculum development and professional learning) shows evidence of collaborative structures.	4 3 2 1	
		The collaborative team's work is a vital component of the district professional learning plan.	4 3 2 1	
		District and site schedules permit job-embedded professional learning and time for collaboration during the school day.	4 3 2 1	
		Professional learning opportunities align to district or site mission, vision, values, and goals.	4 3 2 1	
		After new professional learning, teachers and collaborative teams engage in evidence-based goal setting and action for the next unit.	4 3 2 1	
		All collaborative team members work to activate the vision and support the team's work through peer accountability.	4 3 2 1	
		District- and site-level leaders provide a professional development plan that includes multiple delivery systems with activities differentiated for the various learning needs of participants.	4 3 2 1	
		District and site leaders develop and implement a professional learning plan that addresses the needs identified by quantitative and qualitative data analysis. Professional learning is discipline specific and job embedded but also emphasizes a whole-school approach to learning.	4 3 2 1	
		The mathematics leadership team evaluates professional learning by examining participants' reactions, the degree of their learning, their use of the professional learning content, the degree of support and change in the organization resulting from the professional learning, and the effect of the professional learning on students' achievement and learning.	4 3 2 1	

continued on next page ⇨

Figure 1.4: Mathematics program audit.

Key of Mathematics Leadership	Mathematics Leadership Actions	Statements	Self-Rating	Comments
	Develop highly skilled and highly effective mathematics leaders.	Site-level leaders ensure that teachers assigned to work with low-performing students are experienced and have high expectations for student achievement. Evidence shows that these teachers have successfully accelerated low-achieving students and the teachers have a strong desire to continue working with these students.	4 3 2 1	
		District-level leaders create multiple opportunities to develop teacher leaders through professional learning and support from team and instructional leaders.	4 3 2 1	
		District-level leaders provide supportive conditions for teacher leaders to consistently collaborate and engage in reflective practices.	4 3 2 1	
		Site-level leaders consistently select highly engaging and effective teachers to serve as instructional team leaders.	4 3 2 1	
	Build the capacity of site-based administrators and district leaders.	District and site leaders develop and implement a professional learning plan that addresses the needs identified by quantitative and qualitative data analysis. Professional learning is discipline specific and job embedded, and also emphasizes a whole-school approach to learning.	4 3 2 1	
		The site-based leadership team requires team members to use the professional learning standards and resources in collaboration with district-level leadership, and ensure that all professional learning results in improving all students' learning.	4 3 2 1	
		District mathematics leaders ensure that all site-based leaders participate in ongoing mathematics leadership development.	4 3 2 1	
Develop systems for activating the vision.	Engage high-leverage team actions.	Mathematics collaborative teams, site leaders, and district teams consistently analyze data and student work to systematically answer the four critical questions of a professional learning community culture (DuFour, DuFour, Eaker, Many, & Mattos, 2016). 1. What do we want students to know and be able to do? 2. How will we know if they know it? 3. How will we respond if they don't know it? 4. How will we respond if they do know it?	4 3 2 1	
		Mathematics collaborative teams receive feedback regarding their effectiveness in promoting strong collaboration versus cooperation.	4 3 2 1	

Key of Mathematics Leadership	Mathematics Leadership Actions	Statements	Self-Rating	Comments
	Create and implement well-designed and articulated curriculum and assessments.	Essential learning standards are clearly articulated for each course, unit, and lesson and describe both what students should understand and be able to do (content and mathematical practice standards).	4 3 2 1	
		Essential learning standards support horizontal and vertical learning progressions. Resources support the development of standards with an equal intensity of conceptual understanding, procedural fluency, and application (mathematical rigor).	4 3 2 1	
		Curriculum provides opportunities for all students to access rich mathematical tasks via the Standards for Mathematical Practice.	4 3 2 1	
		Mathematical tasks promote reasoning and problem solving. Tasks vary and address multiple levels of cognitive demand.	4 3 2 1	
		District leaders, in conjunction with teachers, design assessment blueprints provided to all teachers. Teachers use these same blueprints to frame unit plans and for daily lesson planning.	4 3 2 1	
		The curriculum, instructional resources, and assessments align. This alignment is clear to teachers, students, and parents, and the curriculum is transparent to all stakeholders.	4 3 2 1	
		District and site-based assessments are balanced in cognitive demand.	4 3 2 1	
		Assessments vary in the type of questions and are not solely procedural.	4 3 2 1	
		Students receive timely feedback on their progress in the content and the development of the Standards for Mathematical Practice.	4 3 2 1	
		Common assessments are created before a unit of instruction and reviewed during and after the unit to ensure they align to the instructional blueprint and assess the essential learning targets, both content and process requirements.	4 3 2 1	
		District leaders articulate clear, nonnegotiable actions defining high-quality assessment practices.	4 3 2 1	
		Mathematics teams collaboratively score student work, establish strong inter-rater reliability, and use the results to provide specific feedback for all stakeholders.	4 3 2 1	
		Collaborative teams engage students in the assessment cycle as part of continuous improvement. Feedback and action are required elements of the assessment cycle.	4 3 2 1	
		All stakeholders have a clear understanding of effective formative assessment processes that result in teacher and student action through evidence gathering and feedback.	4 3 2 1	

continued on next page ⇨

Key of Mathematics Leadership	Mathematics Leadership Actions	Statements	Self-Rating	Comments
	Monitor consistent expectations for exemplary instruction.	Communication in the mathematics classroom is vital to students sharing their understanding of concepts and procedures. Students engage in high levels of discourse every day to develop meaningful understanding of mathematics.	4 3 2 1	
		Differentiation is evident in flexible grouping, lesson design, and mathematical tasks.	4 3 2 1	
		Districts and sites develop and monitor intervention models to ensure all students have access to core instruction and tiered interventions.	4 3 2 1	
		The Standards for Mathematical Practice are observable during every classroom walkthrough, and students can describe which Mathematical Practice they are developing.	4 3 2 1	
		Teachers consistently implement the curriculum to the depth of each essential learning standard. Site and district leaders observe the intended curriculum daily.	4 3 2 1	
		Teachers employ research-informed instructional strategies consistently and use and connect mathematical representations.	4 3 2 1	
		Teachers design lessons to build procedural fluency from conceptual understanding for application. Teachers support students' productive struggle in learning mathematics.	4 3 2 1	
		District-level leaders, in conjunction with site-level leaders, ensure they provide dedicated time for interaction between teachers and intervention program staff to ensure continuity of instruction.	4 3 2 1	

Key of Mathematics Leadership	Mathematics Leadership Actions	Statements	Self-Rating	Comments
Empower the vision of family and community engagement.	Activate the student voice to check alignment between vision and reality.	Student voices are prevalent and honored throughout the mathematics program. District and site-based leaders make regular efforts to gather insights from students through interviews or surveys. The student voice serves as a catalyst for program improvement.	4 3 2 1	
	Empower families as informed advocates.	Parent and guardian voices are prevalent and honored throughout the mathematics program. District and site-based leaders make regular efforts to develop parents and guardians as advocates and to ensure parent participation in professional development, curriculum development, and advisory groups.	4 3 2 1	
		District- and site-level leadership teams have a well-defined process for gathering and responding to feedback on practices for involving parents and families in student achievement.	4 3 2 1	
		District- and site-level leadership teams have a systematic process for analyzing data and reasons for parents' and families' noninvolvement in student achievement.	4 3 2 1	
		The site-level MLT has a process to inform parents and families about school programs and student progress. The process fosters two-way communication and ensures participation is representative of the school community.	4 3 2 1	
	Build and engage a strong network of partnerships.	Community voices are prevalent and honored throughout the mathematics program. District and site-based leaders make regular efforts to activate community stakeholders to promote the love of mathematics (for example, through hosting community fairs, developing student intern programs, serving as mentors and role models, and so on).	4 3 2 1	
		Additional staff (such as counselors, support staff, paraeducators, intervention specialists, administration, and so on) take ownership of and establish collective capacity for ensuring improved student achievement.	4 3 2 1	
		The site-level leadership team collects data on the school climate and takes steps to make the climate welcoming and invitational for all visitors.	4 3 2 1	

Visit go.SolutionTree.com/leadership for a free reproducible version of this figure.

The facilitator should charge the MLT members to develop a list of stakeholders that they will invite to participate. Students, families, teachers, staff, administration, community members, and partners from institutions of higher education are all possible audit participants. Challenge the MLT members to brainstorm various opportunities to engage stakeholders. For example, MLT members might engage stakeholders in the audit process during school staff meetings, monthly mathematics department meetings, mathematics leadership meetings, PTA meetings, or church or community meetings, or at home using an online version of the audit. Work with MLT members to brainstorm various methods for communicating the audit. Examples include the school system website, a weekly newsletter, social media or a blog, or local newspapers. Finally, challenge your team to think of strategies for collecting the audit data. Consider using multiple methods of data collection, from traditional pencil-and-paper methods to online surveys, to be as inclusive as possible. Once the team members understand the task at hand, communicate clear agreements about the time frame for data collection. Select a reasonable time frame so that team members have a realistic opportunity to gather data from a wide range of stakeholders. Finally, send your MLT members out into the community and into schools to collect information that will guide the vision process.

Move From Vision to Action

Effective mathematics leaders work hard to create a culture of transparency, trust, and collaborative problem solving. Recruiting and empowering a diverse leadership team committed to equity and excellence for all students demonstrates commitment to that pursuit. Further, engaging the MLT in the meaningful work that accompanies the mathematics program audit informs the vision process and subsequent strategic planning. This work steers the mathematics program on a pathway of continuous improvement and ultimately leads to increased student achievement. Table 1.1 describes the relationships among district-, site-, and team-level engagement in taking stock of the mathematics program.

Table 1.1: Mathematics Leadership Commitments for Taking Stock of Your Mathematics Program's Health

District's Role	Site-Level Leader's Role	Collaborative Team's Role
Form an MLT with stakeholders representing all student groups and the community.	Form a site-level MLT responsible for representing the school's voice in the mathematics program.	Apprise all team members of district mathematics leadership actions and initiatives and provide feedback to the site-level MLT.
Facilitate analysis and revision of the mathematics program audit.	Facilitate analysis and revision of the mathematics program audit for site-based staff.	Submit team recommendations for revisions for the mathematics program audit to the lead facilitator of the MLT.
Charge MLT members to collect data using the mathematics program audit.	Gather site-level data to include in the mathematics program audit.	Provide evidence and artifacts to support the mathematics program audit data collection process.

*Visit **go.SolutionTree.com/leadership** for a free reproducible version of this table.*

The results from the mathematics program audit (figure 1.4, page 12) illuminate the program's strengths and opportunities. Chapter 2 shows MLTs how to take the next step and use that information to reimagine their vision for teaching and learning mathematics.

Develop a Collaborative Vision for an Exemplary Mathematics Program

The greatest danger for most of us is not that our aim is too high and we miss it, but that it is too low and we reach it.

—Michelangelo

In this chapter, you will learn how to leverage the data collected from the audit to collaboratively develop a common vision for exemplary mathematics teaching and learning. To ensure that the vision reflects research and best practices for exemplary mathematics teaching and learning, you will explore professional learning models focused on building the capacity of MLT members. Finally, you will learn how to engage MLT members in the development of SMART goals written to activate the vision.

A collaboratively developed and clearly articulated vision guides every successful organization. For mathematics leaders, the collaborative design of a compelling vision for an exemplary mathematics program that inspires action is essential. In *The Five Disciplines of PLC Leaders*, Timothy D. Kanold (2011) explains the vision as the force that "moves the school organization beyond the question of *why* we exist to the question of *what* we should become" (p. 11). Thomas J. Sergiovanni (2006) also captures the vision's importance, describing it as "more than catchy prose, more than inspirational words" (p. 26). The vision "states publicly what is important, why it is important, what our obligations are, and how we get there" (p. 26). Sergiovanni's description of vision as social "contract, even covenants" provides an action-oriented perspective for the effective mathematics leader (p. 26).

The vision is evident in all aspects of the mathematics program. It serves to inform strategic planning, shape the design of professional development programs, improve the quality of classroom instruction, influence the course program of studies, and enhance communication with all stakeholders.

> ### Why Is the Vision So Important?
>
> - *A vision provides clear direction.*
> - *A vision inspires collective action toward common goals.*
> - *A vision focuses thinking, especially when facing difficult decisions.*

We define a *vision statement* in this book as a statement that aims to elevate the quality of mathematics teaching and learning resulting in high levels of student learning as well as high levels of staff and community engagement. The vision statement itself must be more than words on a sign or office letterhead.

Evaluate the Strength of Your Current Vision

As mathematics program leaders, it is our responsibility to lead the collaborative development of the vision, clearly communicate it to stakeholders, and design actions to attain it. The first step in this process is to assess the current vision for exemplary mathematics teaching and learning. In chapter 1, we compared our personal vision for exemplary mathematics teaching and learning to that of members of the mathematics community. This process is a quick, surface-level litmus test of the *strength* of the existing vision. The vision's influence on the actions of stakeholders determines its strength. Unless your school or district has recently engaged in a vision-setting process, chances are there is a great deal of variance between the mathematics leader's personal vision and that described by others. But don't be discouraged. A vision statement has a life cycle of about five years. Changes in policy, leadership, research findings, and culture make it necessary to revisit, revise, and rewrite the mathematics vision periodically. When considering whether the mathematics vision needs an update, take a few minutes to reflect on the statements in figure 2.1.

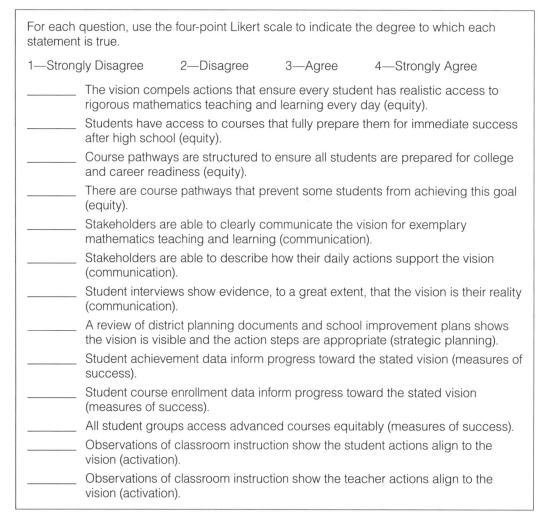

For each question, use the four-point Likert scale to indicate the degree to which each statement is true.

1—Strongly Disagree   2—Disagree   3—Agree   4—Strongly Agree

_____ The vision compels actions that ensure every student has realistic access to rigorous mathematics teaching and learning every day (equity).

_____ Students have access to courses that fully prepare them for immediate success after high school (equity).

_____ Course pathways are structured to ensure all students are prepared for college and career readiness (equity).

_____ There are course pathways that prevent some students from achieving this goal (equity).

_____ Stakeholders are able to clearly communicate the vision for exemplary mathematics teaching and learning (communication).

_____ Stakeholders are able to describe how their daily actions support the vision (communication).

_____ Student interviews show evidence, to a great extent, that the vision is their reality (communication).

_____ A review of district planning documents and school improvement plans shows the vision is visible and the action steps are appropriate (strategic planning).

_____ Student achievement data inform progress toward the stated vision (measures of success).

_____ Student course enrollment data inform progress toward the stated vision (measures of success).

_____ All student groups access advanced courses equitably (measures of success).

_____ Observations of classroom instruction show the student actions align to the vision (activation).

_____ Observations of classroom instruction show the teacher actions align to the vision (activation).

Figure 2.1: Testing the *strength* of your vision (self-reflection).

*Visit **go.SolutionTree.com/leadership** for a free reproducible version of this figure.*

Which of the five main areas are identified as a strength of your vision? Which of the five main areas are opportunities for growth? We designed the checkpoints in figure 2.1 to provide mathematics leaders with insights into five indicators of the strength of the vision. These indicators determine the following.

- The degree to which the vision attends to important issues of *equity and access* in the mathematics program (chapter 2)

- The degree to which stakeholders *communicate* and understand the vision (chapter 2)

- The degree to which *strategic planning* documents reflect the vision (chapter 2)

- The degree to which stakeholders *activate* the vision in mathematics classrooms (chapters 4–12)

- The degree to which clear *measures of success* provide evidence to help stakeholders realize the vision (chapter 3)

When considering the statements in figure 2.1, leaders should ask themselves how their current mathematics vision fared. For which indicators was the vision strong? For which indicators was it weak? Based on the answers to these questions, mathematics leaders will want to engage the MLT in a process of revising or rewriting the vision for exemplary mathematics teaching and learning. Throughout that process, it will be important for leaders to keep these questions and strength indicators in mind. They will serve as guideposts to ensure that the mathematics team creates a vision worth pursuing.

Prepare the MLT for the Vision-Setting Process

The next important step in establishing a vision is to engage the MLT in the vision-setting process. When setting out to create or revise a vision for the program, be sure to take time to help MLT members understand *why* they are engaging in this process. Sergiovanni (2006) notes, "Defining a vision for your school (district) should be a product of many thoughtful conversations within your school (district) and within your community" (p. 28). MLT members engage in these conversations as they collect and analyze data from the mathematics program audit (figure 1.4, page 12). The feedback they gather should provide them with ideas about what is important to the stakeholders in the mathematics community. During the next MLT meeting, give team members adequate time to share what they have learned through their interactions with stakeholders.

The MLT leader's responsibility is to focus the team on ideas and philosophies aligned to research, committed to equity and access, and that result in increased student learning. In *Beyond the Common Core: A Handbook for Mathematics in a PLC at Work™, High School*, Toncheff and Kanold (2015) challenge leaders to continually ask, "How do you know that your defined vision for mathematics instruction and assessment represents the 'right things' to pursue that are worthy of your best energy and effort?" (p. 2). Posing this question to the MLT will provide mathematics leaders with the context for building the capacity of the team. Before the team can formally develop a vision, its members must understand issues of equity and access in mathematics

---

Traditional Barriers to Equity and Access

- *Absence of a district vision committing to mathematics success for all students*
- *Course progressions with rigid tracks*
- *Low expectations of staff who possess fixed mindsets about the capacity of student learning (Dweck, 2006)*
- *One-size-fits-all classroom instruction*
- *Absence of supporting structure to provide accommodations for struggling students*

education. They must also possess a deep, common understanding of mathematics teaching and learning that is supported by research.

② *Build the MLT's Understanding of Equity and Access Issues*

Since the beginning of the 21st century, people have given increased attention to issues of equity and access in mathematics education. In *Principles and Standards for School Mathematics*, the National Council of Teachers of Mathematics (NCTM, 2000) describes equity not as "identical instruction" but instead as a demand to provide "reasonable and appropriate accommodations . . . to promote access and attainment" for all students (p. 12). NCTM's call for action to address issues of equity was timely indeed. A year later, the 2001 reauthorization of the Elementary and Secondary Education Act (ESEA), rebranded as No Child Left Behind, brought into focus the disparities in opportunity among student groups. No Child Left Behind required school districts to demonstrate adequate yearly progress for all students and for each student group. In 2015, the Every Student Succeeds Act (ESSA) reauthorized the ESEA, and it continues to support equity by upholding critical protections for the United States' disadvantaged and high-need students. Close analysis of the first sets of student achievement data revealed that students in Asian American or Caucasian student groups were earning significantly higher mathematics scores on standardized assessments than their African American and Hispanic counterparts. Further, students receiving special education services, English learners services, or free and reduced meals were not realizing academic gains proportional to their peers. Leaders in mathematics education engaged in root-cause analysis with a greater focus on equity realized that, contrary to popular historical beliefs, there are a number of gap-reducing actions available to schools and districts. Douglas Reeves (2006) explains:

> *A growing body of research makes it clear poverty and ethnicity are not the primary causal variables related to student achievement. Leadership, teaching, and adult actions matter. Adult variables, including the professional practices of teachers and the decisions leaders make can be more important than demographic variables. (p. xxiii)*

The notions that some students were not born with the capacity to engage in rigorous mathematics and that some students just don't have the support necessary to succeed in mathematics block effective leadership action. An effective mathematics leader must root out unproductive beliefs and implement clearly defined actions that result in greater opportunity for all students. In figure 2.2, we share a list of productive beliefs about equity taken from NCTM's (2014) *Principles to Actions: Ensuring Mathematical Success for All.*

- ◆ Mathematics ability is a function of opportunity, experience, and effort—not of innate intelligence. Mathematics teaching and learning cultivate mathematics abilities. All students are capable of participating and achieving in mathematics, and all deserve support to achieve at the highest levels.

- ◆ Equity is attained when students receive the differentiated supports (for example, time, instruction, curricular materials, programs) necessary to ensure that all students are mathematically successful.

- ◆ Equity—ensuring that all students have access to high-quality curriculum, instruction, and the supports that they need to be successful—applies to all settings.

- ◆ Students who are not fluent in English can learn the language of mathematics at grade level or beyond at the same time that they are learning English when appropriate instructional strategies are used.

- ◆ Effective mathematics instruction leverages students' culture, conditions, and language to support and enhance mathematics learning.

- Effective teaching practices (for example, engaging students with challenging tasks, discourse, and open-ended problem solving) have the potential to open up greater opportunities for higher-order thinking and for raising the mathematics achievement of all students, including poor and low-income students.
- The practice of isolating low-achieving students in low-level or slower-paced mathematics groups should be eliminated.
- All students are capable of making sense of and persevering in solving challenging mathematics problems and should be expected to do so. Many more students, regardless of gender, ethnicity, and socioeconomic status, need to be given the support, confidence, and opportunities to reach much higher levels of mathematical success and interest.

Source: NCTM, 2014.

Figure 2.2: Productive beliefs about access and equity in mathematics.

In *The PRIME Leadership Framework*, the National Council of Supervisors of Mathematics (2008) asserts, "Leaders in mathematics education have an obligation to provide students with a mathematics curriculum and learning experience that prepare them for their future, whatever that may be" (p. 10). This obligation for mathematics leaders begins with strongly rooting the vision in equitable access to rigorous mathematics teaching and learning for all students. To achieve this goal, work with the MLT to develop commitment statements about equity and access. These statements might include the following.

- Ensure that every student receives access to rigorous mathematics instruction every day.
- Ensure that every student learns the mathematics content necessary to place into credit-bearing college courses.
- Ensure that every student participates in advanced mathematics coursework (AP or honors courses).
- Ensure that every high school student graduates having successfully completed two college-level mathematics courses.
- Ensure that every family receives the knowledge and resources necessary to effectively advocate for their child's mathematics experience.

Notice that each of these statements begins with the word *ensure*. Powerful action verbs elevate the mathematics community's commitment to setting high goals.

Build the MLT's Understanding of Mathematics Teaching and Learning

The recent era of reform has amplified discussions about mathematics teaching, learning, and assessment. The Common Core State Standards movement transferred those discussions about standards from the schoolhouse to the soccer field. Discussions about the Common Core made their way into the broader American culture, taking center stage in social media, political debates, YouTube comedy videos, and even beer commercials. Rather than have their spirits dampened by this negative energy, effective mathematics leaders use that energy to focus their communities' attention on research that supports effective teaching and learning.

A natural starting place for this work is to engage the MLT in the exploration of students' classroom experience. Ask team members to imagine a successful mathematics lesson. Ask, "What should students be doing during the mathematics lesson if our goal is for each student to learn at high levels? What specific actions should students take to increase their chance of success? In other words, as aspiring mathematicians, what is their job description?" Compare the team's responses to the following list of learning behaviors defined by the Common Core State Standards as the Standards for Mathematical Practice (National Governors Association Center for Best Practices [NGA] & Council of Chief State School Officers [CCSSO], 2010).

1. *Make sense of problems and persevere in solving them.*

2. *Reason abstractly and quantitatively.*

3. *Construct viable arguments and critique the reasoning of others.*

4. *Model with mathematics.*

5. *Use appropriate tools strategically.*

6. *Attend to precision.*

7. *Look for and make use of structure.*

8. *Look for and express regularity in repeated reasoning.*

Even with controversy surrounding the release of the Common Core State Standards, there is agreement among major mathematics associations that the standards, including the Standards for Mathematical Practice, represent a worthwhile set of understandings that we should strive to develop explicitly with students (Conference Board of the Mathematical Sciences, 2013). There will likely be some discrepancies between the MLT list of student behaviors and the Standards for Mathematical Practice. As MLT leaders, it is critical that we help team members understand how the Standards for Mathematical Practice serve to better prepare students for success after high school.

Once the MLT clearly understands the desired student behaviors, ask the question, "What actions must teachers take to ensure that students are engaged in the Standards for Mathematical Practice each day?" To deepen MLT members' understanding of mathematics teaching and learning, reference NCTM's (2014) *Principles to Actions: Ensuring Mathematical Success for All*. Begin by having team members explore productive and unproductive beliefs for teaching and learning mathematics. It is very likely that members of the team encountered evidence of both productive and unproductive beliefs as they spoke with stakeholders about the mathematics program audit. Take time to explore productive and unproductive beliefs, and then move into a deeper discussion focused on the eight NCTM (2014) Mathematics Teaching Practices.

> **Establish mathematics goals to focus learning:** *Effective teaching of mathematics establishes clear goals for the mathematics that students are learning, situates goals within learning progressions, and uses the goals to guide instructional decisions.*
>
> **Implement tasks that promote reasoning and problem solving:** *Effective teaching of mathematics engages students in solving and discussing tasks that promote mathematical reasoning and problem solving and allow multiple entry points and varied solution strategies.*
>
> **Use and connect mathematical representations:** *Effective teaching of mathematics engages students in making connections among mathematical representations to deepen understanding of mathematics concepts and procedures and as tools for problem solving.*

Facilitate meaningful mathematical discourse: *Effective teaching of mathematics facilitates discourse among students to build shared understanding of mathematical ideas by analyzing and comparing student approaches and arguments.*

Pose purposeful questions: *Effective teaching of mathematics uses purposeful questions to assess and advance students' reasoning and sense making about important mathematical ideas and relationships.*

Build procedural fluency from conceptual understanding: *Effective teaching of mathematics builds fluency with procedures on a foundation of conceptual understanding so that students, over time, become skillful in using procedures flexibly as they solve contextual and mathematical problems.*

Support productive struggle in learning mathematics: *Effective teaching of mathematics consistently provides students, individually and collectively, with opportunities and supports to engage in productive struggle as they grapple with mathematical ideas and relationships.*

Elicit and use evidence of student thinking: *Effective teaching of mathematics uses evidence of student thinking to assess progress toward mathematical understanding and to adjust instruction continually in ways that support and extend learning.*

 NCTM's Mathematics Teaching Practices describe the daily actions and routines of an exemplary mathematics teacher. To ensure that MLT members understand each of NCTM's Mathematics Teaching Practices, engage team members in the knowledge-building activity we describe in figure 2.3.

1. Write each Mathematics Teaching Practice at the top of a large piece of chart paper and hang the papers around the meeting room. Provide each MLT member with one black and one green marker.

2. Display the following questions for the team to consider for each teaching practice.

   a. Why is this teaching practice important to student learning?

   b. What classroom conditions must exist for teachers to fully engage in this teaching practice?

3. Ask pairs of MLT members, one district member with one community member, to visit each piece of chart paper to write one short response to the two questions. Instruct team members to use a black pen to write the response to question 2a and a green pen to write their responses to question 2b.

4. Review the written responses once every pair has had an opportunity to provide insights for each of the questions for each teaching practice.

5. Encourage team members, especially those members with limited exposure to classroom instruction, to pose clarifying questions so that they possess an informed understanding of each teaching practice.

6. To summarize the activity, ask MLT members to describe what students would be doing in classrooms that featured a full commitment to these practices. Encourage team members to highlight specific links to the Standards for Mathematical Practice.

Figure 2.3: Understanding NCTM's Mathematics Teaching Practices.

Strengthening the MLT's understanding of exemplary mathematics teaching and learning is essential to the vision process. Building strong connections between NCTM's Mathematics Teaching Practices and the

Standards for Mathematical Practice will ensure that the vision reflects the research for exemplary mathematics teaching and learning. The Mathematics Teaching Practices represent a core set of high-leverage practices and essential teaching skills necessary to promote deep learning of mathematics. The Standards for Mathematical Practice represent what students should be doing as they interact with and learn mathematics content. Together, these represent the framework and practices critical to supporting student (and teacher) engagement and meaningful mathematics learning (figure 2.4).

Standards for Mathematical Practice (SMP)		Teacher Action Connections	Mathematics Teaching Practices (MTP)	
SMP1	Make sense of problems and persevere in solving them.	Mathematics lessons align to the essential learning standards and teachers clearly communicate them to students (MTP1). Lessons include complex tasks (MTP2), opportunities for visible thinking (MTP8 and MTP4), and intentional questioning (MTP5) to promote deeper mathematical thinking (MTP6). Teachers design lessons from the student's perspective to provide multiple opportunities to make sense of the mathematics (MTP7). To build SMP1, teachers focus on MTP7 and MTP2. To build SMP2, teachers focus on MTP2 and MTP3. To build SMP3, teachers focus on MTP4 and MTP5. To build SMP4, teachers focus on MTP3 and MTP8. To build SMP5, teachers focus on MTP2 and MTP3. To build SMP6, teachers focus on MTP4 and MTP2. To build SMP7 and SMP8, teachers focus on tasks (MTP2).	MTP1	Establish mathematics goals to focus learning.
SMP2	Reason abstractly and quantitatively.		MTP2	Implement tasks that promote reasoning and problem solving.
SMP3	Construct viable arguments and critique the reasoning of others.		MTP3	Use and connect mathematical representations.
SMP4	Model with mathematics.		MTP4	Facilitate meaningful mathematical discourse.
SMP5	Use appropriate tools strategically.		MTP5	Pose purposeful questions.
SMP6	Attend to precision.		MTP6	Build procedural fluency from conceptual understanding.
SMP7	Look for and make use of structure.		MTP7	Support productive struggle in learning mathematics.
SMP8	Look for and express regularity in repeated reasoning.		MTP8	Elicit and use evidence of student thinking.

Figure 2.4: Framework for connecting the student and teaching practices.

Visit go.SolutionTree.com/leadership for a free reproducible version of this figure.

As a summative exercise, work with the MLT to develop commitment statements about teaching and learning. Examples include the following.

- Ensure that every student understands how to engage in the Standards for Mathematical Practice.

- Ensure that every teacher designs lesson experiences that promote students' engagement in the Standards for Mathematical Practice.

- Ensure that every teacher strategically infuses the NCTM (2014) Mathematics Teaching Practices into every lesson.

These commitment statements anchor the mathematics program and focus collaborative team planning sessions, instructional observation and reflection, and professional learning design.

Develop the Vision Statement Collaboratively

After collecting data from the mathematics program audit and strengthening the capacity of the MLT, the pieces are in place to craft a vision statement that will guide the community's thoughts and actions over the next five years. Careful planning and preparation for the MLT vision meeting is essential. During this meeting, team members will:

- Thoroughly analyze and synthesize data collected from the mathematics program audit

- Review relevant student achievement data, student enrollment data, and student engagement data (discipline referrals, suspensions, and dropout rates)

- Review the equity and access commitment statements

- Review the teaching and learning commitment statements

- Craft a vision statement for exemplary mathematics teaching and learning

Be sure to budget plenty of time for this meeting. If the members of the MLT have performed their duties well, then there will be a massive amount of data to sift through. Figure 2.5 (page 28) describes a process for efficiently analyzing and synthesizing data from the audit.

Once MLT members finish analyzing the data, it is time to craft a vision statement that honors the mathematics program's current realities and fuels program improvement. After leaders have taken so much care to provide members of the MLT with the time to understand the components of the mathematics program, it is crucial to provide them with an opportunity for input during this final process. Toncheff and Kanold (2015) share a strategy that challenges team members to succinctly communicate their ideas:

A favorite team exercise we use to capture the vision for instruction and assessment is to ask a team of three to five teachers to draw a circle in the middle of a sheet of poster paper. We ask each team member to write a list (outside of the circle) of three or four vital adult behaviors that reflect his or her vision for instruction and assessment. After brainstorming, the team will have twelve to fifteen vital teacher behaviors. We then ask the team to prepare its vision for mathematics instruction and assessment inside the circle. The vision must represent the vital behaviors each team member has listed in eighteen words or less. (p. 2)

The purpose of this activity is to identify trends, strengths, and weaknesses in the current mathematics program. Each team receives data associated with one section of the mathematics program audit.

1. Prior to the meeting, prepare four data stations: one station for each section of the audit. At each station, provide a summary of all qualitative and quantitative data associated with the assigned audit section. Also provide one set of student achievement data, student enrollment data, student engagement data, and copies of the commitment statements for equity and access and teaching and learning.

2. During the meeting, assign one section of the audit to small, "expert" groups of MLT members for review. If possible, include a student, parent, teacher, administrator, and community member in each group. Multiple perspectives are important.

3. Provide each team with a stack of blank index cards. As the team reviews the data, they should write trends and themes on the index cards—one idea per card. When possible, team members should try to associate, or triangulate, audit data points to the student achievement, enrollment, or engagement data.

4. After the groups have had sufficient time to analyze and synthesize data, create new groups containing at least one member from each expert group. Have team members share their findings, identifying observations, trends, strengths, and weaknesses.

5. Facilitate a discussion and capture consensus ideas on chart paper. These major themes will influence the development of the vision statement *and* the strategic plan to follow.

Figure 2.5: MLT process for data analysis and synthesis.

Engage MLT members in this process and have each group share its final vision. Limiting the group to eighteen words in this exercise helps distill the group's values and beliefs into ideas that matter most. Then challenge the MLT to commit to one shared vision statement that will serve as your district's new vision for exemplary mathematics teaching and learning. For guidance, here are some vision statements taken from mathematics organizations and school districts.

- The National Council of Teachers of Mathematics (NCTM) is the global leader and foremost authority in mathematics education, ensuring that all students have access to the highest quality mathematics teaching and learning. We envision a world where everyone is enthused about mathematics, sees the value and beauty of mathematics, and is empowered by the opportunities mathematics affords.

- The National Council of Supervisors of Mathematics (NCSM) envisions a professional and diverse learning community of educational leaders that ensures every student in every classroom has access to effective mathematics teachers, relevant curricula, culturally responsive pedagogy, and current technology.

- Every student receives and every teacher delivers rigorous mathematics instruction leveraging the NCTM mathematics teaching practices to engage students in the Standards for Mathematical Practice (Howard County Public School System mathematics program, adapted from Dixon, Adams, & Nolan, 2015; Kanold & Larson, 2015; Kanold-McIntyre, Larson, & Briars, 2015; Toncheff & Kanold, 2015).

◆ The Phoenix Union High School District (2013) mathematics program, E² Math:

> *. . . wants to excel in all areas of teaching and learning. We want to be the role model for professional learning communities, collaborative learning for the 21st century for teachers and students, innovative technology, college and career readiness, and a commitment to continual learning. (p. 2)*

Congratulations! You have led a team of diverse stakeholders through a thorough process of collecting data, analyzing them, and developing a collaborative vision statement for exemplary mathematics teaching and learning. Now you will begin the important process of communicating the vision and bringing it to life through strategic planning.

Communicate the Vision

The development of a vision statement is just the beginning. For it to become a reality, mathematics leaders must ensure that all stakeholders understand how to support the vision through clearly defined actions and understand which actions do not support the vision. For example, if the vision statement asserts that all students graduate ready for enrollment in credit-bearing mathematics courses in college, then it is unacceptable for a course pathway to terminate with algebra 1, geometry, integrated mathematics 1, or integrated mathematics 2 as the grade 12 capstone course. Students who complete their studies with one of those courses will simply not be ready for college-level mathematics coursework. So, one action of an effective mathematics leader is to develop course progressions that terminate with students enrolled in at least algebra 2 (integrated mathematics 3). Kanold (2011) describes the process of building understanding as a leader's responsibility to "teach the vision" to stakeholders. He asserts, "Once the vision is declared, you [the leader] begin teaching for understanding of the vision and those expectations. Teaching the vision ensures coherent implementation by all adults in your leadership sphere of influence" (Kanold, 2011, p. 21). This action is challenging enough for school leaders, but as a mathematics leader, you will have to engage the MLT in a strategic planning process to ensure that the vision is present and understood in all aspects, and by all stakeholders, of the mathematics program.

Bring the Vision to Life Through Strategic Planning and Goal Setting

The vision statement compels actions, but which actions? The mathematics leader's responsibility is to facilitate the collaborative development of a strategic plan that clearly describes stakeholder actions that support the vision for exemplary mathematics teaching and learning. The strategic plan should outline clear expectations for:

◆ Supporting the continuous professional growth of teachers (chapter 4)

◆ Developing highly skilled and highly effective mathematics leaders (chapter 5)

◆ Strengthening the capacity of school administrators and central office staff (chapter 6)

◆ Working as a collaborative team within a professional learning community (PLC) culture (chapter 7)

◆ Supporting teaching and learning through well-designed mathematics curriculum and assessments (chapters 8 and 9)

◆ Empowering students, families, and community members as agents for instructional improvement (chapters 10, 11, and 12)

Developing a comprehensive strategic plan that aligns all district actions to the new vision for exemplary mathematics teaching and learning is a daunting task. Fortunately, a well-trained MLT armed with a deep understanding of the mathematics program audit data will support mathematics leaders in this work. Leaders will treat the collaborative strategic planning process as the next opportunity to strengthen the MLT.

Diane Schilder (1997) of the Harvard Graduate School of Education describes the strategic planning process as "an essential first step in the development of a results-based accountability system" and defines the process by addressing the following questions: "Where are we? What do we have to work with? Where do we want to be? How do we get there?".

The MLT's analysis of the program audit data and student achievement, enrollment, and engagement reports positions the team to effectively respond to the first two questions. The development of the vision for exemplary mathematics teaching and learning clearly establishes a response to the third. After answering the first three questions, the leaders will work with the MLT to determine how to answer the fourth. Use the district program audit data analysis to select an area of focus to support MLT members through the planning process. Working through one portion of the plan together helps develop consistent planning expectations that leaders can apply when smaller MLT workgroups tackle other sections of the plan on their own.

Effective strategic plans begin with a set of clearly defined SMART goals. The acronym SMART stands for goals that are specific, measurable, attainable, results oriented, and time bound. Figure 2.6 summarizes the elements of SMART goals as described by Anne Conzemius and Jan O'Neill (2014).

S: Specific

- Goals should be clearly written, easy to understand, and focused.
- It answers the question, What do you want to accomplish and why?

M: Measurable

- The goal can be evaluated quantitatively.
- It answers the question, How will you know you've met with, or are progressing toward, success?

A: Attainable

- The goal stretches the team or organization but is not excessive or impossible to reach.
- It answers the question, How realistic are your expectations?

R: Results Oriented

- The goal develops concrete ideas for how to quantify success.
- It answers the question, Which measures will we use to monitor progress toward the goal?

T: Time Bound

- The goal specifies the time by which the goal is expected to be achieved.
- It answers the question, When?

Source: Adapted from Conzemius & O'Neill, 2014.

Figure 2.6: Summary of SMART goals.

The SMART goal–setting process focuses on the development of reasonable goals based on the question, Where are we now? For example, analysis of the school improvement data might reveal that just 4 percent of the students receiving special education services ultimately participate in an advanced placement (AP) mathematics course by the time they graduate. However, if the district vision is to ensure that all students will participate in an AP course prior to graduation, the MLT will create SMART goals focused on reasonable annual growth toward the vision. A root-cause analysis might reveal that the mathematics course placement process at the end of grade 3 bars access to AP courses. The MLT writes a SMART goal focused on strengthening this process as well as student support systems so that, each year, more students receiving special education services access the mathematics courses that naturally lead to AP courses in high school. The development of SMART goals clarifies to stakeholders how they can work to support a lofty vision. Once the MLT creates SMART goals for the mathematics program, collaborative teams will also create individual team SMART goals and action steps aligned to the district SMART goals. The leader of the MLT ensures that all team members clearly understand how to write SMART goals. Develop understanding by first analyzing a few examples and then engaging the group in a practice writing session. Here are a few examples.

◆ By December, increase the number of teachers explicitly infusing their daily lessons with NCTM's Mathematics Teaching Practices by 25 percent. (This goal supports consistent expectations for exemplary mathematics teaching and learning.)

◆ By May 31, increase the number of students from underrepresented student groups enrolled in AP mathematics courses by 10 percent. (This goal supports the program's vision for equity and access while honoring the complexity of the issue. Ten percent is a reasonable number considering that the target students are already enrolled in course trajectories that do not naturally lead to AP courses.)

◆ By June, increase the number of school administrators effectively using the mathematics instructional talk questions (Dixon, 2015) during pre- and post-observation conferences by 30 percent.

One strategy for increased transparency is to have all site-based leaders submit their SMART goals to the MLT and other school teams at the beginning of the year. This strategy is not designed to ensure compliance alone. It invites a reflective process that could strengthen the goal itself. For example, the MLT could review each goal to ensure vision alignment and then provide feedback to the school for strengthening specific action steps. Another example: site-based leaders could review each other's SMART goals to glean ideas and additional perspectives leading to meaningful improvement. If mathematics leaders are going to ask collaborative teams to write SMART goals in relation to the teaching and learning vision, they must also provide feedback, monitor the teams' progress, and celebrate successes.

Developing SMART goals is the first step in the strategic planning process. The next steps focus on actions that lead toward attaining the goal. Figure 2.7 (page 32) provides an example of a strategic planning design template to guide the MLT's work.

> ### Mathematics Instructional Talk Questions
>
> 1. *Which one or two Standards for Mathematical Practice are the lesson foci?*
> 2. *Why, given the mathematical content of the lesson, are you choosing to focus on these one or two Standards for Mathematical Practice?*
> 3. *What Mathematics Teaching Practices (NCTM, 2014) will you leverage to develop the students' Standards for Mathematical Practice?*

Focus Area	Equity and Access

Data Focus	◆ Enrollment trends for advanced mathematics course pathways
	◆ Analysis of standardized testing data, including the following
	   ◇ Locally developed assessments for grades preK–12
	   ◇ Cognitive Abilities Test (CogAT) in early grades
	   ◇ PSAT, SAT, and ACT
	   ◇ AP potential
	   ◇ State, PARCC, or Smarter Balanced assessments

Baseline	◆ Percentage of students in each student group accessing above-grade-level, honors, gifted and talented, and AP courses
	   ◇ 85 percent of Asian students
	   ◇ 74 percent of Caucasian students
	   ◇ 62 percent of Hispanic students
	   ◇ 58 percent of African American students
	   ◇ 3 percent of students receiving special education services
	   ◇ 8 percent of students receiving English learners services
	   ◇ 29 percent of students receiving free and reduced meals

Root Cause (Why)	◆ Mathematics course placement at the end of grade 4 is a strong indicator of access. Students not on track to participate in advanced programs by grade 4 are far less likely to accelerate to the advanced course progression prior to graduation. ◆ Students entering the school system in middle school or later are fifteen times less likely to be placed in an advanced mathematics course progression. ◆ Course recovery programs and interventions are focused on supporting students performing below grade level, not on supporting acceleration.
SMART Goal	◆ **By May 31, increase the number of students (for underrepresented student groups) enrolled in AP mathematics courses by 10 percent.**

Strategy (What and How)	◆ Clearly establish a purpose for increased student enrollment in advanced mathematics pathways.
	◆ Communicate explicit connections to the district mathematics vision and leverage research while assessing current school culture and belief systems associated with this target.
	   ◇ If necessary, collaborate with schools to design and implement professional learning focused on issues of equity in mathematics education, including productive versus unproductive beliefs (NCTM, 2014).
	   ◇ If necessary, collaborate to design and implement professional learning focused on developing growth mindsets (Dweck, 2006).
	◆ Collaborate with teachers supporting mathematics instruction and student services staff to engage in data discussions focused on enrollment trends and root-cause analysis. See figure 4.3 (page 55) for a learning progression tool to support planning professional learning.
	◆ Develop students', families', and staff's deep understanding of mathematics course pathways.

Focus Area	Equity and Access
	◆ Considering multiple measures, collaborate with staff to identify students demonstrating a capacity for acceleration. 　◇ In September or October: For identified students, reschedule and provide supports after school or during creative scheduling blocks. 　◇ In November or December: For identified students, regroup. Create additional sections of accelerated classes offering a condensed version of the curriculum. 　◇ In January or February: For identified students, provide additional support through after-school or Saturday programs, offering access to content that might be missed when the students are accelerated the following year. 　◇ From March through August: For identified students, collaborate with parents to communicate a summer program of study to support acceleration for the following year. 　◇ Year-round: Collaborate with families to develop an academic plan that includes enrollment in advanced mathematics pathways. ◆ Work with feeder school partners during articulation meetings to review enrollment data and develop placement recommendations to support the attainment of the school improvement plan target. 　◇ After the initial discussions, review placements and make alterations to student schedules when appropriate. ◆ Collaborate with the offices of mathematics to access student-facing online resources to provide additional support and instruction beyond the school day.
Timeline (When)	◆ July–June (see preceding strategies for breakdown)
Implementer (Who)	◆ School administration, student services staff, mathematics team leaders and coaches, mathematics teachers, other teachers supporting mathematics instruction, families, and students ◆ School improvement team ◆ Offices of mathematics ◆ District mathematics leadership team
Resource	◆ District mathematics curricular resources 　◇ Course-specific resources 　◇ Links to external resources ◆ District curriculum staff (offices of mathematics, for example) ◆ MLT members ◆ *Principles to Actions: Ensuring Mathematical Success for All* (NCTM, 2014) ◆ *Mindset: The New Psychology of Success* (Dweck, 2006)
Milestone	◆ Engage in quarterly data discussions to review enrollment data and to review progress.

Figure 2.7: District strategic plan example—supporting equity and access.

*Visit **go.SolutionTree.com/leadership** for a free reproducible version of this figure.*

Notice that this strategic plan focuses on just one specific slice of the mathematics program. By the time the work with the MLT is complete, the team will have two or three specific goals focused on supporting the targeted areas of growth. Developing and activating a strategic plan at this grain size for every facet of

Effective Leadership Tip

As a leader, you may want to collect the site collaborative team's SMART goals electronically (try Google Forms) to quickly evaluate and monitor them. Visit **go.SolutionTree.com /leadership** for a free reproducible version of this type of form.

the mathematics program dilutes the efforts and reduces the chance of successfully meeting the intended goals. So, be realistic with your approach. Use the mathematics program audit and other sources of data to focus the team's energy on what matters most. Then, once you are able to show growth in the target areas, expand the scope of work to include other aspects of the mathematics program. Next, let's review and consider further ways to move the vision into action.

Move From Vision to Action

As an effective mathematics leader, you have worked to strengthen the capacity of the MLT members to serve as effective advocates and change agents for the district mathematics program. Richard DuFour and Robert J. Marzano (2011) offer a summary of this leadership work. They assert "anyone can write a vision statement describing a better future for the organization, but it requires effective leadership to create a *shared* vision that addresses the hopes and dreams of people within the organization" (p. 201). Lead the MLT by arming it with new knowledge and understanding of mathematics teaching and learning, and developing a common vision to inspire the work of teachers and leaders in the district. Guided by the vision and informed by the mathematics program audit, the team develops a strategic plan. It includes SMART goals focused on program improvement for two or three target areas. Over the next five years, the leaders work to teach, monitor, and measure progress toward the vision. The vision guides all of the decisions leaders make, including the design of the program budget, the design of the professional development plan, and the work to grow a PLC culture. Table 2.1 describes the relationship among district-, site-, and team-level engagement in developing a collaborative vision for an exemplary mathematics program.

Table 2.1: Mathematics Leadership Commitments for Developing a Collaborative Vision for an Exemplary Mathematics Program

District's Role	Site-Level Leader's Role	Collaborative Team's Role
Lead the collaborative development of a vision for exemplary mathematics teaching and learning.	Site leaders engage in drafting the vision for high-quality mathematics instruction.	All staff members review the vision for exemplary mathematics teaching and learning and ask clarifying questions.
With the support of the MLT, provide learning opportunities for all stakeholders to teach the vision for high-quality instruction.	Site leaders teach the vision to all staff responsible for teaching mathematics. Throughout the process, leaders develop a professional learning plan to ensure all stakeholders have the skills and knowledge necessary to achieve the vision.	School mathematics educators assess their current state of mathematics teaching and learning to determine how well current practice aligns to the new vision.
Lead the development of a strategic plan guided by SMART goals.	School leaders infuse district mathematics SMART goal plans into the school improvement plan to ensure alignment to the vision.	School mathematics educators enact strategies outlined in the school improvement plan and regularly review data to monitor progress toward the attainment of SMART goals.

*Visit **go.SolutionTree.com/leadership** for a free reproducible version of this table.*

Reflection

Review the Key 1 audit statements regarding effective team actions in figure 2.8 and with the MLT, reflect upon your current strengths and opportunities to grow. Describe specific action steps to support these specific Key 1 statements and begin to craft an action plan to support the MLT's two or three focus area goals. Appendix A (page 169) contains a reproducible template action plan. At the end of each chapter of this book and in coordination with the MLT, record actions and next steps to create a viable action plan to support meeting the district vision.

Key 1: Develop a Collaborative Vision for an Exemplary Mathematics Program	Next Steps
All stakeholders collaboratively develop, clearly articulate, and understand the vision for exemplary mathematics teaching and learning.	
The vision for exemplary mathematics teaching and learning drives strategic planning, SMART goal setting, budgetary expenditures, and professional learning, and includes measures of success.	
All mathematics teachers and leaders engage in productive beliefs that support high expectations for all students.	

Figure 2.8: Key 1—Develop a collaborative vision for an exemplary mathematics program.

*Visit **go.SolutionTree.com/leadership** for a free reproducible version of this figure.*

After you plan, write, and communicate the vision, it's time to turn your attention to the task of identifying how mathematics leaders will evaluate success in meeting the established vision.

3

Establish Measures of Success

What gets measured gets improved.

—Peter Drucker

In chapter 3, you will explore strategies for designing structures to monitor, evaluate, and celebrate progress toward attaining your vision of exemplary mathematics teaching and learning. First, you will learn to teach the MLT how to develop effective measures of success. Then, you will explore strategies for developing cycles of collaborative review. Finally, you will learn why intentional celebration is a valuable leadership action.

Scenario

A motivated group of mathematics leaders is eager to improve the quality of the mathematics learning experience for students. The team begins by investing considerable effort in developing, nurturing, and empowering a collaborative community to engage as catalysts for change. The team possesses a strong vision for equity and access, a vision that they share proudly and loudly. In the early years of the team's work, they carry their vision to the community, empowering families and community members to serve as advocates for their students. Over time, many members of the district mathematics community come to share this vision. The early stages of the Common Core reform initiative test the team's commitment to the vision. Instead of succumbing to the pressure to reject change, the team has engaged students, teachers, and community members in the process of curriculum and assessment development. More than half the teachers in the district choose to participate in curriculum development workshops, a professional learning activity traditionally sought by just a few mathematics teachers.

Further, to celebrate the community's work, the team makes curricular resources available to teachers from around the world. After just a few years, teachers all over North America and in many countries throughout the world use the resources every day. To support implementation of new standards, the team continues to work with the board of education to secure additional resources to provide higher levels of professional development to mathematics teachers in every school. Teachers come together regularly to plan lessons, share great ideas, and learn from each other. This effort results in a strengthening of mathematics leadership capacity across the district. The mathematics program functions like a well-oiled machine.

Consider the leadership exhibited in the real-life scenario.

- *How would you characterize the success of this district's mathematics leader?*

- *What evidence will you use to justify your characterization?*

When we reflect on the team's leadership actions featured in the scenario, we might be compelled to describe the program as highly effective or successful. The truth is we really don't know. And, based on this excerpt, the members of the team don't really know either. In education, a large number of deliberate actions are sometimes the sole indicators of success. The team in the story engaged in productive work that produced a number of observable artifacts that would seem likely to result in high degrees of success. But success for whom? And just how much success is achieved? Effective mathematics leaders dig deeper by questioning the team's performance.

- The team seems to have a strong vision for equity and access. Did the team collaboratively develop that vision?

- It seems great that a lot of people worked on developing a curriculum, but what is the quality of the resources they produced?

- How did the resources the team developed support improved mathematics teaching and learning?

- How did the leadership team know if professional learning actually improved mathematics instruction, and to what degree?

- The team strengthened district leadership capacity, but by how much? Which specific actions resulted in the greatest leadership growth?

- How did all of these actions influence student learning?

- How did the actions increase student enrollment in advanced mathematics courses?

If the leadership team's goal was to improve the students' mathematics learning experience, then it should support its series of well-intended actions with a series of well-designed and clearly articulated performance measures.

When developing SMART goals, it is of paramount importance to develop effective performance measures as indicators of success. Performance measures are statements that support the SMART goal by providing the answers to the questions, How much growth or progress do we intend to achieve? and How will we know when we have achieved it? The answers to these questions influence virtually every leadership decision, including budgeting, purchasing, staffing, resource allocation, and professional development design. Performance measures must be clear statements so that all stakeholders understand how they measure progress. Performance measures must also be relevant. Collecting student engagement data might provide clues as to why students are not accessing AP courses at the intended levels, but the data will not be able to tell you if you are meeting your goal of increasing enrollment in those courses.

The answer to the question, What will we measure? is entirely dependent on the SMART goals you develop. Some of your measures will be straightforward, quantitative measures. Other measures, often qualitative, require some additional attention to achieve clarity. For example, trying to determine a sense of students' motivation in the mathematics classroom will require the MLT to clarify measures of success and develop a scoring tool or rubric to quantify that success. Further, the team will want to establish guidelines for the application of the scoring tool or rubric to achieve a greater degree of validity and reliability. For this example, engaging staff in a process that includes double scoring may serve to decrease the variance in the scoring process. Whatever the measure, work hard to apply it fairly and consistently among all stakeholders. Here are examples of relevant measures that district mathematics leaders might include.

- Increased student achievement on standardized assessments

- Reduction of achievement or opportunity gaps among student groups

- Increased number of students entering college ready for credit-bearing mathematics courses

- Increased levels of student engagement during classroom instruction

- Increased and equitable access to rigorous mathematics courses by all student groups

- Increased levels of students' hope, well-being, and engagement

When the MLT is developing performance measures for the strategic plan, it is important to use common language to support the process. Nothing derails a strategic planning process faster than misunderstanding or miscommunication. It is wise to address a few common misunderstandings prior to writing performance measures. For example, many strategic plans become ineffective because their authors confuse *outputs* with *outcomes*. Outputs are the actions stakeholders will take in pursuit of the stated goal. Outcomes are positive changes that result from the outputs. So when working with the MLT, be sure to clarify that they will develop outputs or actions to attain a specific outcome. Refer to figure 3.1 as an example of output and outcome correlation.

Figure 3.1: Example of output and outcome correlation.

Another common misconception is to confuse *assessments* with *performance measures*. Assessments are tools or systems to collect data. Performance measures involve applying assessments to provide evidence of progress. Examples of assessments include standardized tests, interviews, portfolios, and clinical observation. Examples of performance measures are how much growth students demonstrated on a standardized assessment, how classroom climate improved as evidenced by interviews, and how much more frequently teachers infused their classroom lessons with high-cognitive-demand questions. As the leader, be sure members of your MLT are using terminology correctly and consistently. Take time to discuss expectations and to review examples of well-written performance measures. A small investment of time at this stage of the process ensures that you are able to measure progress toward your targets effectively.

When developing performance measures, collecting data, and sharing data reports, be sure to carefully consider the frequency. Well-designed strategic plans include milestones or benchmarks as indicators of incremental success. Benchmarks provide leaders and the MLT with checkpoints throughout the implementation process. For example, if the SMART goal is, "By May 31, the percentage of students earning a 550 or higher on the mathematics section of the SAT will increase by 15 percent," then an appropriate benchmark might be this: "The number of students earning 550 or higher will increase by 3 percent for each of the June, October, December, January, and March administrations of the SAT."

Benchmarks are associated with performance measures and strategies. If one of the strategies for meeting the SMART goal is to increase student enrollment in the after-school SAT prep program by three hundred students during the goal period, then an appropriate milestone might be, "The number of students enrolled in the quarterly after-school SAT prep programs will increase by sixty students during each of the offered periods (Summer, Fall, Winter, and Spring)."

Setting appropriate milestones assists the MLT in measuring progress along the way, providing leaders and collaborative teams with opportunities to make midcourse corrections.

Inevitably, despite your MLT's careful planning and goal setting, you learn that you are not on track to meet your intended goal. Or, in some cases, you find that you have already met your stated goals. In either case, your reponsibility as a leader is to adjust your targets accordingly. During this phase of review, it is appropriate to adjust performance measures or strategies, or even change course entirely. There are a number of factors influencing your strategic plan; if the plan becomes untenable, you may have to revise or rewrite your SMART goal. This is a natural part of the strategic planning process. When this occurs, work with the MLT to identify root causes and determine whether you can write a different SMART goal to realize this part of the vision. If you do develop another SMART goal, be sure to include clear performance measures.

3 Celebrate Success—A Leadership Action

Throughout your tenure as a mathematics leader, you will engage in very challenging and emotionally charged work. Ensuring that every student receives a rigorous mathematics learning experience is the kind of endeavor that will test your will, discipline, and leadership capacity. Teachers, colleagues, community members, and MLT members will look to you for energy and inspiration when times get tough. Becoming intentional about thoughtful and meaningful celebration is one way to provide that energy and inspiration to your community.

Timothy Kanold (2011) describes the importance of celebration, asserting, "Your ability to turn vision into action is built upon the foundation and trained practice in the discipline of *accountability* and *celebration*" (p. 36). He goes on to say:

> *These two elements of school leadership, accountability and celebration, are tightly interwoven. Both are necessary to drive every continuous improvement effort you will lead. Account-*
> *ability without celebration—of improved results and the adult action that led to those*

results—leads to diminished hope, uncertainty, disengagement, and a general lack of aware-ness that action and implementation of the vision actually make a difference. (p. 36)

As Kanold notes in this explanation, celebration is an intentional leadership action necessary to achieve your vision. There are two main reasons to engage in intentional celebration: (1) celebrating the change you wish to see in others will help influence the community toward that change, and (2) community members engaged in difficult improvement efforts frankly deserve it. Although the reasons to celebrate are clear, what leaders should celebrate is perhaps a bit less apparent. We identify three areas worthy of celebration: (1) change and risk taking, (2) teachers working with struggling students, and (3) the values of the mathematics program.

Celebrating the change you wish to see in others is an important leadership action. Throughout the very difficult change process, a few teachers and leaders step forward and take highly visible professional risks. Sometimes, these risks pay off with desired outcomes. For example, a teacher introduces concrete models that help students understand and explain why the division-of-fractions algorithm actually makes sense. Increased student performance as a result of this risk is worthy of celebration. However, sometimes these risks do not pro-duce immediate student gains. For example, think about a teacher who introduces algebra tiles to help students understand and explain how the FOIL (first, outside, inside, last) method is an application of the distributive property represented as an area model. The teacher observes increases in student frustration and decreases in student achievement. This outcome might not seem worthy of celebration, but the professional risk taken by the teacher certainly is. As the leader, if your goal is to establish and nurture a community that values risk taking for students and teachers alike, then be prepared to celebrate those risks as voraciously as you celebrate gains in district test scores. (In fact, you may want to celebrate the risk taking even more.) When other teachers see that you value risk taking in the classroom, they are more likely to take risks themselves. You want teachers to persevere when taking risks, and you can reinforce that perseverance with celebration.

Another example of celebrating the change you wish to see in others is to recognize teachers of the students with the greatest needs. Many school districts celebrate SAT or AP scores very publicly. But what message do districts send to teachers when they celebrate AP performance while largely ignoring the efforts of teachers teaching mathematics to the students who struggle most? Teachers of struggling students may begin to say, "As soon as I can, I will work toward a change in my teaching schedule so that I can teach AP courses and then be celebrated for my efforts." You certainly don't want exceptional teachers, skilled in reaching reluctant learners, to feel that they need to give up on struggling learners to receive well-deserved recognition. As the leader, find ways to flip the script of traditional high school celebrations. Continue celebrating students' suc-cesses in AP courses, but celebrate the gains made by struggling students in those ninth-grade mathematics courses even more, maybe even three times as much. Then teachers tell themselves, "My district seems to really understand and appreciate how hard I am working to help these struggling students achieve. I will continue to work with these students because I can see how much my work means to the lives of students who are just starting, thanks to me, to meet with success in mathematics." See the difference? Celebrating success is a leadership action that helps move your vision from concept, to action, and finally to realization.

 The other reason to engage in intentional celebration is because community members deserve it. Teachers, leaders, families, and members of the MLT all work hard to do what is best for students. Based on the evolving body of research related to mathematics teaching and learning, stakeholders are likely doing so in different ways or with a different sense of purpose or intentionality and their commitment, by its very nature, requires additional time from stakeholders. As leaders, we have to honor that commitment through meaningful recognition and heartfelt celebration. Many teachers

can go a whole month without hearing how much their work is appreciated. That cannot be characteristic of your mathematics community. Leaders must work to create a community in which teachers never go an entire week (or even an entire day) without meaningful celebration or an expression of appreciation. As the leader, take time to celebrate the actions of those you lead every day. Take time to celebrate the change you observe in others, and take time to show how much you appreciate the community members. Make sure all members of the mathematics community understand that you value them for their contributions. Further, encourage members of the MLT and site-based mathematics leaders to get into the habit of doing the same. You will see, very quickly, that intentional celebration strengthens your community and brings a measure of respect and honor to the exact group of people who have earned and deserve it.

Move From Vision to Action

As an effective mathematics leader, you have worked with the MLT to develop clear performance measures that answer the questions, How much growth or progress do we intend to achieve? and How will we know when we have achieved it? Reporting on the district's progress provides opportunities to celebrate hard-earned gains and the mathematics leaders have worked to develop a culture that celebrates risk taking, professional growth, and the hard work of community members who deserve praise. Table 3.1 describes the relationship among district-, site-, and team-level commitments with developing measures of success and celebrating that success.

Table 3.1: Mathematics Leadership Commitments to Establish Measures of Success

District's Role	Site-Level Leader's Role	Collaborative Team's Role
Lead the development and articulation of performance measures that mark progress toward realizing the vision for exemplary mathematics teaching and learning.	Facilitate data discussions to monitor performance measures and to inform instructional design.	Routinely collect data and monitor progress toward stated goals.
Nurture a culture of celebration, in which all teachers and leaders receive meaningful praise for their work weekly.	Celebrate the efforts of teachers and leaders working hard to improve the mathematics learning experience for students.	Celebrate the efforts of colleagues working hard to improve the mathematics learning experience for students.

*Visit **go.SolutionTree.com/leadership** for a free reproducible version of this table.*

Reflection

Review the Key 1 audit statements regarding establishing measures of success in figure 3.2, and with your MLT, reflect on your current strengths and opportunities to grow. Describe specific action steps to support these Key 1 statements and add the next steps to the reproducible action plan in appendix A (page 169).

Key 1: Establish Measures of Success	Next Steps
The vision of the mathematics program promotes equity and access to rich, meaningful mathematics for all students.	
Mathematics leaders continually monitor the vision of teaching and learning and consistently provide feedback to teachers, administrators, students, and parents.	
Mathematics leaders clearly define, monitor, and celebrate measures of success with stakeholders during the school year.	
Each collaborative team sets SMART goals aligned to the district mathematics vision.	
Student enrollment in advanced coursework (AP, college-level courses, and so on) proportionally represents district demographics.	
The entire system utilizes evidence of data-driven processes. Collaborative teams adapt instruction based on student thinking, use trends in benchmark assessments to modify curriculum, use trends in student performance to create or modify interventions, and use data to drive decision-making processes.	
Mathematics leaders provide meaningful, action-oriented feedback on student performance and clearly communicate it to all stakeholders.	

Figure 3.2: Key 1—Establish measures of success.

*Visit **go.SolutionTree.com/leadership** for a free reproducible version of this figure.*

Next Steps for Mathematics Leaders With Key 1

The big ideas of Key 1 require a collaboratively written and clearly articulated vision for exemplary mathematics teaching and learning. This vision permeates the actions mathematics leaders, site leaders, and collaborative teams take to support increased student achievement. Using figure 3.3 (page 44) and with your MLT, reflect on the level of engagement and implementation for Key 1, establishing a clear vision for mathematics teaching and learning.

Exemplary Evidence of Engagement and Implementation	Strong Evidence of Engagement and Implementation	Partial Evidence of Engagement and Implementation	Limited Evidence of Engagement and Implementation
Through the MLT, a vision for exemplary mathematics teaching and learning is collaboratively developed and strengthened using input from all stakeholders.	Through the MLT, a vision for exemplary mathematics teaching and learning is collaboratively developed.	A vision for exemplary mathematics teaching and learning is developed but is not collaboratively created by all stakeholders or the MLT.	A vision for exemplary mathematics teaching and learning does not exist.
Mathematics leaders teach the vision to all stakeholders and each community member designs effective practices so that he or she can work to realize the vision through his or her actions.	Mathematics leaders teach the vision to all stakeholders so that each community member understands his or her role in realizing the vision.	Mathematics leaders share the vision with all stakeholders.	Mathematics leaders inconsistently share the vision with stakeholders.
All stakeholders consistently engage in processes and implement and refine effective actions aligned to the vision.	All stakeholders routinely engage in processes and implement effective actions aligned to the vision.	Some stakeholders inconsistently engage in processes and implement effective actions aligned to the vision.	Few stakeholders engage in processes or implement effective actions aligned to the vision.
Mathematics leaders and stakeholders collaboratively create processes for infusing the vision into school improvement plans with clear systems for self-monitoring to gauge effective implementation of the vision.	Mathematics leaders create processes for monitoring effective implementation of the vision.	Mathematics leaders create top-down processes for monitoring implementation of the vision at broad levels.	Systems for monitoring exemplary mathematics teaching and learning do not exist.
All stakeholders participate in a pervasive culture of accountability and celebration.	Most stakeholders participate in the existing culture of accountability and celebration.	Some stakeholders participate in the existing culture of accountability and celebration.	A culture of accountability and celebration does not exist.

Figure 3.3: Reflection tool for Key 1.

*Visit **go.SolutionTree.com/leadership** for a free reproducible version of this figure.*

The mathematics leaders' actions in Key 1 are creating a focus for the work of the MLT, collaborative teams, and site-level leaders. After the MLT is empowered and committed to equity and excellence for all students, it develops a vision and a plan for creating a culture of transparency, trust, and creative problem solving. The MLT will develop SMART goals and consistently set measures of success to meet those goals. The district-level leader, site-level leader, teacher leader, and members of collaborative teams will monitor the work toward established goals while creating and nurturing a culture of accountability and celebration.

Once the vision is created and all stakeholders are setting goals aligned to support the vision, it is time to focus on supportive conditions for building capacity through meaningful professional learning. Teachers, collaborative teams, district-level leaders, and site-level leaders will need to engage in continuous professional learning aligned to the teaching and learning vision.

Key 2 Overview:

Support Visionary Professional Learning for Teachers and Teacher Leaders

> *Leadership is about learning that leads to constructive change. Learning is among the participants and therefore occurs collectively. Learning has direction toward a shared purpose. Leading is a shared endeavor. The learning journey must be shared; otherwise, shared purpose and action are never achieved.*
>
> —Linda Lambert

Stakeholders' actions to cooperatively support the vision for teaching and learning are essential to effective mathematics curriculum, instruction, and assessment. In Key 2, we turn to exploring how to build the capacity of site leaders, collaborative teams, and teacher leaders. These are the people who collectively bring the mathematics vision to life. It takes great leadership to build great teams, and one individual cannot implement the vision alone. Jim Kouzes and Barry Posner (2003), who have researched leadership over their careers, describe the importance of collective support and participation to ensuring success:

> *In the thousands of cases we've studied, we've yet to encounter a single example of extraordinary achievement that didn't involve the active participation and support of many people. We've yet to find a single instance in which one talented person—leader or individual contributor—accounted for most, let alone 100 percent, of the success. (p. 22)*

Essential to Key 2 of mathematics leadership is the commitment to creating structures for shared leadership, accountability, and responsibility for continual student *and* adult learning.

The big ideas and essential understandings of Key 2 prepare mathematics leaders to engage in the following leadership actions.

- ◆ Ensure that collaboration is a vital element of continual professional learning through job-embedded learning opportunities for all stakeholders.

- ◆ Align high-quality professional learning to the vision for exemplary mathematics teaching and learning and systematically develop it with input from all stakeholders.

- ◆ Create multiple opportunities to develop and foster mathematics teacher leadership.

- ◆ Conduct ongoing mathematics leadership development for grade-level, course-level, and site-level leaders.

4

Engage Teachers in Worthwhile and Differentiated Professional Learning

Ultimately there are two kinds of schools: learning-enriched schools and learning-impoverished schools. I have yet to see a school where the learning curves . . . of the adults were steep upward and those of the students were not. Teachers and students go hand in hand as learners—or they don't go at all.

—Roland Barth

The vision is complete and all stakeholders have agreed to support it. Leaders and teachers can collectively describe what a good mathematics classroom looks like and have a clear understanding of what they should hear when students are engaged in mathematics. But does every teacher know *how* to create and implement lessons aligned to the essential learning standards using high-quality assessment processes that support the vision for teaching and learning? Raising expectations for student understanding requires an increased level of expectations for teacher learning. When reviewing the vision statement and the collective commitments for teaching and learning mathematics, leaders must intentionally support mathematics teachers and collaborative teams. They must ensure that professional learning provides opportunities to grow for *all* levels of mathematics teachers and leaders. They must ensure that professional learning is high quality and continuous. Professional learning is more than just a set of activities that we want teachers to experience on the next district release day. The reauthorized ESSA (2015) has defined *professional learning* as the following:

> [Activities that] (A) are an integral part of school and local education agency strategies for providing educators (including teachers, principals, other school leaders, specialized instructional support personnel, paraprofessionals, and, as applicable, early childhood

educators) with the knowledge and skills necessary to enable students to succeed in the core academic subjects and to meet challenging State academic standards; and (B) are sustained (not stand-alone, 1-day, and short-term workshops), intensive, collaborative, job-embedded, data-driven, classroom-focused. (p. 295)

The professional growth of classroom teachers and leaders may require them to develop both content knowledge and pedagogical knowledge—with the ultimate goal of increasing student achievement. Highly effective mathematics leaders create systems and structures to support adults' diverse learning needs to enhance collective capacity in meeting all students' diverse learning needs.

In this chapter, you will learn effective strategies for developing collective capacity within the mathematics program as a critical component for continual growth and learning. First, we will explore how mathematics leaders identify learning needs and ensure that professional learning is supported by and aligned to the vision. Mathematics leaders must also plan to build interest and create opportunities to practice and reflect on the new learning. Intentional planning is required to prioritize and build learning progression. You're crafting a thorough three- to five-year plan for building collective capacity to meet the vision for teaching and learning mathematics.

At the beginning of the next professional learning session, ask the participants, What will make our time together today a successful learning experience? Give participants time to reflect on the question and then have them share their responses with the person beside them. As authors, we have asked this question over the years and are still amazed at the variety of answers—and the assumptions or predispositions evident in the responses. When planning professional learning, take into account that one size does not necessarily fit all. Participants need to understand the purpose of professional learning to value the experience, realize its benefits for them and their students, and learn what they will need to do differently. Mathematics leaders need to articulate the purpose and consider a differentiated professional learning plan to meet the diverse learning needs of educators, mathematics team leaders, other leaders, and peers. Mathematics leaders also need to plan multiple opportunities for engagement through vertical grade-level, site-level, and district-level collaboration.

> ### Effective Leadership Tip
>
> *As a leader, you need to articulate the purpose and consider a differentiated professional learning plan to meet the diverse learning needs of educators, the mathematics team and other leaders, and peers.*

Collaboration is a vital element of continual professional learning and capacity building. Michael Fullan (2011) describes the power of collaborative teams:

Time and again we see the power of collective capacity. When the group is mobilized with focus and specificity, it can accomplish amazing results. . . . The collaborative, sometimes known as professional learning communities, get these results because not only are leaders being influential, but peers are supporting and pressuring each other to do better. (p. 9)

NCTM (2014) reiterates that professionalism is an essential element of an exemplary mathematics program due to the tendency of educators to "hold themselves and their colleagues accountable for the mathematical success of every student and for their personal and collective professional growth toward effective teaching and learning of mathematics" (p. 99).

The importance of developing collective capacity within the mathematics program is critical to continual growth and learning. Shifting the focus between support of each individual teacher and support of the collective whole is an essential leadership skill for improving the entire mathematics program. To begin the intentional planning, we shift our attention to aligning professional learning to the district vision.

Align Professional Learning With Specific Learning Needs

Before mathematics leaders send out an advertisement or plan a professional learning opportunity, effective mathematics leaders begin aligning professional learning opportunities to the district and site mathematics department mission, vision, values, and goals. With the MLT, analyze the current action steps listed in appendix A (or the gaps in the audit in figure 1.4, page 12). What learning opportunities do the action steps require? Leaders consider the following questions before crafting professional learning opportunities.

- What mathematical content knowledge for teachers and leaders is necessary to meet our student achievement goals?

- What specific instructional strategies do we want to ensure all teachers and leaders fully understand and employ (strengthening pedagogy)?

- What part of our vision for exemplary teaching and learning do we not meet (strengthening accountability)?

- Does the faculty have the capacity to notice, analyze, and respond to students' mathematical thinking (strengthening assessment)?

- Do teachers' mindsets help or hinder student K–12 progression toward advanced mathematics coursework (strengthening beliefs)?

As you and your MLT reflect upon these questions, discuss what specific professional learning is needed to support the action steps. When mathematics programs have multiple learning needs, it is important to provide focus for teachers and teacher teams.

Be cautious of initiative fatigue. Trying to change too many things at once could actually result in changing nothing at all. A solid mathematics professional learning plan pays attention to potential initiative overload. When planning, leaders take into account the daily demands of the profession, including recent professional learning initiatives and the staff's current workload. Effective mathematics leaders will want to carefully plan professional learning progressions to support the successful implementation of the professional learning plan. Ask MLT members to brainstorm all of the professional learning needs in figure 4.1 (page 52) and prioritize them according to which year the professional learning will be introduced and mastered.

Professional learning needed	
Who needs the training?	
Who will provide the training?	
How is the professional learning connected to the mission, vision, values, and goals?	
Time frame of professional learning	
First year	
Second year	
Third year	
Fourth year	
Fifth year	

Figure 4.1: Professional learning planning tool.

Visit **go.SolutionTree.com/leadership** *for a free reproducible version of this figure.*

Well-thought-out professional learning plans should clearly illustrate initiatives that span three to five years to ensure all stakeholders understand that every action supports the overarching vision. A thorough blueprint for professional learning should be crafted collaboratively by the MLT and communicated transparently to all stakeholders.

Scenario

A district crafts the following vision statement.

We want to excel in all areas of teaching and learning. We want to be the role model of collaborative learning for teachers and students.

The mathematics leadership team identifies cooperative learning as a promising practice and a focus area for collaborative teams to increase student-to-student discourse. The MLT plans to provide training in cooperative learning for teachers, time for teachers to learn new structures over the course of a school year, a space to share ideas and improve structures, and training for site leaders to guide the development of support systems to monitor and sustain cooperative learning.

Figure 4.2 is an example of the district's professional learning plan and the implementation sequencing of more meaningful student-to-student discourse.

Professional learning needed	Cooperative learning structures to support structured student-to-student discourse
Who needs the training?	Teachers new to the district in the last five years Teachers who participated in previous years (refresher)
Who will provide the training?	District mathematics coach and site-level instructional coach
How is the professional learning connected to the mission, vision, values, and goals?	Our vision is to become a role model for collaborative learning for students.
Time frame of professional learning	Two to three years .
First year	Introduction Create library of strategy examples Curriculum teams write lesson plan to model specific structures
Second year	Instructional rounds and lesson study
Third year	Training for new faculty Monitoring to support areas of challenge

Figure 4.2: Professional learning plan example.

Achieving a change in instructional practice cannot occur overnight. Therefore, professional development plans should support incremental growth of the community over time. Mathematics leaders must first identify the learning need and then plan how to build interest and create opportunities to practice and reflect on the new learning. Utilizing the following five-step creative process from Mihaly Csikszentmihalyi (1996), mathematics leaders plan for and embrace the necessary steps to support district goals.

1. **Preparation:** becoming immersed in problematic issues that are interesting and arouse curiosity
2. **Incubation:** having ideas churning around below the threshold of consciousness
3. **Insight:** having the "Aha!" moment when the puzzle starts to fall together
4. **Evaluation:** deciding if the insight is valuable and worth pursuing
5. **Elaboration:** translating this insight into its final form

What professional learning supports your vision statements? Figure 4.3 (page 54) is a professional learning progression example that uses the five steps of the creative process to develop a district's shared understanding of differentiated instruction. Using the same phases of planning and the planning tool in figure 4.1 (page 52), your MLT can develop a learning plan to support a specific learning need. Go to appendix A (page 169) for a reproducible blank template.

Instructional Vision: Move collaborative teams away from providing direct instruction for all students to providing differentiated instruction.	
Step Considerations	**Plan for Professional Learning**
Step 1: Preparation ◆ Define key terms. ◆ Develop common understanding. ◆ Create measurable targets. ◆ Conduct research. **Questions to Address** ◆ How does this new learning connect to what we have already learned? ◆ Do we have a shared understanding?	◆ Define differentiation. ◆ Research differentiation. ◆ Describe what differentiation looks like in a classroom. ◆ List specific differentiation strategies. ◆ Provide research to inform shared understanding of differentiation. ◆ Look for entry points into the differentiation learning progression. ◆ Identify what teachers and leaders already know about differentiation.
Step 2: Incubation ◆ Compare various understandings of the topic. ◆ Develop a common understanding and possible solutions. ◆ Analyze measurable targets. ◆ Research and discuss the topic, possible solutions, and targets. **Questions to Address** ◆ What better ideas and practices can we generate? ◆ How will our team integrate this new learning?	◆ Identify different types of differentiation to try as a collaborative team. ◆ Brainstorm how to apply researched solutions/strategies. ◆ Set SMART goals with measurable action steps. ◆ Design lessons with differentiation. ◆ Share strategies for differentiation. ◆ Plan learning opportunities for teachers across sites to share teams' progress.
Step 3: Insight ◆ Analyze various aspects of the topic. ◆ Deploy the new initiatives or changes. ◆ Collect data and explore how to read them. ◆ Start to use new practices. **Question to Address** ◆ How might we support implementation?	◆ Compare student work using differentiation strategies. ◆ Implement action steps tied to SMART goals. ◆ Implement lessons with differentiation. ◆ Engage in action research, lesson studies, and instructional rounds.

Step Considerations	Plan for Professional Learning
Step 4: Evaluation • Analyze the various stages of the new initiative or change. • Collect data and explore how to analyze and use them to change practice. • Use new practices. • Create feedback loops to analyze implementation, measure targets, and make changes to fit individual needs. **Questions to Address** • How well is this practice connected to successful outcomes? • How well is this practice working?	• Collect evidence of student thinking after employing the differentiation strategy. • Reflect on student data from different differentiation strategies. • Collect instructional data so teams can reflect on differentiation strategies. • Complete lessons and tasks that exemplify differentiation. • Provide feedback to peers on implementation.
Step 5: Elaboration • Analyze predictive and reactive data. • Use feedback loops. • Use technology and strategies at a mastery level. **Questions to Address** • How might the idea connect to other applications? • Can we use the idea in other capacities?	• Connect differentiation to developing the Standards for Mathematical Practice (or other content and pedagogy practices) as a team. • Embed differentiation into team practices. • Reflect consistently as a team on the successes and challenges of implementing differentiation strategies.

Sources: Adapted from Armstrong, 2014; Csikszentmihalyi, 1996.

Figure 4.3: Professional learning progression.

Please note that the collaborative team's work is a vital component of the professional learning plan. If the professional learning plan includes opportunities for new learning and no expectation that the collaborative team develops and self-monitors the new content or pedagogy, we limit capacity building and, worse, lose the time we spent fostering teacher learning.

Differentiate Professional Learning

Mathematics leaders must understand that the needs of collaborative teams and individual teachers are different. Recognizing that, leaders must provide differentiated professional learning that honors those differences, strengthening both the individual team members and the whole team simultaneously. Adult learners need voice and

> **Effective Leadership Tip**
>
> *As a leader, share your five-year plan digitally to embrace feedback as a continual learning process. Visit https://goo.gl/SLgvr0 for an example of a five-year plan. The link https://goo.gl/nE7QRb takes you to a reflection on a five-year plan. Finally, like the example located at http://goo.gl/NoPYbR, you could write a blog post.*

choice, just as students do with differentiation strategies. Once you have identified professional learning priorities, provide several levels of support. Some team members will be early adopters and embrace new learning, while other collaborative teams will need multiple opportunities to engage. Figure 4.4 is a learning menu example from which collaborative teams and individual teachers can choose their level of support.

Team Learning	Individual Learning
◆ Focusing on mathematics teaching practices	◆ Using lesson design and focused work on instructional shifts
◆ Planning to select, implement, and support mathematical tasks	◆ Building understanding of student Standards for Mathematical Practice, processes, and standards
◆ Designing lessons	◆ Using practice-forward mathematics tasks to intentionally develop the Standards for Mathematical Practice
◆ Developing an educator toolkit for instructional strategies	
◆ Studying lessons	◆ Employing student-to-student discourse
◆ Conducting instructional rounds	◆ Using video self-reflection
◆ Using PLC progression of learning	◆ Employing mathematical instruction look-fors to gain observational feedback
◆ Using instruction artifacts for before, during, and after the unit	◆ Discussing content (mathematics gatherings)
◆ Looking at student work	
◆ Hosting content discussions (mathematics gatherings)	◆ Providing curriculum training
◆ Providing curriculum training	◆ Developing assessment
◆ Developing assessments	◆ Providing technology training
◆ Providing technology training	◆ Providing instructional resource training
◆ Aligning teams vertically (across grade levels)	◆ Modeling lessons
	◆ Coplanning
◆ Hosting book clubs	◆ Using collaborative coaching (prepare, plan, teach the lesson, observe, and debrief)
◆ Planning units	

Figure 4.4: Menu of mathematics job-embedded professional development example.

Refusing to engage in new learning is not an option; the menu creates an individualized approach to supporting diverse learning needs.

Collaborative teams, site-level leaders, and district leaders will also create a plan of action for the school year to model transparency. The plan lays out three expectations for teacher professional learning.

1. Professional learning models alignment to the district and site vision for mathematics teaching and learning.

2. The district and site provide collaborative teams choices in their professional learning that will support necessary action steps to meet their SMART goal.

3. The district and MLT provide site leaders with an arsenal of professional learning opportunities to align them with teacher needs.

Appendix C (page 189) supplies a district professional learning calendar example with descriptions. When reviewing the plan, notice the alignment between the district vision and the specific learning opportunities, as well as the diversity within the types of learning. By the same token, mathematics leaders also need to attend to the quality of these opportunities.

Think about the last professional learning session that you attended—what made it memorable or what would you have done differently to make it more meaningful? When planning professional learning, mathematics leaders need to certify that the experience will be meaningful and high quality. Learning Forward's (2011) Standards for Professional Learning identify seven specific characteristics of quality professional learning. They include learning communities, leadership, resources, data, learning designs, implementation, and outcomes. When crafting the professional learning plan, work with your MLT to concentrate on each characteristic by answering the questions in table 4.1.

Table 4.1: Questions for Consideration Aligned to the Learning Forward (2011) Standards for Professional Learning

Characteristics of Quality Professional Learning	Questions to Consider When Planning
Learning Communities	How will we engage collaborative teams in professional learning? How will we ensure that professional learning aligns to our mission, vision, values, and goals?
Leadership	Who will lead the professional learning? How will we build capacity? What other systems will we need to support professional learning?
Resources	What are our priorities? How will we monitor and provide feedback to teachers and site leaders when implementing the new learning?
Data	What data will we use to inform our professional learning priorities? What variety of data will we use to inform our plan? How will we evaluate the success of professional learning?
Learning Designs	What is the best learning design to support the learning plan (for example, face-to-face meetings, an online environment, or in workshops; during district professional development days, summer, or extended time, and so on)? What experiences will support participants in learning? How will we differentiate the plan to meet the needs of diverse learners?
Implementation	How will teachers and collaborative teams engage in evidence-based goal setting and action for the next unit? What are the intended long-term goals?
Outcomes	What are the defined learning outcomes for the participants? How will the new professional learning impact students' learning? Are the outcomes for students aligned to the professional learning plan?

Source: Adapted from Learning Forward, 2011.

*Visit **go.SolutionTree.com/leadership** for a free reproducible version of this table.*

After new learning, teachers and collaborative teams set evidence-based goals and take action on an upcoming unit of instruction. To activate new learning, teachers and collaborative teams need time. The time needed to apply new learning varies greatly depending on the task. Evidence of growth might not be observable by the end of an instructional unit, or even several months, a full school year, or several years.

For example, consider a teacher assigned to teach an AP course for the first time. The first year of teaching the course feels like a race to get through the content and understand the depth, coherence, and rigor of the course. Sometimes the teacher might teach a course for two or three years before grasping the expectations of the AP curriculum. The application of new learning requires ample time to incubate, grow, and solidify through multiple learning opportunities, conversations, and explorations.

The mathematics professional learning plan should provide teachers with opportunities during the school day for job-embedded professional learning and collaboration. Educators can use this collaboration time for action research, lesson studies, instructional rounds, and leveraging a mathematics coach's or mentor teacher's support to test out the new learning and take risks in a safe environment. Just as teachers encourage students to embrace mistakes and develop a growth mindset, leaders must urge teachers and teacher leaders in the same way. Securing collaborative team time is valuable and supports the team's work to activate the vision in a culture of peer accountability.

Build a Culture of Continuous Learning

The following section is adapted from Barnes, 2015.

Mathematics leaders constantly search for creative structures to support multiple district mathematics goals and initiatives. Effective leaders create innovative professional learning structures focused on the following goals.

- Build a closely knit community of teachers and leaders who see themselves as the experts they aspire to be and cultivate a spirit of "Together, we can do anything."

- Build a culture of facilitative leadership.

- Develop systems to ensure equitable access to rigorous mathematics for all students.

- Improve the quality of mathematics teaching and learning in every classroom by providing timely professional learning to stakeholders.

- Strengthen teachers' understanding of new content standards.

- Strengthen teachers' understanding of effective pedagogy.

- Engage students in the design and implementation of professional learning initiatives.

- Engage the mathematics community in the design and implementation of professional learning initiatives.

- Build the leadership capacity of system leaders and site-based mathematics leaders and administrators.

- Build the leadership capacity of emerging mathematics leaders.

- Spotlight outstanding practitioners and their best ideas.

- Celebrate the work of the mathematics community and its members.

As one can imagine, trying to build a new professional learning structure that serves all of these purposes is daunting. Here is an example of how one district pushed its professional learning to a new level.

The Math Gatherings

The mathematics leadership team in the Howard County Public School System (HCPSS) develops a professional learning system called math gatherings. *The district mathematics office hosts these gatherings, which are monthly professional learning events. Teachers, students, and leaders from each of the thirty-three secondary schools in the district lead them collaboratively. Each month, members of the mathematics community receive invitations to attend all or part of a three-hour math gathering to network, collaboratively plan lessons or assessments, watch and critique mathematics teaching in action, or learn new ideas from their peers. To help tailor teachers' and leaders' individual learning experiences, HCPSS presents math gatherings in a variety of learning formats, such as the learning lab, the collaborative planning hub, and the miniconference.*

The learning lab is a live teaching event during which a featured teacher engages students in a minilesson or task. Participants meet prior to the lesson to preview the task and learn about the focus of the lesson they will observe, taking note of the intended Standards for Mathematical Practice (NGA & CCSSO, 2010), the intended Mathematics Teaching Practices (NCTM, 2014), and the intended content standard. After the orientation, teachers enter the classroom and observe the lesson. After the lesson, participants question the students and the teacher. Students also have the opportunity to ask questions of the teacher or the process observers.

The collaborative planning hub is a space for teams of course-alike teachers to plan collaboratively. Course-level lead teachers facilitate a brief overview of the upcoming major content strands. Teams use systemic planning tools and templates to design resources to support instruction for those content strands. The MLT encourages teams to share their planned resources on the district's open-source curricular resources site (HCPSS, n.d.).

The miniconference is a series of conference-style sessions that provide opportunities for teachers to learn from other teachers or teacher leaders. The sessions focus on content development through the use of research-informed pedagogy. Participants have the opportunity to improve skills, gain knowledge, and receive resources, which immediately supports their classroom instruction.

The math gatherings have been a signature series of events for the mathematics program of the Howard County Public School System. Over the first three years of the initiative, the district hosted more than twenty gatherings. Between 20 percent and 50 percent of the secondary mathematics teaching staff attended the sessions, and more than fifty unique members of the mathematics community—about 18 percent— served in a leadership capacity. Howard County leaders observed, as a significant measure of progress, the emergence of a highly connected, yet interdependent, team of professionals that values continual learning (Barnes, Wray, & Novak, 2015). The observation of progress was supported by:

- *An increase in the number of mathematics teachers seeking school-based or district-level mathematics leadership positions*

- *An increase in the number of students who have access to rigorous mathematics programming at all levels due to the identification and support of caring professionals*

- *An increase in student awareness of and engagement with the Standards for Mathematical Practice during mathematics lessons*

Once the professional learning plan is in action, the MLT needs to constantly evaluate the process and the impact on teacher and student learning, and adjust or revise the plan. The MLT examines:

- Participants' reactions

- The degree of participants' learning

- Participants' use of the professional learning content

- The degree of support and change in the organization resulting from professional learning

- The effect of professional learning on students' learning and achievement

Feedback from all stakeholders is critical to sustain the plan. All participants appreciate a voice in the process. When creating the action steps for professional learning in appendix A (page 169), be sure to include an evaluation component.

Move From Vision to Action

To review, the MLT plans critical steps when supporting professional learning to meet the vision of teaching and learning mathematics, including prioritizing the professional learning, crafting a thorough three- to five-year plan, and demanding high-quality professional learning experiences. Table 4.2 describes the relationships and roles among district-, site-, and team-level commitments to engage teachers in worthwhile and differentiated professional learning.

Table 4.2: Mathematics Leadership Commitments to Engage Teachers in Worthwhile and Differentiated Professional Learning

District's Role	Site-Level Leader's Role	Collaborative Team's Role
Establish multiple systems to support collaboration as a vital element of continual professional learning.	Monitor and provide feedback to grade-level or course-based collaborative teams to support continual learning.	Value collaboration as a means for continual learning.
Work with the district mathematics leadership team to align professional learning opportunities to the district vision.	Ensure collaborative teams and site leaders engage in opportunities for professional learning that support alignment with district vision.	Grade- and course-level team leaders work with team members to evaluate current learning opportunities and align teams' action steps and professional learning to support the district vision.
Create a systemic plan for professional learning that attends to progression of learning and focuses on building the capacity of all stakeholders.	Ensure collaborative teams engage in professional learning and provide systemic support for learning progressions to build team capacity.	Evaluate and reflect on grade- and course-level teams' progress in professional learning and request additional support when needed.
Provide high-quality professional learning and consistently evaluate, revise, and revisit it when needed.	Attend high-quality professional learning and consistently provide feedback to adapt or revise the professional learning plan when needed.	Engage in high-quality professional learning with the collaborative team and consistently provide feedback to adapt or revise the professional learning plan when needed.

*Visit **go.SolutionTree.com/leadership** for a free reproducible version of this table.*

Reflection

Review the Key 2 statements about engaging teachers in worthwhile and differentiated professional learning in figure 4.5 and with your MLT, reflect on your current strengths and opportunities to grow. Describe specific next steps to support Key 2 in relation to professional learning.

Key 2: Engage Teachers in Worthwhile and Differentiated Professional Learning	Next Steps
Collaboration is a vital element of continual professional learning. Every part of the mathematics program (curriculum development, professional learning, and so on) shows evidence of collaborative structures.	
The collaborative team's work is a vital component of the district professional learning plan.	
District and site schedules permit job-embedded professional learning and time for collaboration during the school day.	
Professional learning opportunities align to the district or site mission, vision, values, and goals.	
After new professional learning, teachers and collaborative teams engage in evidence-based goal setting and action for the next unit.	
All collaborative team members work to activate the vision and support the team's work through peer accountability.	
District- and site-level leaders provide a professional development plan that includes multiple delivery systems with activities differentiated for the various learning needs of participants.	
District- and site-level leaders develop and implement a professional learning plan that addresses the needs identified by quantitative and qualitative data analysis. Professional development is discipline specific and job embedded but also emphasizes a whole-school approach to learning.	
The mathematics leadership team evaluates professional learning by examining participants' reactions, the degree of their learning, their use of the professional learning content, the degree of support and change in the organization resulting from the professional learning, and the effect of the professional learning on students' achievement and learning.	

Figure 4.5: Key 2—Engage teachers in worthwhile and differentiated professional learning.

Visit go.SolutionTree.com/leadership for a free reproducible version of this figure.

When crafting the action steps with the MLT, add ideas for creating a professional learning plan aligned to the vision and strategies for implementing meaningful professional learning for teachers to your action plan (appendix A, page 169). Be sure to include specific accountability measures so that district and site-based leaders clearly understand how to monitor the impact of professional learning on student learning. Once the MLT develops a clear action plan for teacher professional learning, it is ready to focus on creating similar opportunities for teacher leaders, site leaders, and district-level leaders. Chapter 5 explains this work in further detail.

5 | Develop Highly Skilled and Highly Effective Mathematics Leaders

It turns out that leadership not only matters: it is second only to teaching among school-related factors in its impact on student learning.

—Wallace Foundation

In this chapter, you will explore strategies for building capacity with existing and emerging mathematics leaders. First, you will learn how to strengthen and grow site-based mathematics leaders. Then, you will explore how to clearly define leadership roles and actions. Finally, you will learn how to design systems of communication that enable designed actions, important messages, and feedback to flow freely among schools, communities, and the district office.

Imagine a team of mathematics teachers conversing about an upcoming unit of instruction and their common assessment. What did you visualize? Did you see a collaborative team having a robust discussion and coming to consensus following agreed-on norms, or did you see a team of teachers struggling to find consensus, speaking over each other, and unwilling to listen to their peers? If you visualized the first scenario, most likely you saw a team with a leader, someone who drives meaningful conversation and holds the team accountable for meeting its goals. The team leader builds rapport with the team, encourages trust in the process of team consensus, and supports all team members' growth with content and pedagogical knowledge. Developing effective team leaders is a priority for building collective capacity within a professional learning community for mathematics teaching and learning.

Collaborative team leaders are vital to support the program's vision through shared responsibility and roles. Educational and organizational research supports this instrumental role (Elmore, 2004; Kotter, 1996; Marzano & Waters, 2009; Sergiovanni, 2005). In a K–8 setting, this may consist of grade-level team leaders together supporting their collaborative teams to meet the district vision. In a secondary setting, course-level team leaders share the responsibility of creating exemplar common assessments and ensuring their collaborative team understands the depth of each essential learning standard. In a small-school setting with singleton teachers—the only ones who teach that grade or course level—vertical teams or grade-band teams attend to students' learning progressions. Sites may have department chairs, instructional leaders, or coaches who work jointly with the team leaders and collaborative teams. Whatever the setting, creating a structure for a supportive mathematics leadership team is vital for building capacity.

Support Mathematics Leadership at All Levels

If the collaborative team is an engine for change, the team leader is the engineer. Strong mathematics programs contain several layers of sustained teacher leadership support. The MLT is the guiding coalition, in addition to the district-level (teachers from across multiple sites) and site-level (teachers from a single site) collaborative teams. Figure 5.1 is a visual representation of the district mathematics leadership structure at Phoenix Union High School District, an urban high school district in Phoenix, Arizona.

Shared leadership	District mathematics leadership team				
Districtwide teams	Curriculum teams (which create exemplar artifacts)		Teacher leader team (team leaders from every site within a district)	Singleton collaborative teams	
Site-level teams	Technology integration team	Vertical articulation team	Site-level teacher leader	Site-level course-level team	Site-level intervention team

Figure 5.1: Phoenix Union High School District mathematics shared leadership model.

Figure 5.1 models systematic collaboration between both site-level and district-level collaborative teams and cross-pollinates teams at all levels. Singleton teachers receive opportunities to collaborate with course-alike teachers across the district, both face to face in monthly meetings and virtually in more frequent interactions. Site-level teams create collaboration opportunities to attend to students' experiences in each grade level and build a progression of learning for technology and the vertical articulation of essential learning standards. Team leaders find support at both the district level and site level. They participate in district-level professional learning where they collaborate with similar grade- or course-level leaders and then drill down to specific site-level concerns with their individual site MLTs. The important part of creating leadership structures is deciding *how* to support teacher leadership throughout the system. With your MLT, complete the questions in figure 5.2.

1. How do we identify teacher leaders? What criteria do we use to select teacher leaders for collaborative teams or districtwide collaborative teams?

2. What support do collaborative teams or districtwide collaborative teams provide for teacher leadership? How frequently?

3. What incentives can we provide to team leaders for their service?

4. How do we give feedback to collaborative team leaders on their progress? How do we monitor and celebrate the teams for meeting their SMART goal?

Figure 5.2: Teacher leader reflection.

Visit **go.SolutionTree.com/leadership** *for a free reproducible version of this figure.*

When seeking candidates for exemplary teacher leaders, simply look for teachers who have varied experience. However, team leaders do not have to be experts in all areas or have all the answers. They do need the willingness to serve others, the aptitude to solve problems, the ability to create collective capacity within the team, and most of all, the relational skills to manage the complexities of team leadership. After the MLT has selected the teacher leaders and the structures for collaboration, the next step is to build common understandings of each role and leadership capacity within each role.

In conjunction with the Council of Chief State School Officers, the Teacher Leadership Exploratory Consortium (2010) developed Teacher Leader Model Standards consisting of seven domains that describe the diverse and varied dimensions of teacher leadership:

> *Domain I: Fostering a Collaborative Culture to Support Educator Development and Student Learning*
>
> *Domain II: Accessing and Using Research to Improve Practice and Student Achievement*
>
> *Domain III: Promoting Professional Learning for Continuous Improvement*
>
> *Domain IV: Facilitating Improvements in Instruction and Student Learning*
>
> *Domain V: Using Assessments and Data for School and District Improvement*
>
> *Domain VI: Improving Outreach and Collaboration with Families and Community*
>
> *Domain VII: Advocating for Student Learning and the Profession* (p. 2)

These standards for teacher leadership provide a framework that helps educators plan diverse learning opportunities to develop teacher leadership. Robert Eaker and Janel Keating (2009) describe the expectation for team leaders and the professional learning support they need:

> *Considerable thought must also be given to the kind of training and support team leaders need in order to be successful. If we expect team leaders to perform their duties at a high level, they deserve the support, resources, and training necessary to successfully do the job they are asked to do.*

To build teacher leadership that works, mathematics leaders need to clarify the purpose of teacher leadership, clearly define teacher roles, and ensure sufficient time, support, and resources.

Because improving student learning frequently requires changing teacher practice, team leaders need to work collaboratively with colleagues to support these changes. Teacher leaders act as team advocates, but as Cindy Harrison and Joellen Killion (2007) observe, they often perform many additional roles. Teachers demonstrate leadership in a variety of capacities, including but not limited to resource provider, instructional support specialist, curriculum expert, mentor, and data coach (Harrison & Killion, 2007).

Team leaders who are just beginning to develop a collaborative culture commonly ask, How do I deal with the team member who will not do _____? Regardless of what the team leader asks of his or her team, whether it is to bring their data to the team meeting, share artifact examples, or complete team tasks, the leader needs support on managing growth, change, and disengaged team members. Because improving students' mathematics learning frequently involves doing things differently from how they have been done in the past, team leaders should receive professional learning opportunities on managing the change process. In *Managing Complex Change*, Delores Ambrose (1987) presents a framework for evaluating change initiatives. To successfully manage change, teams must have vision, skills and knowledge, incentive, resources, and an action plan. For example, if a team lacks vision, the team may be confused about where it must focus. If a team lacks skills and knowledge, either content or pedagogical, the members will experience anxiety about the unknown. If a team lacks incentive, the team will feel that it has no purpose and resist change. If a team lacks resources, members believe they do not have what they need to accomplish the vision. Lastly, if there is no action plan, teams will feel like they are going nowhere fast (Ambrose, 1987). Working with team leaders, use the framework as an opportunity for reflection. Begin the conversation with your MLT by completing figure 5.3 to identify current gaps in support and possible solutions to fill them.

Vision for Mathematics Teaching and Learning	Skills and Knowledge for Content and Pedagogy	Purpose or Value—Why Are We Doing This?	Resources—Do We Have What We Need to Accomplish the Vision?	Action Plan—Do We Know What Needs to Be Done?

Figure 5.3: Evaluating the change process.

*Visit **go.SolutionTree.com/leadership** for a free reproducible version of this figure.*

Remember: change is a process, not an event. Leaders must arm team leaders with the vision of teaching and learning; the purpose of the change; resources, skills, and knowledge to implement the change; and a valid action plan to support the process. Once the MLT has identified the components necessary to support teacher leaders managing change, the next step is to ensure continual learning opportunities for teachers and teacher leaders.

Develop Teachers and Future Mathematics Leaders

Teaching is complex. Adding leadership responsibilities to the mix can overwhelm the most experienced and effective teacher. DuFour and Marzano (2011) state, "Leadership is ultimately about the ability to influence others" (p. 3). Mathematics leaders must commit to developing teachers and future mathematics leaders and provide opportunities for their continual growth. To be influential, they need avenues to learn from each other and learn how to facilitate team meetings effectively.

> ## Scenario
>
> During the first year of implementing the new curriculum, the district mathematics specialist knows that the teachers and collaborative teams will need additional support for creating new artifacts and making sense of the curriculum. With the support of the MLT, the specialist arranges to have all teachers meet together quarterly throughout the school year to share expertise, strengths, and challenges, as well as to provide continual professional learning with the required instructional shifts. The site-level leaders are concerned about finding substitute coverage; however, they are able to commit to the plan. The team leaders and site leaders provide input on the agenda for the first meeting. The session begins with a reflection component, and teachers from across the district share their strengths and challenges. Then, the entire group plans next steps to overcome the challenges. The teachers and leaders also participate in professional learning to support the instructional shifts. After the meeting, the specialist sends a summary email to all site-level leaders, team leaders, and teachers to clarify the next steps, the teams' commitments, and specific learning that teachers are going to test in the next month.
>
> Additionally, with the support of the MLT and site-level leaders, the team leaders also meet three times throughout the school year to discuss current challenges and implementation success. During the team leaders' training, discussions center on the current reality of student learning, progress toward SMART goals, intentional celebrations, and leadership skills. Team leaders share their own learning and learn from their peers. As the school year progresses, team leaders and teachers both report that having time to reflect, plan, and learn from each other has impacted their teams' overall performance during the new curriculum's first year.

This scenario models the power of shared leadership. Imagine the power of a collaborative team built of the strongest teacher leaders who are willing to serve others and work side by side with district- and site-level leadership to embrace the required changes. Tap into this power by building multiple team structures and developing teacher leaders.

Building shared leadership is vital for meeting the vision for teaching and learning mathematics. Transparency in the process is also critical, so we shift to effective communication that promotes clear understanding of all actions.

The most accomplished district leaders, site leaders, principals, instructional coaches, and teacher leaders use communication to systematically reinforce the vision for teaching and learning mathematics in their buildings and in their learning teams. Mathematics leaders strategically create a system of shared leadership, where all components complement each other and open communication thrives throughout the system. This communication stems from multiple opportunities to engage with peers at each individual site, across sites, and outside the district boundaries with site- and district-level leaders. Thinking back to the scenario, if the specialist did not communicate the anticipated outcome and desired actions for team learning, site-level leaders would not be able to follow up with the teams and team leaders.

Think about the current communication structures among the collaborative teams, site-level leadership, and district-level leadership and answer the following questions to identify current opportunities for collaboration and improved communication.

- ◆ What are the current opportunities for engaging teachers in collaborative teams?
- ◆ Is there a balance between site-level and districtwide opportunities?
- ◆ Are the opportunities elective or required?
- ◆ How do collaborative teams communicate their efforts to site- and district-level leaders and vice versa?

Feedback is a crucial element of team communication for team leaders as they lead collaborative teams.

Move From Vision to Action

Mathematics leadership exists at many levels. A strong mathematics program develops a shared leadership model with collaboration across every level. All mathematics leaders within the system work together to manage the complexities of teaching and learning mathematics through open communication and intentional supports. Table 5.1 describes the relationship among district-, site-, and team-level commitments in developing highly skilled and highly effective mathematics leaders.

Table 5.1: Mathematics Leadership Commitments to Develop Highly Skilled and Highly Effective Mathematics Leaders

District's Role	Site-Level Leader's Role	Collaborative Team's Role
Include in the district professional learning plan a variety of capacity-building learning opportunities for teacher leaders that support the PLC process.	Identify potential teacher leaders and build capacity by supporting engagement with shared leadership opportunities.	Share team responsibilities and work cohesively to equally support the team members and the team leaders.
Create a systemic model that incorporates shared leadership across multiple layers in the district.	Support mathematics teachers' participation in all aspects of the systemic shared leadership model to represent site voices.	Ensure that the team's voice is present in all layers of the shared leadership model.
Prioritize open communication by providing multiple engagement opportunities for all stakeholders.	Regularly schedule meetings with team leaders, coaches, and teacher leaders to discuss current strengths and challenges.	Consistently evaluate current progress and share results with other stakeholders to build shared knowledge.

*Visit **go.SolutionTree.com/leadership** for a free reproducible version of this table.*

Reflection

Review the Key 2 audit statements for the actions to develop highly skilled and highly effective mathematics leaders in figure 5.4, and with your MLT, reflect upon your current strengths and opportunities to grow. Describe specific action steps to support these Key 2 statements and add the next steps to your action plan. (See appendix A, page 169, for the action plan template.)

Key 2: Develop Highly Skilled and Highly Effective Mathematics Leaders	Next Steps
Site-level leaders ensure that teachers working with low-performing students are experienced and have high expectations for student achievement. Evidence shows that these teachers have successfully accelerated low-achieving students and the teachers have a strong desire to continue working with these students.	
District-level leadership creates multiple opportunities to develop teacher leaders through professional learning, team leader support, and instructional leader support.	
District-level leadership provides supportive conditions for teacher leaders to consistently collaborate and engage in reflective practices.	
Site-level leaders consistently select highly engaging and highly effective teachers to serve as instructional team leaders.	

Figure 5.4: Key 2—Develop highly skilled and highly effective mathematics leaders.

*Visit **go.SolutionTree.com/leadership** for a free reproducible version of this figure.*

Once you have added professional learning action steps to support building capacity for teacher leaders to the action plan, you are ready to focus on creating similar opportunities for site- and district-level leaders. Chapter 6 discusses the actions mathematics leaders can take to promote these opportunities.

6

Build the Capacity of Site-Based Administrators and District Leaders

Before you are a leader, success is all about growing yourself. When you become a leader, success is all about growing others.

—Jack Welch

Mathematics leaders who hope to effect positive instructional change must become experts at developing mathematics leadership in the places that matter most—the school and the boardroom. Mathematics leaders like you work hard to create and serve a collaborative community of stakeholders working to achieve a common vision. You build the capacity of teachers, site-based mathematics leaders, families, and community partners by engaging them in the MLT. But to support an effective districtwide mathematics program, mathematics leaders must develop and encourage the leadership capacity of site administrators and district leaders.

In this chapter, you will learn how to build the mathematics leadership capacity of site-based administrators so they may advance the vision for exemplary mathematics teaching and learning in schools every day. You will also learn how to build the mathematics leadership capacity of your colleagues in central office leadership positions so that they learn how to better support mathematics teaching and learning for all students. First, we'll explore the role of site-based administrators in leading instruction. Then, we'll turn our attention to professional learning geared toward site-based administrators and district leaders. The chapter concludes with practical ways to move the vision into action using the information this chapter presents, and encourages MLTs to reflect on their progress.

The Site-Based Administrator as Mathematics Instructional Leader

The site administrator fills the important role of instructional leader. But as any site administrator will attest, the unique demands of each instructional program complicate the effective performance of an instructional leader's duties. For example, a high school principal might serve as the instructional leader for as many as twenty-five instructional programs. How can he or she expect to become an expert in mathematics if he or she also has to become an expert in music, health, science, world languages, and social studies, to name just a few? Site-based administrators try to balance their understanding of each curricular program with the demands on their time of leading and managing the school. Thus, mathematics leaders' responsibility is to find ways to partner with and engage site-based administrators in professional learning designed to improve their mathematics leadership capacity so that they can:

- ◆ Support the growth of mathematics teachers and site-based mathematics leaders
- ◆ Improve the quality of conversations with teachers about mathematics instruction
- ◆ Improve the quality of formative feedback provided to mathematics teachers about observed instruction
- ◆ Provide leadership to collaborative planning teams working in a PLC culture
- ◆ Support the vision for exemplary mathematics teaching and learning

Timothy D. Kanold, Diane J. Briars, and Skip Fennell (2012) summarize the role of a site-based administrator as a mathematics instructional leader as follows:

> *Understanding the nature of high-quality mathematics instruction, and what teachers and students should be doing in the classroom, is essential for your role as instructional leader of your school. Such understanding is the basis for monitoring and evaluating instruction, assessing what teachers need to improve their instruction, and designing and supporting appropriate professional development. (p. 21)*

To meet these expectations, site-based administrators rely on district mathematics leaders to provide the skills and knowledge to lead their schools' mathematics program effectively and confidently.

Professional Learning for Site-Based Administrators

When considering the design of a professional learning plan for site-based administrators, district mathematics leaders need to answer the question, How can we provide administrators with effective skills, knowledge, and resources to support the vision for exemplary mathematics teaching and learning with fidelity while respecting the demands of their schedule? To answer that question, district mathematics leaders need to engage site-based leaders in professional learning that strengthens their capacity to support *all* programs, not just mathematics. District mathematics leaders compete for the attention of site administrators. Developing experiences with transferable learning outcomes through the context of mathematics is a strategy for supporting administrators' work while still achieving program goals. Figure 6.1 provides some examples of professional learning experiences that support the growth of site-based administrators.

> ### *Effective Leadership Tip*
>
> *Develop experiences with transferable learning outcomes through the context of mathematics in order to support administrators' work while still achieving program goals.*

Professional Learning Goal: Support exemplary mathematics teaching and learning through classroom observation.

Overview: The goal of this series of learning experiences is to focus the administrator's attention on key elements of exemplary mathematics teaching and learning during classroom observations. Site-based administrators spend a great deal of time monitoring instruction. When they monitor mathematics instruction, they should focus on the same elements that the district mathematics program leader would focus on.

Key Questions	Key Activities

◆ What do exemplary mathematics teaching and learning look like?
◆ What are the desired student actions?
◆ What are the desired teacher actions?
	◆ Work with the MLT to develop a look-for tool that focuses on collecting evidence of student engagement in the Standards for Mathematical Practice. With mathematics teachers and site-based leaders, district mathematics leaders conduct informal classroom visits and compare evidence collected using the tool.
	
	◆ District and site-based mathematics leaders conduct informal classroom visits and collect and discuss evidence of teacher engagement in the National Council of Teachers of Mathematics' (2014) Mathematics Teaching Practices.
	
	◆ Site-based mathematics leaders conduct informal classroom visits to collect and discuss evidence of student engagement in the Standards for Mathematical Practice and teacher engagement in the NCTM Mathematics Teaching Practices with a school administrator from another district school.
	
	◆ District mathematics leaders review case studies (written or video) to discuss evidence of student engagement in the Standards for Mathematical Practice and teacher engagement in the NCTM Mathematics Teaching Practices with a cadre of school-based administrators.
	
	◆ District or site-based mathematics leaders organize a book study to read, discuss, and try activities presented in the following books with a cadre of school-based administrators.
	   ◇ *Principles to Actions: Ensuring Mathematical Success for All* (NCTM, 2014)
	   ◇ *What Principals Need to Know About Teaching and Learning Mathematics* (Kanold et al., 2012)

Professional Learning Goal: Support exemplary mathematics teaching and learning through instructional conversations.

Overview: The goal of this series of learning activities is to improve the quality of instructional conversations and formative feedback provided by the site-based administrator to the mathematics teacher. Site-based administrators spend a great deal of time engaged in instructional conversations. When they talk about mathematics teaching and learning, they should focus on the same key questions as the district mathematics leader.

Figure 6.1: Examples of professional learning for site-based administrators.

continued on next page ⇨

Key Questions	Key Activities

◆ How can site-based administrators improve mathematics teaching and learning through instructional conversations and content-focused coaching?
 	
◆ How can site-based administrators improve the quality of formative feedback provided to mathematics teachers after classroom visits?
	◆ Mathematics leaders are process observers and practice using the mathematics instructional talk questions (Dixon, 2015) with mathematics teachers after informal classroom observations.
	
	   ◇ Which Standard for Mathematical Practice is the focus of the lesson?
	
	   ◇ Why, given the mathematical content of the lesson, did you choose a particular Standard for Mathematical Practice?
	
	   ◇ What Mathematics Teaching Practices (NCTM, 2014) will you leverage to develop the chosen Standard for Mathematical Practice?
	
	   ◇ What student evidence did observers expect to see, and did the observations prove whether students learned the desired outcome for the day?
	
	◆ District or site-based mathematics leaders practice providing formative feedback that elicits teacher action focused on student engagement in the Standards for Mathematical Practice or teacher engagement in the NCTM Mathematics Teaching Practices.
	
	◆ Engage a cadre of site-based administrators in formal, content-focused coaching training. Conduct coaching labs to practice coaching conversations.
	
	◆ District or site-based mathematics leaders organize a book study to read, discuss, and try activities presented in the following books with a cadre of site-based administrators.
	
	   ◇ *Embedded Formative Assessment* (Wiliam, 2011)
	
	   ◇ *Content-Focused Coaching: Transforming Mathematics Lessons* (West & Staub, 2003)

Professional Learning Goal: Support collaborative mathematics teams working in a PLC culture.

Overview: The goal of this series of learning activities is to improve the site-based administrator's leadership of collaborative teams working in a PLC culture. Site-based administrators are leaders of site-based PLCs. District mathematics leaders want administrators to support, monitor, and provide feedback to collaborative teams as they engage in high-leverage team actions (HLTAs) that will be described in detail in chapter 7.

Key Questions	Key Activities

◆ What supporting structures must exist for collaborative teams to function effectively?
 	
◆ How will site-based administrators build the team's capacity with the HLTAs?
	◆ Engage a cadre of site-based administrators in the formal study of each of the HLTAs. Partner with effective teams from across the district to engage administrators in simulations designed to strengthen skills and knowledge of a target HLTA.
	
	◆ Provide professional learning for leading data conversations with a cadre of site-based administrators.
	
	◆ Organize a book study to read, discuss, and try activities presented in the following books with a cadre of site-based administrators.
	
	   ◇ *Common Core Mathematics in a PLC at Work™, Leader's Guide* (Kanold & Larson, 2012)
	
	   ◇ *Beyond the Common Core: A Handbook for Mathematics in a PLC at Work™, High School* (Toncheff & Kanold, 2015)
	
	   ◇ *The Five Disciplines of PLC Leaders* (Kanold, 2011)

Developing the mathematics leadership capacity of site-based administrators is an essential leadership action. Effective mathematics leaders provide administrators with the skills, knowledge, tools, and resources to advance the vision for exemplary mathematics teaching and learning every day.

Professional Learning for District Leaders

Effective district mathematics leaders also seek opportunities to teach the district vision for mathematics teaching and learning to colleagues in the district office. Activating any vision is a collaborative effort. The following suggestions may help district mathematics leaders succeed in doing so.

- Secure financial resources to support exemplary mathematics teaching and learning.

- Secure financial resources to support the professional growth of mathematics teachers and school leaders.

- Recruit, hire, and retain staff members who possess the skills, knowledge, and dispositions necessary to support the district's vision.

- Support and train preservice teachers working in district schools.

- Leverage partnerships with other curricular programs to develop cross-curricular resources to deepen students' understanding of the relevance of mathematics through application.

Before setting out to build the mathematics leadership capacity of other district leaders, district mathematics leaders need to identify target leadership groups and clearly define the outcome for each group. Figure 6.2 (page 76) illustrates some examples of professional learning experiences that support the growth of various district leaders.

Enlisting district leaders in the cause of advancing the vision for mathematics teaching and learning is an essential leadership action. Here are additional ways to spread the mathematics message.

- Host a mathematics leadership gathering (see the math gatherings referenced in chapter 4).

- Conduct live webinars.

- Host online chats or tweetups (Twitter meetings).

- Write blog posts.

- Produce weekly podcasts or videocasts.

Think of creative ways to engage site-based administrators and district leaders. Chances are these leaders have great ideas to share about improving the mathematics community. As district mathematics leaders, it is our responsibility to provide professional learning experiences to leaders who can support the mathematics vision with their day-to-day actions. Strengthening the mathematics leadership capacity of site-based administrators ensures that the vision is alive and well even when the district mathematics leaders are not on site. It also reinforces the commitment to aligning financial and human resources to the district's mathematics vision.

Leadership Group: Superintendent and board of education members

Anticipated Outcomes: For this leadership group, district mathematics leaders build key understandings about shifts in mathematics teaching and learning, research-based district positions on various topics, mathematics curriculum reform, and college- and career-readiness initiatives.

Key Activities:

- Analyze shifts in mathematics teaching and learning (Achieve the Core, n.d.).
- Examine select position statements from the National Council of Teachers of Mathematics (NCTM, 2016) and the National Council of Supervisors of Mathematics (NCSM, 2016) in order to develop systemwide positions on issues of equity and access, assessment, and teaching and learning.
- The superintendent and board of education members, together with district mathematics leaders and site-based administrators, conduct informal classroom visits to observe exemplary mathematics instruction. Engage all observers in a discussion about observed behaviors.
- Working with the superintendent and board of education, district mathematics leaders develop talking points for mathematics instruction and assessment. Take time to illustrate the district's vision and mission for exemplary mathematics teaching and learning. The superintendent, board of education members, and district mathematics leaders, working with local journalists, conduct simulated interviews to practice using the talking points.
- Working with the superintendent and board of education, develop a five-year plan for mathematics growth, highlighting the need to secure financial and human resources when applicable.

Leadership Group: Office of human resources

Anticipated Outcomes: For this leadership group, you will build key understandings about shifts in mathematics teaching and learning, develop a profile for the ideal mathematics teacher candidate, and strengthen structures for recruiting, hiring, and retaining highly qualified and highly effective mathematics teacher candidates.

Key Activities:

- Analyze shifts in mathematics teaching and learning (Achieve the Core, n.d.).
- Partnering with district mathematics leaders and site-based administrators, develop a profile for the ideal mathematics teacher candidate. Clearly define in the profile the skills, knowledge, and mindset that best fit the district's vision for exemplary mathematics teaching and learning.
- Develop and test a set of interview questions to support the following.
  - District-level curriculum interviews
  - School-level interviews
  - Mathematics leadership interviews
- Partner with institutions of higher education and share expectations for prospective teacher candidates. Design professional learning for teacher interns currently working with students.

Leadership Group: Professional learning staff

Anticipated Outcomes: For this leadership group, you will build key understandings about the vision for exemplary teaching and learning, leadership development strategic plans, and SMART goals focused on equity and access.

Key Activities:

♦ Work with identified staff to develop professional learning focused on common expectations for mindsets, culturally relevant mathematics pedagogy, and social justice.

♦ Work with the MLT to develop and communicate clear mathematics leadership pathways (for example, from teachers as leaders, to site-based mathematics leadership, to district-level mathematics leadership, and to upper-level leadership, such as school administration and curriculum office leadership). Clarify desired experiences and qualifications for progression through the leadership ranks.

♦ Develop a customized training program for mathematics coaching and mentoring.

♦ Connect mathematics professional learning to overarching district initiatives to unify districtwide learning and growth (for example, building literacy, establishing PLC collaborative teams, designing and implementing quality common assessments, developing students' critical-thinking skills in all courses, connecting ELA capacities, linking the Standards for Mathematical Practice and the Next Generation Science Standards, and other areas that may be district foci; (NGA & CCSSO, 2010; Next Generation Science Standards Lead States, 2013).

Leadership Group: Other curricular program leaders

Anticipated Outcomes: For this leadership group, aim to build a common understanding of effective teaching and learning for all curricular programs. In addition, work collaboratively to develop cross-curricular resources to highlight mathematical relevance and increase meaningful applications of mathematics in all classrooms.

Key Activities:

♦ Partner with teachers from multiple curricular programs to develop tasks that feature the application of mathematics in a real-world context. Work with students and develop a set of student work to support professional learning for teachers who infuse their lessons with these tasks.

♦ Develop a common tool in conjunction with site-based administrators to use in all classrooms to gather evidence of desired teaching behaviors and student learning. Test this tool during collaborative classroom visits.

Figure 6.2: Examples of professional learning for district leaders.

Move From Vision to Action

Building the mathematics leadership capacity of site-based administrators and district leadership teams strengthens and expands the stewardship of the vision for exemplary mathematics teaching and learning. Empower leaders to work on mathematics instructional improvement with a trained eye and an informed voice. We attain visions through everyday work in schools. The commitment to building leadership capacity increases the chance of meeting district goals. Table 6.1 (page 78) describes the relationship among district-, site-, and team-level efforts to build the capacity of site-based administrators and district leaders.

Table 6.1: Mathematics Leadership Commitments to Build the Capacity of Site-Based Administrators and District Leaders

District's Role	Site-Level Leader's Role	Collaborative Team's Role
Develop a professional learning plan to train site-based administrators to do the following. • Collect evidence of student engagement in the Standards for Mathematical Practice. • Collect evidence of teacher engagement in the Mathematics Teaching Practices. • Engage in meaningful instructional conversations. • Improve the quality of formative feedback provided to teachers after classroom visits.	Engage in professional learning to observe classrooms effectively, improve instructional conversations, and provide formative feedback to teachers.	Routinely invite site-based leaders into mathematics classrooms to contribute to their professional learning and to provide opportunities for teachers and site-based leaders to receive instructional feedback.
Develop a professional learning plan to train district leaders to do the following. • Advocate for exemplary mathematics teaching and learning. • Make informed decisions about allocation of funds to support mathematics programming. • Ensure that recruited teacher candidates hold beliefs aligned to the district vision for exemplary mathematics teaching and learning.	Develop an understanding of the big ideas of the professional learning plan in order to do the following. • Advocate for exemplary mathematics teaching and learning. • Encourage decisions regarding allocation of funds to support mathematics programming. • Ensure that potential teacher candidates' beliefs align to the district and site vision for exemplary mathematics teaching and learning.	Routinely invite district-level leaders into mathematics classrooms to contribute to their professional learning and to provide opportunities for teachers and site-based leaders to receive instructional feedback.

*Visit **go.SolutionTree.com/leadership** for a free reproducible version of this table.*

Reflection

Review the Key 2 audit statements on building the capacity of site-based administrators and district leaders in figure 6.3, and with your MLT, reflect on your current strengths and opportunities to grow. Describe specific action steps to support these specific Key 2 statements and add the next steps to your action plan (see appendix A, page 169).

Key 2: Build the Capacity of Site-Based Administrators and District Leaders	Next Steps
District and site leaders develop and implement a professional learning plan that addresses the needs identified by quantitative and qualitative data analysis. Professional learning is discipline specific and job embedded, and also emphasizes a whole-school approach to learning.	
The site-based leadership team requires team members to use the professional learning standards and resources in collaboration with district-level leadership and ensure that all professional learning results in improving all students' learning.	
District mathematics leaders ensure that all site-based leaders participate in ongoing mathematics leadership development.	

Figure 6.3: Key 2—Build the capacity of site-based administrators and district leaders.

*Visit **go.SolutionTree.com/leadership** for a free reproducible version of this figure.*

Next Steps for Mathematics Leaders With Key 2

The big ideas of Key 2 include *how* to build the capacity of site leaders, collaborative teams, and teacher leaders who collectively bring the mathematics vision to life. Mathematics leaders consistently pursue structures for professional learning that develop shared leadership for continual student and adult learning. Using figure 6.4, with your MLT, reflect on the level of engagement and implementation necessary for Key 2, "Supporting visionary professional learning for teachers and teacher leaders."

Exemplary Evidence of Engagement and Implementation	Strong Evidence of Engagement and Implementation	Partial Evidence of Engagement and Implementation	Limited Evidence of Engagement and Implementation
All teachers, site-based leaders, and district leaders demonstrate a commitment to continual professional learning and leadership development.	Most teachers, site-based leaders, and district leaders demonstrate a commitment to continual professional learning and leadership development.	Some teachers, site-based leaders, and district leaders demonstrate a commitment to continual professional learning and leadership development.	Few teachers, site-based leaders, and district leaders demonstrate a commitment to continual professional learning and leadership development.

Figure 6.4: Reflection tool for Key 2.

continued on next page ⇨

Exemplary Evidence of Engagement and Implementation	Strong Evidence of Engagement and Implementation	Partial Evidence of Engagement and Implementation	Limited Evidence of Engagement and Implementation
Mathematics leaders systematically develop professional learning experiences designed to strengthen leadership capacity and align to the mathematics vision with input from all stakeholders.	Mathematics leaders develop professional learning experiences designed to strengthen leadership capacity and align to the mathematics vision.	Mathematics leaders develop professional learning experiences designed to strengthen leadership capacity, but they do not strategically align to the mathematics vision.	Mathematics leaders do not develop professional learning experiences designed to strengthen leadership capacity.
Mathematics leaders collaboratively design professional learning experiences focused on leadership development using feedback from various stakeholders.	Mathematics leaders differentiate professional learning experiences focused on leadership development to meet the needs of various stakeholders.	Mathematics leaders do not differentiate professional learning experiences focused on leadership development to meet the needs of various stakeholders.	Mathematics leaders do not design professional learning experiences focused on leadership development.
Mathematics leaders respond to feedback from stakeholders and provide multiple opportunities for them to develop and foster mathematics leadership.	Mathematics leaders provide multiple opportunities for stakeholders to develop and foster mathematics leadership.	Mathematics leaders provide few opportunities for stakeholders to develop and foster mathematics leadership.	Mathematics leaders provide very few or no opportunities for stakeholders to develop and foster mathematics leadership.

*Visit **go.SolutionTree.com/leadership** for a free reproducible version of this figure.*

The mathematics leaders' action in Key 2 helps strengthen the capacity of the teachers and leaders charged with activating your vision for exemplary mathematics teaching and learning. The design and implementation of a professional learning plan must be comprehensive and strategic. The plan must provide differentiated skills and knowledge to support the growth of teachers, site-based leaders, district leaders, and community members. These stakeholders, armed with new skills and knowledge, are better able to understand exactly which action they must take to ensure the vision's realization.

Highly strained stakeholders deserve structures that support their continued learning through the application of new knowledge. In Key 3, you will learn how to create structures that support collaborative teams working in a PLC culture; how to create well-articulated, focused, and coherent curricular frameworks; and how to develop a culture of assessment.

Key 3 Overview:

Develop Systems for Activating the Vision

Begin with the end in mind.
—Stephen R. Covey

A strong relationship between effective teaching and learning is essential to a solid mathematics program vision. In Key 3, we explore *how* to activate the vision and share strategies for developing systems that support it. Once all stakeholders understand the common vision, district leaders need to guarantee systems are in place to monitor, evaluate, and revise districtwide and site-based goals and action steps. This key promotes reflective practices to ensure instructional actions align to the vision.

The big ideas and essential understandings of Key 3 prepare mathematics leaders to engage in the following leadership actions.

- Establish structures for collaborative teams to engage in high-quality, research-affirmed actions that focus on answering the four critical questions of a professional learning community (DuFour et al., 2016):

    a. What do we want students to know and be able to do?

    b. How will we know if they know it?

    c. How will we respond if they don't know it?

    d. How will we respond if they do know it?

- Create a viable curriculum and establish a framework for continual reflection to close the gap between the intended and enacted curriculum.

- Engage all stakeholders in a culture focused on learning, where all stakeholders build strong relationships through meaningful mathematics assessment processes with feedback and action.

Leverage Collaborative Team Actions

> *Believing that all students have innate capacity and that academic ability can be grown is a definitional element of professional learning communities.*
>
> —Jonathon Saphier

As mentioned in chapter 5, the collaborative team is the engine for change. Supporting collaborative teams with *how* to activate the vision will provide fuel for the engine. Providing time, space, and systematic feedback for continual job-embedded learning will sustain improved student achievement.

 Teacher participation in collaborative teams is crucial to realizing the MLT's developed vision. Districts and sites that operate as professional learning communities (PLCs), especially those that have established a PLC at Work™ culture as outlined by DuFour et al. (2016), are equipped to effectively meet the demands of teaching and learning mathematics. Teachers engaged in these actions are changing teaching and learning status quo.

Collaborative teams focused on meeting new goals for curriculum, instruction, and assessment require teachers to act *differently* (the input) to increase student learning (the output). Change can be difficult, and leading change is even more complex. Chip Heath and Dan Heath (2010), in their research on change, find that regardless of whether the change is individual, organizational, or societal, it always requires an answer to a common question: Can we get people to act in a new way?

In this chapter, you will learn strategies to model and support research-affirmed collaborative team actions. You will also learn how to provide supportive conditions to develop effective teams. First, we will explore the high-leverage team actions to answer the four critical questions of a PLC culture. Then we will examine progression from the first team meeting to meaningful collaboration and explore specific strategies that move teams toward the expected vision for teaching and learning mathematics.

The expectations and vision for teaching and learning mathematics may look different from teachers' own experiences as K–12 students. If we think about our personal experiences, what do we remember about learning mathematics? If we were to close our eyes, we might visualize a teacher at the front of the room, writing a very complex problem with a thorough solution as all students take copious notes. But how was the teacher thinking about the mathematics? Most likely, the teacher thought more about the mathematics that he or she needed to teach than what mathematics the students learned. Local, state, provincial, and national standards' increased emphasis on focused, coherent, and rigorous content changes the expectations for mathematics teaching and learning. To meet the demands of the standards and ensure mathematics success for all, the *typical* teaching that we imagined earlier must transform into *motivational* and *engaging* mathematics instruction focused on student understanding.

Support for Teacher Collaboration

District- and site-level leaders provide the most promising practice of job-embedded professional learning when they support collaborative teams' research-affirmed actions (Dixon et al., 2015; Kanold & Larson, 2015; Kanold-McIntyre et al., 2015; Toncheff & Kanold, 2015). Teacher participation in collaborative teams focuses on improving students' learning of mathematics, working collectively to support a common goal, sharing resources, and supporting all team members' growth as they navigate changing aspects of teaching and learning mathematics. Mathematics leaders must provide supportive conditions for this level of collaboration. NCSM (2014) states, "Supportive conditions are the non-negotiable messages and program characteristics that ensure the teachers, leaders, and parents are pulling in the same direction to see that every student can and will successfully learn mathematics" (p. 12).

> **Effective Leadership Tip**
>
> *As a leader, you must provide supportive conditions for collaborative teams to focus on improving students' learning of mathematics, working collectively to support a common goal, sharing resources, and supporting all team members' growth as they navigate changing aspects of teaching and learning mathematics.*

Collaborative teams build vital shared knowledge and support all team members with understanding the instructional and assessment shifts they need to master to realize the vision for teaching and learning mathematics. Collaborative teams begin their work together by answering the four critical questions of a PLC and continue to focus on these questions on a unit-by-unit basis (Dixon et al., 2015; DuFour et al., 2016; Kanold & Larson, 2015; Kanold-McIntyre et al., 2015; Toncheff & Kanold, 2015).

1. What do we want students to know and be able to do?

2. How will we know if they know it?

3. How will we respond if they don't know it?

4. How will we respond if they do know it?

For our purposes in this book, the unit of instruction is the natural cycle of time for meaningful analysis, planning, reflection, and action for each collaborative team within a district. For most teams, a unit of instruction, or a chunk of mathematical content, should take approximately two to three weeks (Dixon et al., 2015; Kanold & Larson, 2015; Kanold-McIntyre et al., 2015; Toncheff & Kanold, 2015). Before, during, and after the unit of instruction, collaborative teams plan and practice high-leverage team actions (HLTAs) that align to the four critical questions, which we outline in figure 7.1.

High-Leverage Team Actions	**1. What do we want students to know and be able to do?**	**2. How will we know if they know it?**	**3. How will we respond if they don't know it?**	**4. How will we respond if they do know it?**
Before-the-Unit Team Actions				
HLTA 1. Making sense of the agreed-on essential learning standards (content and practices) and pacing	■			
HLTA 2. Identifying higher-level-cognitive-demand mathematical tasks	■	◧		
HLTA 3. Developing common assessment instruments	◧	■		
HLTA 4. Developing scoring rubrics and proficiency expectations for the common assessment instruments		◧		
HLTA 5. Planning and using common homework assignments	◧	■	◧	◧
During-the-Unit Team Actions				
HLTA 6. Using higher-level-cognitive-demand mathematical tasks effectively	◧	■		
HLTA 7. Using in-class formative assessment processes effectively	◧	◧	■	■
HLTA 8. Using a lesson-design process for lesson planning and collective team inquiry	■	■	■	■
After-the-Unit Team Actions				
HLTA 9. Ensuring evidence-based student goal setting and action for the next unit of study			■	■
HLTA 10. Ensuring evidence-based adult goal setting and action for the next unit of study			■	■

■ = Fully addressed with high-leverage team action

◧ = Partially addressed with high-leverage team action

Source: Toncheff & Kanold, 2015, p. 4. Used with permission.

Figure 7.1: High-leverage team actions aligned to the four critical questions of a PLC.

Support for teacher collaboration is essential to activate the vision. Mathematics leaders must ask, What high-leverage team actions are you focusing on to get different outcomes? Think about the variety of teams mathematics leaders currently serve. When teachers first meet in their collaborative teams, do they consistently focus on answering the four critical questions? Do they align their SMART goals and actions to support meeting the district vision for teaching and learning mathematics? How do they engage in the unit-by-unit HLTAs? With the MLT, use figure 7.2 to reflect on the current reality of mathematics collaborative teams and identify strengths and opportunities for growth. Be sure to include evidence of each HLTA and specific actions that have been observed.

Evidence of High-Leverage Team Actions	Site Team	Site Team	Site Team
Team focuses on making sense of the agreed-on essential learning standards (content and practices) and pacing.			
Team identifies higher-level-cognitive-demand mathematical tasks to use during the unit.			
Team develops common assessment instruments.			
Team develops common scoring rubrics and proficiency expectations for the common assessment instruments.			
Team plans and uses common homework assignments.			
Team effectively implements higher-level-cognitive-demand mathematical tasks.			
Team consistently uses in-class formative assessment processes effectively.			
Team uses a lesson-design process for lesson planning and collective team inquiry.			
Team creates structures to ensure evidence-based student goal setting and action for the next unit of study.			
Team uses evidence-based adult goal setting and action for the next unit of study.			

Figure 7.2: Observations of collaborative teams' current engagement in the ten HLTAs.

*Visit **go.SolutionTree.com/leadership** for a free reproducible version of this figure.*

When reviewing trends across the collaborative teams, the MLT, with support from the district and site leaders, can use these data to inform professional learning. Not only must mathematics leaders model the HLTAs, they must also provide the conditions necessary to support the HLTAs before, during, and after the unit. Professional learning and clear communication about the HLTAs can help ensure that collaborative teams practice the HLTAs in alignment with the district's vision for mathematics teaching and learning. First and foremost, collaborative teams must be aware of the HLTAs. They must understand how to engage in these research-affirmed actions and meet the expectations of evidence gathering, analysis, and collective inquiry. However, to accomplish these tasks effectively, teams need to know how to work together collaboratively. Let's take a look at how teams can move beyond mere cooperation and become truly collaborative as they work together to improve mathematics teaching and learning.

Effective Collaborative Teams

When teachers first collaborate, do they immediately begin to trust each other, share all their ideas, and look at student work to adapt instruction? Not usually. So, how can district- and site-based mathematics leaders encourage teams to collaborate meaningfully? First, mathematics leaders need to understand the stages collaborative teams experience as they work together. Teacher collaboration is an essential aspect of a PLC; however, what some may consider collaboration might actually be cooperation or coordination (Grover, 1996). The initial phase is *cooperation*. Cooperation is about getting along while sharing ideas and touching the surface level of HLTAs. It is an appropriate starting point, allowing them to establish trust through open conversations about teaching and learning. When teams begin digging into the HLTAs, creating common assessments together, scoring rubrics collectively, and establishing common grading expectations, they begin *coordinating* as a team. During this phase, the team collectively makes decisions about what evidence is needed for students to be proficient and begins to review data from the assessment instruments. Teams advance to the final phase, *collaboration*, when they use the common assessment instrument evidence to adapt their instruction, reflect on student learning, and set goals for the next unit of instruction. Parry Graham and William Ferriter (2008) offer the useful framework in table 7.1 that details seven stages of collaborative team development within three phases: cooperation, coordination, and collaboration.

Table 7.1: The Seven Stages of a Collaborative Team

Phases of Collaboration	Stages	Question That Defines Each Stage
Cooperation	Stage 1: Filling the time	What exactly are we supposed to do?
	Stage 2: Sharing personal practice	What is everyone doing in his or her classroom?
	Stage 3: Planning, planning, planning	What should we be teaching and how do we lighten the load for each other?
Coordination	Stage 4: Developing common assessments	What does proficiency on the essential learning standards look like?
	Stage 5: Analyzing student learning	Are students learning what they are supposed to be learning?
Collaboration	Stage 6: Adapting instruction to student needs	How can we adjust instruction to help both those students struggling and students already exceeding expectations?
	Stage 7: Reflecting on instruction	Which instructional practices are most effective with our students?

Sources: Adapted from Graham & Ferriter, 2008; Kanold & Larson, 2012.

Mathematics leaders must clearly communicate how collaborative teams advance to the collaboration stage. Equally important, they must create structures to provide the support and feedback the teams need to advance. As teams grow and share knowledge, team members begin to take collective responsibility for all students in their entire grade or course instead of only those in their own classes. To encourage teams to deepen their collaborative practices, mathematics leaders can build opportunities for reflective practices into as many activities as possible, including professional learning and daily or weekly collaborative team time. With the MLT, read through the scenarios in figure 7.3 and discuss which one best represents which stage (refer to stages in table 7.1, page 87). Describe what evidence supports your designation.

Scenario 1: Grade 8 Mathematics Team

There are four members on the team. Two team members, Kris and Anne, are walking down the hallway when they see Fernando, another member of their team. Kris says, "Anne and I were thinking we should meet to discuss what we are going to do for the unit on functions starting next week. I have some activities I used last year that should work." Fernando responds, "Sure, sounds like a plan. I'm heading to the mathematics office and I will let our team leader, Juli, know that we are going to meet. Should we meet Thursday morning?" Kris and Anne agree.

Scenario 2: Grade 3 Mathematics Team

This team of four comprises Jason, Jessica, Jaime, and the team leader, Shaun. They meet on Monday to revise the unit assessment they are going to use for multiplication. Prior to this meeting, each has reviewed the test to see if it assesses all concepts and to determine if questions are well written with plausible distractors. During this session, they finalize the number of questions they will include for each concept and balance the level of cognitive demand of the items. Three out of four members use the common assessments. Jason does not use the common assessments because he teaches the bilingual section of the course. During a previous team meeting in the fall, Jason did not attend the meeting when the team discussed the results of students' tests and Jessica did not bring her results.

Scenario 3: High School Geometry Team

There are six members on the geometry team. The team has been using common unit assessments and has just ended the unit on transformations. In order to identify students' areas of mastery and areas of needed improvement, each member has brought to the team meeting his or her graded class set of the assessment to analyze student work together. The team leader reviews the protocol for looking at student work. All members completed the data analysis for their individual classes and submitted the response via a Google Docs form prior to the meeting. The purpose of the team meeting is to discuss their trends as a team. They share ideas for interventions they can do as a team and as individual teachers. They also discuss the recursive materials they will need to create to re-engage students who have not demonstrated proficiency in the concepts before the next assessment. The team is unsure how to get campus administration involved with planning and executing a couple of the team's interventions, so the team leader decides to discuss the ideas with the principal before the next meeting.

Figure 7.3: Collaborative team scenarios.

Identifying the present stage and phase of the teams' collaboration is not as important as discerning what *support* the teams need to move forward. In scenario 1, it is easy to see the team is truly in the cooperation phase of a collaborative team. The team is beginning to share ideas and resources, yet they have not discussed why the activities are *best* for the essential learning standards and what evidence of student learning they will use to make their decisions. Feedback to the team will need to include specific actions or activities that focus their next steps and promote collaborative team growth. For instance, we could tell them to look at an upcoming unit and create a common assessment to ensure that they all have a common expectation of mastery. But whatever the feedback, a structure to provide it must be in place.

Practice giving feedback to the third-grade mathematics team in scenario 2 described in figure 7.3. Use the feedback tool in figure 7.4 to record the feedback.

Team:	Date:
Current strengths	**Current focus, challenges, and concerns**
Observed HLTA	**Which critical question did the team and its actions answer?** ☐ 1. What do we want students to know and be able to do? ☐ 2. How will we know if they know it? ☐ 3. How will we respond if they don't know it? ☐ 4. How will we respond if they do know it?
Suggested next steps for team	**Observer questions to probe for clarification**
Team reflection: To be completed by team members during feedback debrief	

Figure 7.4: Feedback tool for collaborative teams.

*Visit **go.SolutionTree.com/leadership** for a free reproducible version of this figure.*

Mathematics leaders, who support collaborative teams to become strong collaborators, in turn, do not need to focus solely on monitoring teams; they instead strive to be partners in collaboration. Mathematics leaders will work in conjunction with site-level leaders and collaborative teams to identify tools or structures to support the team's growth. Recall the eighth-grade mathematics team in scenario 1 in figure 7.3. As the team members share their practices, the team shows strong evidence of stages 1–3 in the cooperation phase. Once mathematics leaders observe and understand the level of team engagement, they

Table 7.2: Analysis Tool for Collaborative Teams

Stage	Questions That Define the Stage	Description of the Stage	Guidance on Moving Forward	Specific Tasks and Actions to Move to Next Stage
Stage 1: Filling the Time	What exactly are we supposed to do? Why are we meeting? Is this going to be worth my time?	• Teams in this stage may believe in the collaborative process but lack clear guidelines or experiences regarding what they need to focus on during collaboration time. • Team members believe that student learning is based primarily on student effort, motivation, and family conditions. • Teams have not explicitly identified what students should know, understand, and be able to do, both defining the essential learning standards and focused Standards for Mathematical Practice. • Team members have limited awareness of what and when other teachers are teaching, what they expect their students to learn, or how they assess that learning. • The site administrator is not clear about his or her expectations for the teams. • This stage is often characterized by frustration, bewilderment, and a desire to go back to what was comfortable.	• Provide clear guidelines and work expectations for teams in this stage. Identify specific tasks for the team, use agendas, create norms, and determine collective commitments. • Create collaborative structures to provide the crucial foundation for teams. • Generate the essential standards for the next unit, decide on the length of the unit, and plan a unit assessment.	• List the artifacts that need to be completed when engaging in the before-the-unit HLTAs (i.e., common unit tasks, common assessments and scoring rubrics, common independent practice). • Create norms for collaboration. • Assign a team leader to create an agenda and take minutes. • Assign a timekeeper during the meeting to ensure the team stays on task. • Create a team vision. • Write a SMART goal and action plan. • Build consensus for team expectations and team actions by completing the "Critical Issues for Team Consideration". (Visit **go.SolutionTree.com/PLCbooks** to access this activity from *Learning by Doing, Third Edition* [DuFour et al., 2016].)
Stage 2: Sharing Personal Practice	What is everyone doing in her or his classroom? What relevant activities do other teachers use for this unit?	• Teachers have identified some essential learning standards and have a general pacing plan, but there is limited mutual accountability. • The team has not established regular collaboration time. • Teachers in this stage may be genuinely interested in what other teachers are doing, hoping to pick up new ideas. • Talking about teaching feels like collaboration but does not include an in-depth look at student learning. • Teachers' opinions and decisions are not based on evidence of student learning and assessment results.	• Promote meaningful work by requiring team members to arrive at collaborative decisions regarding curriculum, assessment, or instruction. • Reorient milestones and goals from an individual focus to a collective focus. • Discuss shared accountability. • Build collaboration schedules into the school calendar.	• Dedicate time to begin engaging in the before-the-unit HLTAs. Choose to design a common assessment, common high-cognitive-demand tasks, and common independent practice. • Assign a common assignment, assessment, or task and share examples of student work. • Create a common rubric or scoring guide for an assignment, assessment, or task. • Grade one assignment, assessment, or task together. Score independently and then compare results to determine whether grades are fair and equitable.

Stage	Critical questions	Description		Actions
Stage 3: Planning, Planning, Planning	What content should we be teaching, and how should we pace this unit? How do we lighten the load for each other? Have we planned a rich lesson collaboratively?	• Teachers use a team approach to plan lessons together. Instead of planning all lessons for the unit by themselves, members take responsibility for sets of lessons and share their planning work with others. • Teams often may be uncomfortable with shared planning and fail to focus on results. Teacher attention remains centered on teaching rather than learning.	• Use student achievement data in the planning process. • Ask teachers, Are students learning what you want them to learn? How do you know they are learning?	Before-the-unit actions • Determine the essential learning standards for a unit. • Identify and create common tasks for a unit. • Create a common unit plan. • Create a common lesson. • Choose a high-level task and discuss the best way to use the task.
Stage 4: Developing Common Assessments	How do you know students learned? What does mastery look like? What does student proficiency look like?	• Shared assessments require teachers to define exactly what students should learn and what evidence is necessary to document success. • Some team members may avoid common assessments and steer clear of difficult conversations, but common assessments are essential if teams are to shift their focus from teaching to learning. • The site-based administrator expects teams to use data and monitor progress to drive instructional decisions and interventions.	• Consider having teacher leaders and site-based administrators moderate difficult conversations and model strategies for joint decision making. • Spend time on discussing the critical differences between assessments of learning and for learning. • Provide professional learning to ensure teachers develop critical skills for improving assessment practices.	Before-the-unit and after-the-unit actions • Determine how to use student self-reflection and engage students in after-the-unit actions. • Determine criteria for proficiency. • Develop common unit assessments and common formative assessments. • Determine a scoring guide or rubric for a common assignment, assessment, or task.
Stage 5: Analyzing Student Learning	Are students learning what they are supposed to be learning? What does it mean for students to demonstrate understanding of the learning targets?	• Collaborative teams begin to shift their focus from teaching to learning. • Teachers spend time looking at and dissecting student work, analyzing the strengths and areas of improvement for each student. • Teachers use assessment results to recommend students for generic interventions, such as after-school programs. • Teams may be very motivated and driven by results in this stage. However, openly sharing their own students' assessment results with their team may put teachers in a delicate position and may elicit an intensely personal response. • Collective intelligence provides a never-ending source of solutions for addressing shared challenges.	• Provide structures and tools for effective data analysis. This stage requires emotional support and patience. • Create safe environments in which to examine results together. Separate the person from the practice. • Encourage site leaders to model a data-oriented approach and shared reflection on their own work.	During-the-unit and after-the-unit actions • Use protocols for analyzing student work, and focus on improving student performance beyond the percentage of proficient students. • Use a learning management system (LMS) or data tool to analyze team performance and make adjustments to future learning. • Ask the team, How will we re-engage students in the content they do not understand? • Catalog available interventions and have teams decide how they can evaluate the individual interventions' effectiveness.

continued on next page ⇨

Stage	Questions That Define the Stage	Description of the Stage	Guidance on Moving Forward	Specific Tasks and Actions to Move to Next Stage
Stage 6: Adapting Instruction to Student Needs	How can we adjust instruction to help those students struggling and those exceeding expectations?	• Teachers, teacher leaders, and site leaders collectively commit to helping all students improve and learn. Team members' behaviors represent this commitment. • Teams typically perform at high levels and take collective responsibility for student success rather than success as individuals. Teams set SMART goals and revisit them periodically. • Teams focus on building a systematic and progressively more intense pyramid of interventions. • Teams use data to make decisions about providing initial instruction and tiers of intervention. • The site administrator fully engages in the processes and provides the supportive conditions for the team to focus on student learning.	• Pose reflective, provocative questions to the team to explore various approaches to intervention and enrichment. • Provide professional learning opportunities for developing interventions. • Refine the progress-monitoring cycle. • Learn and use SMART goals. • Explicitly involve students in their own learning by providing multiple opportunities for formative assessment with feedback and action.	Before-, mid-, and after-the-unit actions • Create differentiation structures. • Deepen collective understanding of differentiation. • For planned tasks, create questions that promote a student's deeper understanding of mathematics (assessing and advancing questions; Kanold & Larson, 2012). • Analyze tiered interventions, such as those in an RTI framework.
Stage 7: Using the Continual Learning Cycle	Which of our instructional and assessment practices are most effective with our students?	• Teams embrace the continual learning cycle and keep honing instruction and assessments. • Teams' professional learning processes come full circle, connecting learning back to teaching. • Teams engage in deep reflection, tackling innovative projects such as action research and lesson study. • Teachers observe other classrooms, videotape instruction, intentionally invite others into the group, and develop their teams' success into a school culture. • Within their classrooms, teachers organize students as "student learning communities" that share many of the same elements as teacher learning teams.	• Encourage and support teams' explorations of the teaching–learning connection. • Support teachers' peer observations. • Provide release time for special projects. • Facilitate cross-team conversations. • Expand the team culture schoolwide and districtwide.	During-the-unit and after-the-unit actions • Conduct a lesson study. • Analyze student work and discuss next steps for instruction and student resources. • Perform walkthroughs to observe team members. • Analyze data. • Observe peers in instructional rounds. • Design lessons focused on NCTM's (2014) Mathematics Teaching Practices in figure 2.3 (page 25).

can differentiate their support and offer learning experiences to support the team's growth. Refer to table 7.2 (page 90) to review the collaborative teams' stages and the questions, suggestions for teams to move forward, actions, and tools aligned to each stage to support team growth.

When observing collaborative teams in action, pay attention to their actions and what stage seems most prevalent. There are times when teams need to be in the planning stage; however, if planning or artifact development are the *only* team actions being observed, that is a concern. The key to using this tool is to be aware of the teams' current reality and strengths, and to provide feedback and potential next steps to each team. That way they can move to the truly collaborative stage.

Effective Leadership Tip *While establishing and developing collaborative teams, consider implications of instructional, curricular, and assessment demands.*	# Move From Vision to Action Not all teams are created equal. As with any collaborative team, mathematics teacher teams also need support and guidance to become *effective* teams. As mathematics leaders establish and develop collaborative teams, they must consider the implications of instructional, curricular, and assessment demands. They must create a plan to involve teams in effective collaboration, practice high-leverage team actions, and provide opportunities to learn from colleagues to promote equity

and access to meaningful mathematics. Table 7.3 describes the relationship among district-, site-, and team-level practices of leveraging team actions.

Table 7.3: Mathematics Leadership Commitments to Leverage Team Actions

District's Role	Site-Level Leader's Role	Collaborative Team's Role
Provide opportunities for all grade-level or course-based collaborative teams in every school to understand and practice the high-leverage team actions.	Monitor and provide feedback to grade-level or course-based collaborative teams to ensure they practice the high-leverage team actions.	Work with team members to practice research-affirmed, high-leverage team actions to answer the four critical questions of a PLC.
District mathematics leaders work with the MLT and site leaders to understand how collaborative teams grow and evolve from cooperation, to coordination, to highly effective collaborative teams.	Understand the seven stages of collaborative teams and provide resources (such as time, tools, resources, and guidance) to move each grade-level or course-based team forward through the stages.	Reflect with team members on their current collaborative team stage and identify specific action steps to move forward.
Create systems that provide ongoing feedback to site leaders and grade-level or course-based team leaders on each collaborative team's stage and progress.	Use systematic structures that provide feedback to each grade-level or course-based collaborative team to promote their collaborative growth and understanding of highly effective NCTM Mathematics Teaching Practices.	Work collaboratively together with team members to evaluate feedback and ensure SMART goal action steps support opportunities for personal growth and improvement.

continued on next page ⇨

District's Role	Site-Level Leader's Role	Collaborative Team's Role
Develop several scheduling models for schools to support the infusion of collaborative planning time into the schedule.	Site-based leaders review district scheduling models to determine which model will be adopted to ensure the inclusion of collaborative planning time.	Create an agenda for collaborative team time to intentionally plan before-, during-, and after-the-unit high-leverage team actions.

*Visit **go.SolutionTree.com/leadership** for a free reproducible version of this table.*

Visit www.allthingsplc.info for additional up-to-date resources on creating and sustaining effective collaborative teams. (Visit **go.SolutionTree.com/leadership** for live links to the websites mentioned in this book.)

Reflection

Review the Key 3 audit statements about high-leverage team actions in figure 7.5, and with your MLT, reflect on your current strengths and opportunities to grow. Describe specific action steps to support these Key 3 statements, and add them to your action plan created from the template in appendix A (page 169).

Key 3: Engage High-Leverage Team Actions	Next Steps
Mathematics collaborative teams, site leaders, and district teams consistently analyze data and student work to systematically answer the four critical questions of a professional learning community culture. 1. What do we want students to know and be able to do? 2. How will we know if they know it? 3. How will we respond if they don't know it? 4. How will we respond if they do know it?	
Mathematics collaborative teams receive feedback regarding their effectiveness in promoting strong collaboration versus cooperation.	

Figure 7.5: Key 3—Engage high-leverage team actions.

*Visit **go.SolutionTree.com/leadership** for a free reproducible version of this figure.*

Collaborative teams are the driving force behind activating the vision. Next, chapter 8 provides examples and strategies to meet the district and site curricular, assessment, and instructional vision.

8

Create and Implement Well-Designed and Articulated Curriculum and Assessments

An excellent mathematics program includes a curriculum that develops important mathematics along coherent learning progressions and develops connections among areas of mathematical study and between mathematics and the real world.

—National Council of Teachers of Mathematics

A strong vision for teaching and learning mathematics includes a curriculum that engages students in developing conceptual understanding. This curriculum is the foundation for developing procedural fluency through strategic problem solving and adaptive reasoning (NCTM, 2000, 2009). This engaging curriculum also consistently develops students' mathematical habits of mind (NGA & CCSSO, 2010).

At the heart of a strong mathematics curriculum is the development of content via the Standards for Mathematical Practice, which represent what students are *doing* as they are learning mathematics. In this chapter, we'll explore how to coach teams and teachers to move beyond standards and textbooks to design a guaranteed and viable curriculum (Marzano, 2003). We will examine strategies for making curriculum visible to all stakeholders and building support systems to close the gap between the intended and the assessed curriculum. We will also delve into high-quality assessment practices for both teachers and students.

① Visible Curriculum

Curriculum leadership involves more than just having a written curriculum available in a binder or on a website. It goes beyond providing a set of standards and a textbook. Mathematics leaders must start by defining the purpose of curriculum and setting clear expectations about what is and what is not curriculum.

> ## *Two Types of Experience With Curriculum*
>
> *Teacher A, a new mathematics teacher, meets with the department chair a few days before she is to report to work. The department chair hands her the textbook and a shiny new binder that shows each standard for the course aligned to a quarter or semester and the location where the standards appear in the textbook. She is fully armed with the district curriculum and is told, "Go forth and teach." She sits with her book over the next two days and creates a scope and sequence for the course.*
>
> *Teacher B, another new mathematics teacher, meets with her collaborative team a few days before school starts. They share a Google Docs folder with the upcoming common unit assessments, a yearlong calendar for the course, common homework assignments, and lesson examples to assist with her first few days. She also receives a hard copy of the instructional resources for the year.*

In the scenario for teacher A, the district-defined curriculum is a list of standards correlated to the textbook, with the textbook as the complete curriculum. However, teacher B's team has a completely different understanding of curriculum. Effective mathematics leaders ensure that all stakeholders agree on what curriculum is. Perhaps due to budget cuts and limited funds, some districts have not prioritized purchasing new textbooks, leading teachers to proclaim that since there is no current textbook—or no textbook at all—there is no curriculum.

For our purposes in this book, *curriculum* refers to the specific unit-by-unit essential learning standards derived from local, state, provincial, or national standards. Curriculum shapes the essential learning standards for each unit into a coherent and focused progression of learning through effective and engaging instruction and assessment processes (Dixon et al., 2015; Kanold & Larson, 2015; Kanold-McIntyre et al., 2015; Toncheff & Kanold, 2015; Wiggins & McTighe, 2005). In the simplest terms, curriculum is a description of what, why, and how students should learn mathematics. Stevenson and Stigler (1992) note in *The Learning Gap*:

> *Daunted by the length of most textbooks and knowing that the children's future teachers will be likely to return to the material, American teachers often omit some topics. Different topics are omitted by different teachers, thereby making it impossible for the children's later teacher to know what has been covered at earlier grades—they cannot be sure what their students know and what they do not. (p. 140)*

 If our vision is equitable mathematics learning for all students, mathematics leaders will establish collaborative structures for developing and understanding the guaranteed and viable curriculum, and this curriculum is visible to all stakeholders. A *guaranteed and viable curriculum* is one that gives students access to the same essential learning regardless of who teaches the class, and it allows adequate time to teach the content (Marzano, 2003). As teachers create the guaranteed and viable curriculum collaboratively, they address the following questions.

- What is the curriculum and what components does it include?
- What are teachers', site leaders', and district leaders' roles in implementing the curriculum?

- How do we make the curriculum transparent to all teachers and site leaders to ensure equity with implementation?

- What are the essential learning standards for each course and unit of instruction?

- What is the focus, depth, and coherence of each essential learning standard?

- How do we support beginning teachers and those new to the course or grade level? How do we convey a clear understanding of each essential learning standard's purpose and how each standard connects to the overall big ideas of the unit or course?

Strong mathematics programs make curriculum transparent to all stakeholders by creating opportunities for all teachers to develop the curriculum, articulating and cementing teachers' understanding of the content. Let's look at how district- and site-level mathematics leaders can coach collaborative teams as they develop the curriculum. First, we'll examine how they determine essential learning standards for each course or grade level. Then, we'll see how district, site, and collaborative teams use the essential standards to plan units, and how they can support daily lesson planning to meet the demands of the curriculum.

District-level leaders, site-level leaders, and collaborative teams all have roles in clarifying the essential learning standards for each course or grade level. District- and site-level leaders provide opportunities for teachers to make sense of the agreed-on essential learning standards. Mathematics leaders ensure the essential learning standards coherently adhere to meaningful mathematical learning progressions and build upon each other from unit to unit and year to year. To focus the essential learning standards to a manageable scope, collaborative teams collectively respond to the first PLC critical question, What do we want students to know and be able to do (DuFour, DuFour, & Eaker, 2008)?

> **Effective Leadership Tip**
>
> *As a leader, to make your curriculum visible, you may want to share your curriculum digitally and embrace feedback as a continual learning process. Visit https://hcpss.instructure.com /courses/125 for an example of an open-sourced curriculum hosted by the Howard County Public School System.*

Mathematics leaders should consider during their observations whether teams race through the standards just to cover them and if they discuss their expectations for proficiency for each essential learning standard. Mathematics leaders also need to observe the extent to which teachers understand the content connections between grade levels. For example, when eighth-grade teachers introduce the concept of functions, do the ninth-grade teachers of algebra 1 and integrated mathematics 1 build on the concepts from eighth grade? If the team does not make connections, the ninth-grade team may assume that functions are a new concept in ninth grade and create an entire unit that is most likely review, not new content that extends students' understanding of functions. Teachers generally understand their specific grade-level or course-level content; however, they do not always fully grasp natural connections to the prerequisite and future content. NCSM (2014) states, "A coherent curriculum must carefully connect learning within and across grades so students bridge knowledge from previous years to new understanding" (p. 25). To help teachers and collaborative teams develop a strong understanding of their curriculum, district mathematics leaders must create opportunities for various planning perspectives, including the following.

- **Grade-level standards:** How will you align essential learning standards to create instructional units that build a sound and coherent K–12 curriculum?

◆ **Unit-by-unit essential learning standards:** What is the best way to guide students through the content of this particular unit of study?

◆ **Vertical progression:** How do the essential learning standards for a course connect to what students have previously learned and what they will learn in the future?

◆ **Commitments to other content areas:** How can teachers leverage connections with other content areas to deepen meaning?

◆ **Adequate time for engagement:** How much time do we provide to guide all stakeholders' ongoing review and revision of the district curriculum?

Prioritizing essential learning standards should not take place in isolation. Teachers and collaborative teams require guidance and support to develop their understanding of the essential learning standards and the Standards for Mathematical Practice. Working with your MLT, answer the questions in figure 8.1 to identify next steps to make the curriculum transparent to all stakeholders.

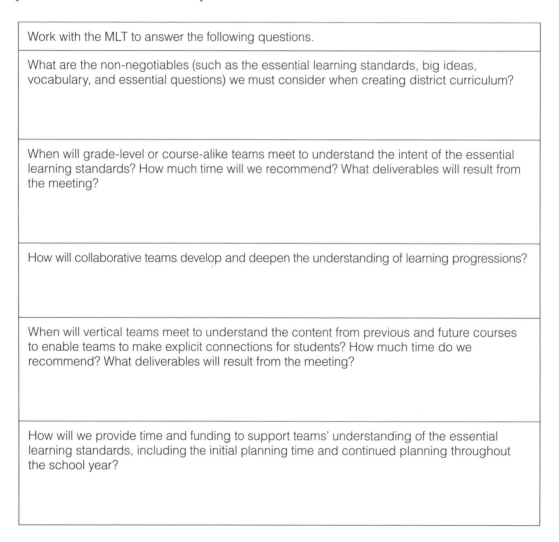

Figure 8.1: Tool for planning curriculum and supporting teams' understanding of essential learning standards.

Visit go.SolutionTree.com/leadership for a free reproducible version of this figure.

A systemic example is listed in table 8.1 and models how Phoenix Union High School District engaged multiple stakeholders in implementing the new curriculum.

Table 8.1: Systemic Example of Engaging Multiple Stakeholders

Team Type	Team Meeting Frequency and Responsibilities	Method of Sharing Artifacts
District curriculum teams: Course-alike teachers from across the district or surrounding districts	Teams meet quarterly to review unit assessments and create daily lessons.	Teams post artifacts on the district server and send updates to all teachers.
Site-level teams: Specific course-level team members	Teams meet weekly and engage in before-, during-, and after- HLTAs.	Teams post artifacts to the district server in site-specific folders to share with all district teachers.
Professional learning teams: All teachers who attend professional learning	Teams meet throughout the school year and demonstrate new learning by sharing lessons, mathematical tasks, and student work examples.	Teams post artifacts on the district server in professional learning folders to build shared knowledge.
Districtwide singleton teacher team: Course-alike teachers from across the district or surrounding districts	Teams meet monthly and engage in before-, during-, and after-HLTAs.	Teams post artifacts on the district server and send updates to all teachers.

Using the responses from the planning tool in figure 8.1, the MLT identifies current curricular needs and creates structures and systems for curriculum collaboration. Effective mathematics leaders ensure that teachers, collaborative teams, and site-level leaders have a common understanding of the intended curriculum. This shared understanding strikes a balance and closes the gap between the intended curriculum (or written curriculum) and the implemented curriculum (or the curriculum that is actually taught; Ball & Cohen, 1996; Porter & Smithson, 2001).

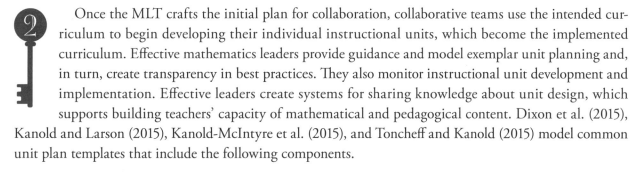

Once the MLT crafts the initial plan for collaboration, collaborative teams use the intended curriculum to begin developing their individual instructional units, which become the implemented curriculum. Effective mathematics leaders provide guidance and model exemplar unit planning and, in turn, create transparency in best practices. They also monitor instructional unit development and implementation. Effective leaders create systems for sharing knowledge about unit design, which supports building teachers' capacity of mathematical and pedagogical content. Dixon et al. (2015), Kanold and Larson (2015), Kanold-McIntyre et al. (2015), and Toncheff and Kanold (2015) model common unit plan templates that include the following components.

♦ **Essential learning standards for the unit:** What are the unit's priority standards and what standards support the priority standards?

♦ **Targeted Standards for Mathematical Practice or process standards:** What evidence observed during the unit will develop the targeted mathematical habits of mind?

♦ **Time frame of the unit:** What are the common pacing expectations for this unit?

♦ **Purpose and overview of the essential learning standards:** What are the big ideas of this unit?

◆ **Enduring understandings and essential questions:** How does the unit connect the overarching understandings of the unit to the questions that we want students to be able to answer at the end of the unit?

◆ **Prior knowledge:** What prior knowledge and skills do teachers need to weave throughout the unit as a means of filling instructional gaps while deepening understanding?

◆ **Key vocabulary:** What specific mathematics vocabulary do students need during the instructional unit?

◆ **Assessment evidence:** What formative assessment processes will best assess student proficiency in the essential learning standards?

◆ **Daily learning experiences:** What mathematical tasks do we use to teach the essential learning standards? What suggested teaching strategies, procedures, differentiation, integration of technology, and notes to teachers strengthen the implementation of the unit?

Effective mathematics leaders support collaborative teams by articulating the essential learning standards in a unit plan. As W. James Popham (2009) observes, it is also important to pay attention to the grain size of the standard and how each standard connects to the learning progression of the unit. Popham (2009) explains:

> *The grain size of an instructional objective refers to the breadth of the outcome teachers seek from students. An example of large grain size would be when a student can generate an original, effective, persuasive essay. That's a significant instructional outcome, and it might take a full semester of school for students to accomplish it. An objective with a small grain size might deal with a less demanding outcome. Objectives with small grain size might be achieved in a single class period. (p. 16)*

Think back to teacher A in the scenario near the beginning of this chapter (page 96). Would her students benefit from the collective knowledge of all grade-level teachers teaching algebra 1? The grain size of planning, from the big ideas of the unit to the smaller, specific, daily learning outcomes, builds collective capacity for both novice and veteran teachers. They can work together to implement a solid unit of instruction, limiting the variance from teacher to teacher.

Visit **go.SolutionTree.com/leadership** to see examples of completed units.

◆ **K–5 example:** "Figure 1.5: Sample Unit Plan Progression of Content for Applying Properties of Operations as Strategies to Multiply for Grade 3" (Dixon et al., 2015)

◆ **Middle school example:** "Figure 1.6: Sample Unit Progression for Geometry Across Standards" (Kanold-McIntyre et al., 2015)

◆ **High school example:** "Figure 1.6: Sample Unit Plan Progression of Content for a Quadratic Functions Unit of Study" (Toncheff & Kanold, 2015)

② Assessed Curriculum

Another component of curriculum is the assessed curriculum. Before designing learning experiences, teachers and teams begin planning the assessments and defining proficiency of the guaranteed and viable curriculum. We start with the end in mind. Effective mathematics teachers use evidence of student thinking to assess the depth of student understanding and knowledge and then adjust instruction to promote a deeper understanding of the content (NCTM, 2014). Assessments are the bridge between teaching and learning. The fourth principle of NCSM's (2008) *The PRIME Leadership Framework* states that leaders need to "ensure timely, accurate monitoring of student learning and adjustment of teacher instruction for improved student learning" (p. 4). Mathematics assessment leadership requires more than ensuring collaborative teams assess student learning. Leaders need to pay attention to *how* teacher teams do so by observing how they respond to the following questions.

- What does proficiency look like? Do all collaborative teams have the same expectations for each essential learning standard? What evidence do collaborative teams look for when answering PLC critical question 2, How will we know when students have learned the content?

> **Effective Leadership Tip**
>
> *As a leader, you need to pay attention to how teacher teams assess student learning.*

- When are students supposed to demonstrate proficiency? Some standards appear multiple times throughout the grade level or course, and teams must be clear what the learning progression will be at each point during the school year. Do all teachers understand the intended learning progression?

- How do collaborative teams know that their assessments align to the essential learning standards? Do teams truly assess the intent of each standard?

- How do collaborative teams use the assessment evidence as an integral component of instruction?

- How do teachers and students use feedback from assessment evidence?

- How equitable is the scoring of the common assessments?

- What formative assessment processes and structures do collaborative teams use to continually monitor students' learning and inform feedback for teachers and students?

As you reflect on the questions, identify areas of strength and opportunities to grow as a mathematics program. A priority leadership assessment action is to ensure teachers and collaborative teams agree on essential standards proficiency. They must agree on the evidence of student thinking and the best tool to use to evaluate student understanding.

Defining Proficiency

When discussing mastery and proficiency, teams must analyze the essential learning standards for a course, note when teachers introduce them, and then determine when to expect proficiency of each standard. A proficiency map is one tool that supports this conversation. It tracks this process as teams place the state standards under the column of the unit and indicate when team members expect students to be proficient. This proficiency map also supports long-term and content progression planning as teams note the time frame of each unit and the related strand or domain. For example, say a second-grade team is starting its proficiency conversation and planning curriculum units. Consider the second-grade example in table 8.2 (page 102). After comparing the district scope and sequence and the major clusters from the Smarter Balanced Assessment Consortium (SBAC) and the California Framework for Mathematics (California State Board of Education, 2015), the team notices that the district's scope and sequence emphasize proficiency of the major clusters only during the first two trimesters (or first six chapters). Through this comparison, a collaborative team would be able to address specific questions about proficiency and realize that there are several priority essential standards that need to be included in units during the second and third trimesters to guarantee students have multiple opportunities to demonstrate their understanding of the big ideas.

Table 8.2: Second-Grade Proficiency Map Example (Trimester Map)

Grade 2016–2017	Unit 1 Addition 20 Days	Unit 2 Addition Problem Solving 10 Days	Unit 3 Subtraction 14 Days	Unit 4 Place Value 15 Days	Unit 5 Addition and Subtraction 26 Days	Unit 6 Money and Graphing 15 Days	Unit 7 Addition and Subtraction 25 Days	Unit 8 Measurement 15 Days	Unit 9 Shapes, Symmetry, and Area 20 Days
OA	**2.OA.2** Fluently add within 20 **2.OA.3** Odd or even **2.OA.4** Use addition with rectangular arrays	**2.OA.1** Use addition within 100 (only to 20) to solve one-step and two-step problems	**2.OA.2** Fluently subtract within 20 **2.OA.3** Write an equation **2.OA.6** Use repeated subtraction		**2.OA.1** Use addition within 100 to solve one-step and two-step problems				
NBT				**2.NBT.1** Three-digit numbers **2.NBT.2** Skip count **2.NBT.3** Read and write numbers to 1,000 **2.NBT.4** Compare three-digit numbers	**2.NBT.5** Fluently add and subtract within 100 **2.NBT.6** Add up to four two-digit numbers **2.NBT.9** Explain why strategies work		**2.NBT.7** Add and subtract within 1,000 **2.NBT.8** Mentally add and subtract 10 or 100		

Grade 2016–2017	Unit 1 Addition 20 Days	Unit 2 Addition Problem Solving 10 Days	Unit 3 Subtraction 14 Days	Unit 4 Place Value 15 Days	Unit 5 Addition and Subtraction 26 Days	Unit 6 Money and Graphing 15 Days	Unit 7 Addition and Subtraction 25 Days	Unit 8 Measurement 15 Days	Unit 9 Shapes, Symmetry, and Area 20 Days
MD					2.MD.6 Represent numbers as lengths from 0 on a number line diagram	2.MD.8 Money 2.MD.10 Draw a picture graph and a bar graph		2.MD.1 2.MD.2 2.MD.3 Measure and estimate lengths 2.MD.4 2.MD.5 Relate addition and subtraction to length 2.MD.7 Time 2.MD.9 Measurement data	
G									2.G.1 Recognize and draw shapes 2.G.2 Partition a rectangle into rows and columns 2.G.3 Partition circles and rectangles

OA = Operations and Algebraic Thinking; NBT = Number and Operations in Base Ten; MD = Measurement and Data; G = Geometry

Mathematics leaders must guide and support collaborative teams when developing proficiency maps. This course overview and the visual representation detailing how essential standards are connected within a course are both vital for making instructional and assessment decisions. When collaborative teams understand agreed-upon levels of proficiency, they make more informed decisions when creating unit assessments.

It is not possible to assess every essential learning standard on an end-of-unit assessment or district benchmark assessment, such as a criterion-referenced exam, final exam, midterm, quarterly assessment, or module assessment. Collaborative teams decide on important questions to assess students' knowledge and understanding, and mathematics leaders ensure that students are assessed on what matters versus what is easy to assess.

With technology, teachers can easily scan an assessment using multiple-choice, single-response, or right-or-wrong types of answers. These types of assessments are perfect to check for understanding quickly and offer immediate feedback on the number of correct and incorrect items. However, teachers *and* students need feedback on what students are learning so both parties can take specific actions to re-engage in the content. Research suggests that consistently limiting assessment evidence to standardized test results does not equate to higher levels of student achievement (Wiliam, 2013). Instead, collaborative teams need to create dynamic assessments to evaluate student thinking and focus on the specific feedback teachers and students need to respond appropriately. Effective mathematics leaders provide collaboration time for similar grade- or course-level team members and leaders during the summer, after school, or on the weekends to discuss, create, and evaluate meaningful assessments and build assessment literacy.

In addition, mathematics leaders must consider three questions as they coach collaborative teams to design dynamic assessments that accurately evaluate students' learning and yield specific feedback.

1. Do collaborative teams design assessments to collect evidence of students' learning?

2. Do assessment items align to the essential learning standards, and are they clear indicators of student understanding?

3. Do the items assess essential learning standards at the appropriate cognitive demand?

To assist teachers and teams as they design assessments, effective mathematics leaders use several activities, practices, and tools to help build assessment literacy, develop understanding of balanced assessments, and improve assessment processes. Some of these may include evaluating assessment quality, creating exemplar assessment items, and using assessment blueprints. Let's look at each of these in depth.

As part of a visible curriculum, districts can provide exemplar assessments for collaborative teams as a starting point for assessment conversations. When collaborative teams first begin to explore higher expectations of any new curriculum, they might struggle with describing proficiency of the essential learning standards. What is the depth of understanding for each essential learning standard? What type of questions would elicit evidence of student thinking? District mathematics leaders can support districtwide collaboration time focused on crafting exemplar assessments. Using the Assessment Instrument—Quality Evaluation Tool (Dixon et al., 2015; Kanold & Larson, 2015; Kanold-McIntyre et al., 2015; Toncheff & Kanold, 2015), mathematics leaders can model how to evaluate assessments and revise as needed. The tool requires teams to evaluate assessments using the following criteria.

- Essential learning standards are clear and listed in student-friendly terms somewhere on the assessment to ensure students can evaluate their results tied to the essential learning standards.

- Assessment is neat, orderly, and includes enough space for students to work and teachers to provide feedback.

- There is a balance of higher- and lower-level-cognitive-demand tasks tied to the essential learning standards.

- Directions are clear and precise.

- There are a variety of assessment *task* formats that assess both the content standards and the Standards for Mathematical Practice.

- Vocabulary is fair and clearly understood by teachers and students, and students must attend to precision with constructed responses or performance tasks in order to succeed.

- Teams complete the assessment as if they were a student and follow the ratio of 1:3 (one minute for a teacher to three minutes for a student) to ensure that they can complete the test in the allotted time.

- Scoring rubric is evident to students and collaborative team members.

With your MLT, consider any additional criteria you would include in evaluating assessments. Exemplar assessments and scoring rubrics support both struggling teams and highly effective teams and help them understand and embrace the mathematics assessment vision.

Once collaborative teams evaluate and discuss the quality of exemplar assessments, have teams practice writing and scoring quality assessment items to build their knowledge of the specific standards and improve their assessment skills. Begin by identifying the essential learning standards that students consistently struggle with on district assessments or standards that collaborative teams consider hard to teach, and select two or three standards or clusters per grade level. After collaborative teams have made sense of these identified learning standards, ask them to create assessment task examples using a variety of cognitive demands (Smith & Stein, 1998). Teams may complete the task electronically using a collaborative tool such as Google Docs, Edmodo, Blackboard, or the district LMS. Have teams submit their examples and describe the level of cognitive demand using the descriptors from appendix B (page 187), which is a cognitive-demand-level task-analysis guide.

At times, students struggle with essential learning standards because the teacher doesn't understand the language of a particular standard. Consider the following example of how a team of fifth-grade teachers can address a misunderstood standard and create assessment item examples using this process (see figure 8.2, page 106).

> *5.NF.5 Interpret multiplication as scaling (resizing), by:*
>
> a. *Comparing the size of a product to the size of one factor on the basis of the size of the other factor, without performing the indicated multiplication.*
>
> b. *Explaining why multiplying a given number by a fraction greater than 1 results in a product greater than the given number (recognizing multiplication by whole numbers greater than 1 as a familiar case); explaining why multiplying a given number by a fraction less than 1 results in a product smaller than the given number; and relating the principle of fraction equivalence a / b = (n × a) / (n × b) to the effect of multiplying a / b by 1. (NGA & CCSSO, 2010, p. 36)*

A team or multiple teams across the district can collaboratively discuss the standards, write assessment item examples, evaluate the level of cognitive demand, and submit their work to their peers or mathematics leaders for feedback. Through this level of collaboration, the teachers are able to craft items that assess student proficiency *and* also develop a deeper understanding of the intent of each essential learning standard.

Essential Learning Standard (Student Friendly)	Lower-Level-Cognitive-Demand Example	Higher-Level-Cognitive-Demand Example
I can compare the size of a product to the size of its factors (without performing multiplication).	$\frac{1}{2} \times 3\frac{1}{8} = ?$ Will the answer be more than or less than $3\frac{1}{8}$? We feel that is lower cognitive demand because is it purely procedural with no explanation.	$\frac{1}{2} \times 3\frac{1}{8} = ?$ Will the answer be more than or less than $3\frac{1}{8}$? Explain why and create a model to explain your thinking. We raised the cognitive demand by asking the students to explain their thinking. It is still procedural but we are asking them to connect their responses to their understanding of multiplying fractions.
I can explain the result of multiplying a given number by a fraction greater than and less than 1.	Determine the answer using estimation. 1. $792 \times 9{,}999$ 2. $\frac{1}{2} \times 9{,}999$ 3. $1\frac{3}{4} \times 9{,}999$ We feel that is lower cognitive demand because it is purely procedural with no explanation.	Luke has a calculator that will only display numbers less than or equal to 999,999,999. Which of the following products will his calculator display? Explain. 1. $792 \times 999{,}999{,}999$ 2. $\frac{1}{2} \times 999{,}999{,}999$ 3. $1\frac{3}{4} \times 999{,}999{,}999$ 4. $0.67 \times 999{,}999{,}999$ (Illustrative Mathematics, n.d.) We feel this is a higher-cognitive-demand task because it focuses students' attention on the use of procedures for the purpose of developing an understanding of multiplying a given number and the impact on the result (more than or less than the second factor).

Figure 8.2: Lower-level- and higher-level-cognitive-demand discussion tool example.

When working with teachers and collaborative teams, providing time and space to make sense of expected student learning is necessary for closing the gap between the intended (written curriculum), enacted (what is taught), and assessed curricula. Once teachers and collaborative teams understand the intent of the standards, the expectations for proficiency, and how to create high-quality assessments aligned to the essential standards, we can begin to offer guidance for district-level assessments.

Effective Leadership Tip

As a leader, when creating district assessment blueprints, utilize the complexity of thinking that is aligned to state, provincial, or national assessments.

Assessment blueprints of district assessments (such as district final exams, midterms, benchmark assessments, and so on) provide another way mathematics leaders can support teams' understanding of balanced assessments. Blueprints are created with teachers and mathematics leaders to ensure that district-level assessments value teacher input. Assessment blueprints should include each assessment item's complexity; that informs teachers and collaborative teams of the assessment expectations. Then, teams review the blueprints to make sound assessment decisions about cognitive demand when they create their unit assessments. Figure 8.3 (page 108) is a benchmark assessment blueprint example for third-grade trimester assessments. The example school uses Webb's Depth of Knowledge (DOK) model to classify the complexity of thinking (Webb, 1997).

When third-grade collaborative teams begin creating their unit assessments, they can ensure they assess students at the appropriate cognitive level by referring to the district assessment blueprints. In figure 8.3, there were six DOK 3 items on the trimester assessment. Teams can quickly review their unit assessments to identify DOK 3 items that students will experience prior to the district trimester assessments. If teachers never expose students to higher-cognitive-demand tasks during a unit of instruction, they poorly prepare them for summative assessments.

Once the district assessment blueprints are created, collaborative teams use the same structure to create unit assessment blueprints to ensure alignment from team to team within a district. The unit assessment blueprints can include detail about the focus Standards for Mathematical Practice. Figure 8.4 (page 109) is a unit assessment blueprint example for a geometry unit on transformations. In this assessment blueprint, teams also consider the intended Mathematical Practice (see figure 2.3, page 125).

The team used this tool to review its first attempt at creating its assessment and came to three important realizations: (1) the assessment overemphasized DOK 2 items, (2) the variety in the DOK did not align to the district blueprint, and (3) it needed a few more items on certain standards or a performance task that encompassed multiple standards to truly assess proficiency of the essential learning standards. Both district assessment blueprints and site-level unit assessment blueprints support collaborative teams by building assessment capacity and ensure equity in meeting the assessment vision.

Once the assessment and description of proficiency are clear, and leaders have established plans and support for providing specific feedback with a common purpose to all stakeholders, we turn our attention to powerful feedback and assessment processes that engage and motivate all stakeholders.

The Importance of Feedback and Action

Once collaborative teams create high-quality assessments, they must receive support from mathematics leaders to engage students in the assessment cycle. When students view their assessment scores, they often respond in the following ways.

- They see if they did better than their classmates.

- They go home and tell their parents.

- They put the assessment in the closest receptacle—their desk, a folder, the trash can.

- They pat themselves on the back for a job well done or cringe at the results and hope for a better showing next time.

Some of these scenarios are exciting for students and others are discouraging because students often do not embrace assessments as a next step toward improving their learning. Research shows that classroom assessments that provide accurate, descriptive feedback to students, involve them in the assessment process, and activate them as their own learning advocates positively affect learning (Black & Wiliam, 1998; Hattie,

Big Idea for First Trimester District Assessment	Targeted Standards	Depth of Knowledge Level 1	Depth of Knowledge Level 2	Depth of Knowledge Level 3	Number of Items on Assessment	Total Number of Points
Place Value	**3.NBT.1:** Use place value understanding to round whole numbers to the nearest 10 or 100. **3.NBT.2:** Fluently add and subtract within 1000 using strategies and algorithms based on place value, properties of operations, and/or the relationship between addition and subtraction. **3.NBT.3:** Multiply one-digit whole numbers by multiples of 10 in the range 10–90 using strategies based on place value and properties of operations.	2	2	2	6	14
Addition	**3.NBT.2:** Fluently add and subtract within 1000 using strategies and algorithms based on place value, properties of operations, and/or the relationship between addition and subtraction. **3.OA.9:** Identify arithmetic patterns (including patterns in the addition table or multiplication table), and explain them using properties of operations.	2	2	1	5	8
Subtraction	**3.OA.8:** Solve two-step word problems using the four operations. **3.NBT.2:** Fluently add and subtract within 1000 using strategies and algorithms based on place value, properties of operations, and/or the relationship between addition and subtraction.	1	2	1	4	7
Multiplication	**3.OA.1:** Interpret products of whole numbers. **3.OA.3:** Use multiplication within 100 to solve word problems in situations involving equal groups, arrays, and measurement quantities and use unknowns to represent the problem. **3.OA.5:** Apply properties of operations as strategies to multiply. **3.OA.8:** Solve two-step problems using multiplication and addition/subtraction. Represent these problems using equations.	2	3	2	7	16
	DOK Total	7	9	6	22	45
	Percent of Each Level of DOK on the Assessment	32 percent	41 percent	27 percent	100 percent	

Figure 8.3: Trimester district assessment blueprint example.

Big Idea or Cluster	Essential Learning Standard	Question Number	Points	Intended Standards for Mathematical Practice	Depth of Knowledge Level
Experiment with transformations in the plane.	G-CO.2: Represent transformations in the plane using, for example, transparencies and geometry software; describe transformations as functions that take points in the plane as inputs and give other points as outputs. Compare transformations that preserve distance and angle to those that do not (for example, translation versus horizontal stretch).	1	2	3, 7	2
		2	2	7	1
		3	3	3, 7	2
		4	3	3, 7	2
Experiment with transformations in the plane.	G-CO.3: Given a rectangle, parallelogram, trapezoid, or regular polygon, describe the rotations and reflections that carry it onto itself.	5	3	1	1
Experiment with transformations in the plane.	G-CO.4: Develop definitions of rotations, reflections, and translations in terms of angles, circles, perpendicular lines, parallel lines, and line segments.	6	2	6, 7, 8	2
Experiment with transformations in the plane.		7	4	3, 7, 8	3
		8	2	1, 3, 7	2
		9	2	1, 3, 7	2
Experiment with transformations in the plane.	G-CO.5: Given a geometric figure and a rotation, reflection, or translation, draw the transformed figure using, for example, graph paper, tracing paper, or geometry software. Specify a sequence of transformations that will carry a given figure onto another.	10	3	3, 6	2
Experiment with transformations in the plane.		11	2	6, 7	2
Understand congruence in terms of rigid motion.	G-CO.6: Use geometric descriptions of rigid motions to transform figures and to predict the effect of a given rigid motion on a given figure; given two figures, use the definition of congruence in terms of rigid motions to decide if they are congruent.	12	2	3, 8	2
Understand congruence in terms of rigid motion.		13	2	3, 7	2
Understand congruence in terms of rigid motion.		14	3	1, 3	2
Understand congruence in terms of rigid motion.		15	3	2, 3	2
				Depth of Knowledge Level 1	13 percentage points
				Depth of Knowledge Level 2	80 percentage points
				Depth of Knowledge Level 3	7 percentage points

Figure 8.4: Unit assessment blueprint example.

2009; Wiliam, 2011). As part of the assessment vision, effective mathematics leaders create structures for collaborative teams to re-engage students in the essential learning standards, have them set goals, and encourage them to take action on the feedback. Teachers use assessment results to adapt instruction or differentiate re-engagement strategies, and collaborative teams need to foster student investment in the assessment cycle (Vagle, 2015). All stakeholders invest in a culture of collaboration by focusing on student learning and engaging students in the assessment process.

Mathematics leaders support collaborative teams by modeling systems and environments for engaging students in the assessment cycle. One of the characteristics of an exemplar assessment is that it lists the essential learning standards (Briars, Asturias, Foster, & Gale, 2012; Kanold & Larson, 2012; Larson et al., 2012a, 2012b; Zimmermann, Carter, Kanold, & Toncheff, 2012). When students evaluate their feedback *and* tie the results to specific actions to improve their learning, whatever grade or score they receive will not trump what they learned. Leaders can ensure student engagement in self-reflection and action by developing artifacts with the exemplar unit assessments and including them in the written curriculum, such as figure 8.5.

Learning Target	Test Questions	Score	Percent
A-REI.C.5: I can prove that a linear combination (that is, elimination) is valid.	1–4	/13	
A-REI.D.11: I can explain why the x-coordinate of the points where the graphs of the equations $y = f(x)$ and $y = g(x)$ intersect are solutions of the equations $f(x) = g(x)$; find the solutions approximately.	5–7	/15	
F-LE.A.2: I can write a linear function given a pattern, a set of ordered pairs, a graph, or a slope and a point.	8–10	/6	
A-REI.D.12: I can graph the solution set to a system of linear inequalities in two variables.	1–13	/7	

My strengths (the targets I learned):

My areas for growth (the targets I am still learning):

My learning goal and plan:

Figure 8.5: Student assessment form example.

With the MLT, complete the planning tool in figure 8.6 for engaging collaborative teams in student self-assessment practices.

Work with the MLT to answer the following questions.
Do collaborative teams currently provide specific feedback to students tied to essential learning standards or big ideas of a unit of instruction? If not, what support do teams require to embrace this specificity of feedback?
Do we have structures to provide specific feedback to other stakeholders tied to essential learning standards or big ideas of a unit of instruction? If not, what support do teams require to embrace this specificity of feedback?
What structures do teachers need to encourage active student action after they provide feedback?

Figure 8.6: Planning tool for engaging collaborative teams in student self-assessment practices.

*Visit **go.SolutionTree.com/leadership** for a free reproducible version of this figure.*

As collaborative teams begin to create specific feedback for students, they will also have to grapple with the purpose of a grade.

What is the purpose of a grade? If we were to ask a group of teachers, we would most likely receive several different responses. Leading researchers in grading practices have asked this question to teachers and leaders across the United States and have generally found that the responses can be categorized into six categories (Guskey & Bailey, 2001, 2010). Thomas R. Guskey and Jane M. Bailey (2010) describe the categories:

1. *To communicate information about students' achievement in school to parents and others*

2. *To provide information to students for self-evaluation*

3. *To select, identify, or group students for certain educational paths or programs*

4. *To provide incentives for students to learn*

5. *To evaluate the effectiveness of instructional programs*

6. *To provide evidence of students' lack of effort or inappropriate responsibility (pp. 13–14)*

If one of the monitored measures of success (see chapter 3) is grade distribution, then district mathematics leaders need to ensure that teachers and leaders agree on the purpose of a grade. Figure 8.7 (page 112) is a survey example that mathematics leaders sent to all district mathematics teachers in Phoenix Union High School District.

Why do we give grades?

Please take a few minutes and answer the following questions.

My team has equitable grading procedures.*

Grading is consistent from one teacher to the next.

- ☐ 1: Strongly disagree
- ☐ 2: Disagree
- ☐ 3: Agree
- ☐ 4: Strongly agree

Why do we use grades?*

* Required

Figure 8.7: The purpose of a grade survey.

The anonymous responses were gathered, cut into strips, and given to the MLT to sort. Team members sorted them into two categories based on their alignment to the six characteristics: positive or negative grading beliefs (figure 8.8).

Positive Grading Belief Statements	Negative Grading Belief Statements
◆ I want to communicate information about students' achievement in school to parents and others. ◆ I want to provide specific information to students for self-evaluation. ◆ I want to evaluate the effectiveness of instruction.	◆ I want to select, identify, or group students for certain mathematics courses or pathways of learning. ◆ I want to provide incentives for students to learn. ◆ I want students to know that there are consequences for not being responsible or making an effort.

Figure 8.8: Grading beliefs.

If the vision for teaching and learning includes equitable grading practices, this activity highlights any disconnect between teacher actions and grading beliefs. Teachers who use grades for motivation, for punishment, or as a sorting mechanism model examples of negative belief systems for grading. When they use grades in this manner, students come to believe that grading systems are part of an education game. The students quickly turn their focus from learning the content to learning how to work the system. Ultimately, using grades in unproductive ways will not impact student learning (Wormeli, 2006). However, when teachers use grades as feedback to further student learning, they make a positive impact on student learning. Positive grading belief systems promote grades as feedback and require that both teachers and students take action on the feedback (Dixon et al., 2015; Kanold & Larson, 2015; Kanold-McIntyre et al., 2015; Toncheff & Kanold, 2015). With your MLT, ensure consensus on the purpose of grades and create supportive conditions to ensure that collaborative teams communicate feedback that both students and teams will use.

Next Steps for Well-Designed and Articulated Curriculum and Assessments

As a mathematics leader, set aside time to meet with mathematics teachers and collaborative teams and ask these three simple questions.

1. What is curriculum? What makes a good curriculum?

2. What is important for site-level leaders to understand about the curriculum?

3. What can district leaders, site leaders, and teachers do to make it even better?

A note of caution: as a mathematics leader, it is easier to pull together a small pool of representatives from course-alike and grade-level teachers to create curriculum and assessments. District mathematics leaders need to be aware of any action that removes teachers from this process. Developing curriculum is more than picking a set of artifacts. During the *process* of creating curriculum and assessments, team members collaboratively build understanding of the essential learning standards and define proficiency, which in turn increases the capacity of all team members. Be careful not to take away or limit the process of collaborative teams to support each other's understanding of the content and curriculum (DuFour et al., 2016).

Move From Vision to Action

It is important for collaborative teams to build shared understanding of the written and assessed curriculum. As a district mathematics leader, it is equally important to build districtwide opportunities during professional learning or planning to develop a deeper understanding of curriculum. Mathematics leaders will need to engage representatives from each building at each grade or course level. Build shared knowledge as a district team and then ensure that the knowledge will be developed back at the site level with intentional structures. If there are too many schools in a district, think about using a couple of teachers from each site and having them work with collaborative teams in a professional learning setting, where they can facilitate conversations that build shared understanding and simultaneously clarify curriculum artifacts and their purpose in instructional design. Table 8.3 describes the relationship among district-, site-, and team-level engagement in well-designed and articulated curriculum and assessments.

Table 8.3: Mathematics Leadership Commitments for Well-Designed and Articulated Curriculum and Assessments

District's Role	Site-Level Leader's Role	Collaborative Team's Role
Provide opportunities for all stakeholders at every site to have a voice in the development of the guaranteed and viable curriculum (content and the Standards for Mathematical Practice).	Provide supportive conditions for teachers and collaborative teams to understand the intent of the guaranteed and viable curriculum, including time during the school day to learn from others.	Team leaders and course-based, grade-level leaders work with team members to ensure all team members understand the big ideas of the grade or course and define the guaranteed and viable curriculum.

continued on next page ⇨

District's Role	Site-Level Leader's Role	Collaborative Team's Role
Focus on developing the essential learning standards and provide a coherent unit-by-unit progression.	Demonstrate interest in the development of the unit plans and provide supportive conditions for teams to reflect on implementation.	Team leaders and grade-level leaders work with team members to develop a focused, coherent unit plan that develops procedural fluency through conceptual understanding and application.
Provide opportunities for collaborative teams and teacher leaders to validate and reflect on the alignment among the assessments, unit plans, and daily lesson design.	Engage site teams to reflect on the alignment among the assessments, unit plans, and daily lesson design.	Collaborative teams review assessment evidence to ensure that it aligns to the intent of each essential learning standard.
Create systems for vertical teacher leaders and teams to support the development of standards with an equal intensity of conceptual understanding, procedural fluency, and application (mathematical rigor).	Engage grade-level and course-alike teams in vertical articulation to ensure that they meet expected learning outcomes to support student matriculation through meaningful and connected mathematics.	Collaborative teams work with future and previous grade levels and courses to ensure that they connect essential learning standards for prior and future learning.

*Visit **go.SolutionTree.com/leadership** for a free reproducible version of this table.*

Reflection

Review the Key 3 audit statements about well-designed and articulated curriculum and assessments in figure 8.9, and with your MLT, reflect on your current strengths and opportunities to grow.

Key 3: Create and Implement Well-Designed and Articulated Curriculum and Assessments	Next Steps
Essential learning standards are clearly articulated for each course, unit, and lesson; and describe both what students should understand and be able to do (content and mathematical practice standards).	
Essential learning standards support horizontal and vertical learning progressions. Resources support the development of standards with an equal intensity of conceptual understanding, procedural fluency, and application (mathematical rigor).	
Curriculum provides opportunities for all students to access rich mathematical tasks via the Standards for Mathematical Practice.	
Mathematical tasks promote reasoning and problem solving. Tasks vary and address multiple levels of cognitive demand.	

Key 3: Create and Implement Well-Designed and Articulated Curriculum and Assessments	Next Steps
District leaders, with teachers, design assessment blueprints provided to all teachers. Teachers use these same blueprints to frame unit plans and for daily lesson planning.	
There is a clear alignment among the curriculum, instructional resources, and assessments. This alignment is clear to teachers, students, and parents, and the curriculum is transparent to all stakeholders.	
District and site-based assessments are balanced in cognitive demand.	
Assessments vary in the type of questions and are not solely procedural.	
Teachers give students timely feedback on their content progress and the development of the Standards for Mathematical Practice.	
Teams create common assessments before a unit of instruction and review them during and after the unit to ensure the assessment aligns to the instructional blueprint and assesses the essential learning targets, both content and process requirements.	
Mathematics leaders articulate clear, non-negotiable actions in the district defining high-quality assessment practices.	
Mathematics teams collaboratively score student work, establish strong inter-rater reliability, and use the results to provide specific feedback to all stakeholders.	
Collaborative teams engage students in the assessment cycle as part of continual improvement. The assessment cycle requires feedback and action.	
All stakeholders clearly understand effective formative assessment processes that result in teacher and student action through evidence gathering and feedback.	

Figure 8.9: Key 3—Create and implement well-designed and articulated curriculum and assessments.

*Visit **go.SolutionTree.com/leadership** for a free reproducible version of this figure.*

With the MLT, identify specific action steps to realize the curriculum and assessment vision and add them to your action plan developed from the template in appendix A (page 169). Once you have solidified the plan to support high-quality curriculum and assessments, you are ready to focus on monitoring consistent expectations for teaching mathematics, a topic we cover in chapter 9.

9

Monitor Consistent Expectations for Exemplary Instruction

We cannot solve our problems with the same thinking we used when we created them.

—Albert Einstein

Take a minute and think about the best lesson you have observed in action. What key characteristics made the lesson go so well? Are those characteristics present in most daily mathematics lessons? Teaching is a complex act. As the first guiding principle from NCTM's (2014) *Principles to Actions* states, "An excellent mathematics program requires effective teaching that engages students in meaningful learning through individual and collaborative experiences that promote their ability to make sense of mathematical ideas and reason mathematically" (p. 5). Effective mathematics teaching requires that teachers pay attention not only to the content they teach but also to their students' mathematical thinking.

In a collaborative culture, much of teams' daily work focuses on high-quality instruction to create equity and access to meaningful mathematics. Kati Haycock (1998) summarizes the research on the impact of effective teaching practices and concludes, "In the hands of our best teachers, the effects of poverty and institutional racism melt away" (p. 9). Effective teaching practices begin with clear communication of the district vision for high-quality mathematics instruction and the district's expectation that teachers will embody it. Effective mathematics leaders ensure the vision incorporates research-affirmed teaching practices that meet the needs of all learners. Additionally, they intentionally create multiple opportunities for teachers, teams, site-level leaders, and district-level leaders to align instruction with the district's vision. This chapter is designed to help you develop structures to do so.

A Picture of the Vision

Read through the following scenarios in figure 9.1 (page 118).

Which scenario best represents your vision for teaching and learning mathematics? In both scenarios, the teachers implement the intended task for the essential

117

A ninth-grade algebra I team chose the *Almost Total Inequality Task* to assess students' conceptual understanding of the essential learning standard for the unit.

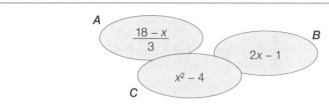

When x is zero, A is greater than both B and C.

- For what other values of x is A the greatest? (Your answer will include that zero value, of course.)
- For what x values is B the greatest? And C?
- Is there a value of x when neither A, B, or C is greater than the other two?

Scenario 1: Mr. Doherty, Grade 9 Algebra I Class

Mr. Doherty's class started a unit on quadratic functions. After a quick check of the previous night's homework, Mr. Doherty begins the lesson with a definition of terms and reviews procedures on solving linear equations and linear inequalities. He then demonstrates how to graph quadratic functions limited to values A and C; he models two or three problems (functions with positive and negative values) while students are taking notes and listening; he assigns twenty similar problems from the students' textbook. As students work individually at their desks applying the procedures to the in-class problems, he walks around the room. Most of his assistance falls into one of two categories: (1) help with solving for x and (2) reminders of how to use the graphing calculator to find the values in the table. As the period ends, Mr. Doherty tells the students to finish working on the twenty problems for homework and to do a word problem (Almost Total Inequality Task).

Scenario 2: Ms. Scott, Grade 9 Algebra I Class

The ninth-grade students in Ms. Scott's class are also working on a unit that involves quadratic functions. As students walk into the room, Ms. Scott directs their attention to the task displayed on the SMART Board (Almost Total Inequality Task) and asks them to begin to work immediately in their small groups. She tells the students that they will have the entire period to work on this task and reminds them that, as usual, they may quietly get whatever paper, tools, or manipulatives they need to complete the task.

Ms. Scott walks around the room, stopping at different groups to listen in on their conversations and to provide support as needed. She notes that students started out by discussing their conjectures and a variety of solution strategies. Some students begin the task by using the guess-and-check strategy. As these students start working through the task, they organize their guess-and-check answers and realize they needed to keep track of the values they have already tried. This leads them to construct a table that identifies the values that they substitute into the three inequalities. Two other groups set up the inequalities and one group uses graphs to find the value of x where A would be the greatest. Students in all of the groups look for patterns and test their conjectures. During this time Ms. Scott circulates among the groups asking such questions as How do you know you have all of the possible solutions?, What values have you tried?, and Do you see a pattern? These questions lead students to see the need to organize their data, make conjectures, and test them out.

As the period draws to a close, none of the groups have completed the task but most are well on their way to discovering the solutions. All students are deeply engaged with the task and actively talk to their partners about how to justify, organize, and communicate their thinking. For homework, Ms. Scott asks students to summarize what they have learned so far from their exploration and what they want to continue to work on in the next class.

Kindly reproduced with the permission of NRICH Source: http://nrich.maths.org/5966.

Figure 9.1: Algebra scenarios.

learning standard; however, Ms. Scott's classroom shows more evidence of effective student-to-student discourse and deeper understanding of the content, and the instruction is more aligned to a strong vision of student-centered instruction.

A strong mathematics program is steeped in closing the gap between the vision and the reality of mathematics instruction. Consider a mathematics program's vision statement: "E² Math wants to excel in all areas of teaching and learning. We want to be the role model for . . . collaborative learning for the 21st century for teachers and students" (Phoenix Union High School District, 2013, p. 2).

Now imagine walking through a classroom in the school whose mathematics program articulated this vision. If instruction has made this vision statement a reality, we would observe students working in groups, making sense of mathematics, and asking each other questions to deepen their understanding. Student-to-student discussions would be more prevalent than teacher-centered discussions, and there would be evidence of collaborative teacher team planning. Is this vision a reality? To activate the instructional vision, it is imperative that all teachers in the district clearly understand expectations and are able to describe the evidence of the vision in action. Use figure 9.2 to summarize the district's vision statement about instruction. With the MLT, describe what observable actions and sounds support the vision.

Vision statement:	
What does this look like?	What does this sound like?

Figure 9.2: Clarifying the expectations for exemplary instruction.

As discussed previously, vision statements must be well articulated and focused. The more specific the vision, the better stakeholders will understand it. Figure 9.3 (page 120) is a completed table for the vision statement example.

Professional learning and ongoing collaboration with district, site, and collaborative team leaders help to articulate the instructional vision. Let's consider how mathematics leaders can monitor the vision's implementation.

Components of Effective Instruction

Teaching mathematics requires understanding mathematics (content knowledge) and instruction that develops student understanding (pedagogical knowledge), as well as integrating the content and pedagogy into meaningful learning for students (Hill, Ball, & Schilling, 2008). Effective mathematics leaders ensure that collaborative teams and teachers implement research-affirmed teaching practices and collaborate to deliver high-quality instruction and solidify deeper understanding of mathematics.

Vision statement: We want to excel in all areas of teaching and learning. We want to be the role model for collaborative learning for teachers and students.	
What does this look like?	**What does this sound like?**
◆ Collaborative teams consistently work together to answer the four critical questions of a PLC. ◆ Site leaders provide time during the school day for teachers to collaborate. ◆ Collaborative teams create lessons that encourage student-to-student discourse. ◆ District- and site-level leaders provide supportive conditions for action research on best practices for collaborative learning.	◆ Team members see evidence of collaboration when they complete instructional rounds. ◆ Students sit in small groups (such as teams of four) and evidence of their thinking is visible throughout the lesson. ◆ Students audibly share their thinking with other students and critique the reasoning of their peers. ◆ Teachers use high-cognitive-demand tasks to allow all students access into meaningful mathematics.

Figure 9.3: Articulated instructional vision statement example.

Review each of the NCTM Mathematics Teaching Practices in figure 9.4. With your MLT, reflect on the observable evidence of implementation or structures that currently exist in your district that support each practice.

National Council of Teachers of Mathematics' Mathematics Teaching Practices: Read each practice and describe observable teacher actions that reflect the practice.	Comments
Establish mathematics goals to focus learning. Effective teaching of mathematics establishes clear goals for the mathematics that students are learning, situates goals within learning progressions, and uses the goals to guide instructional decisions.	
Implement tasks that promote reasoning and problem solving. Effective teaching of mathematics engages students in solving and discussing tasks that promote mathematical reasoning and problem solving and allow multiple entry points and varied solution strategies.	
Use and connect mathematical representations. Effective teaching of mathematics engages students in making connections among mathematical representations to deepen understanding of mathematics concepts and procedures and as tools for problem solving.	
Facilitate meaningful mathematical discourse. Effective teaching of mathematics facilitates discourse among students to build shared understanding of mathematical ideas by analyzing and comparing student approaches and arguments.	

National Council of Teachers of Mathematics' Mathematics Teaching Practices: Read each practice and describe observable teacher actions that reflect the practice.	Comments
Pose purposeful questions. Effective teaching of mathematics uses purposeful questions to assess and advance students' reasoning and sense making about important mathematical ideas and relationships.	
Build procedural fluency from conceptual understanding. Effective teaching of mathematics builds fluency with procedures on a foundation of conceptual understanding so that students, over time, become skillful in using procedures flexibly as they solve contextual and mathematical problems.	
Support productive struggle in learning mathematics. Effective teaching of mathematics consistently provides students, individually and collectively, with opportunities and supports to engage in productive struggle as they grapple with mathematical ideas and relationships.	
Elicit and use evidence of student thinking. Effective teaching of mathematics uses evidence of student thinking to assess progress toward mathematical understanding and to adjust instruction continually in ways that support and extend learning.	

Source: NCTM, 2014.

Figure 9.4: Reflection on NCTM's Mathematics Teaching Practices.

*Visit **go.SolutionTree.com/leadership** for a free reproducible version of this figure.*

As the MLT compares observable actions, the team should consider whether there are specific teaching practices that are more evident than others. By evaluating trends and reflecting on teachers' and collaborative teams' strengths and challenges, effective mathematics leaders can identify specific learning needs and next steps to support closing the gap between the vision and current reality.

As the focus on engaging students with the Standards for Mathematical Practice grows, the expectations for teaching and learning mathematics evolve. The second principle from NCSM's (2008) *The PRIME Leadership Framework* states district leaders should "ensure high expectations and access to meaningful mathematics instruction every day" (p. 21). A strong partnership among district, site, and collaborative teams promotes the latter's efforts in collaborating, sharing, and collecting evidence of student thinking, as well as in reflecting on and adapting instruction in response to student understanding. Figure 9.5 (page 122) provides specific strategies to enrich this partnership and align the vision of teaching and learning with the reality of instruction.

Strategies to Build Instructional Capacity Using NCTM's Mathematics Teaching Practices		
District-Level Leaders	**Site-Level Leaders**	**Collaborative Teams**
Ensure that the district vision aligns with NCTM's Mathematics Teaching Practices. Create opportunities for site-level leaders and collaborative teams to understand expectations for teachers and determine what evidence of student engagement looks like.	Work with site-level leaders to develop a common understanding of NCTM's Mathematics Teaching Practices. Create opportunities for leaders to explore all of NCTM's Mathematics Teaching Practices and observe them through videos, instructional rounds, or scenarios.	Dig deeper into each of the Mathematics Teaching Practices and choose a focus practice. Share evidence of the practice during weekly team time, and create lesson plans specifically aligned to the focus practice. Analyze the focus practice with instructional rounds or action research.

Figure 9.5: Strategies to engage a strong partnership using NCTM's Mathematics Teaching Practices.

Teaching Practices

These examples are a starting point to engage all partners in promising instructional practices. To help your MLT monitor the vision for high-quality instruction, use figure 9.6 as a discussion tool for work focused on NCTM's Mathematics Teaching Practices.

> Directions: Use these questions to identify specific action steps needed to monitor your vision for high-quality instructional practices.
>
> 1. What do site-level leaders currently know about the eight NCTM Mathematics Teaching Practices? What opportunities can we create to engage site-level leaders in understanding each teaching practice and identifying the practices in action?
>
> 2. What do collaborative team leaders currently know about the eight NCTM Mathematics Teaching Practices? What opportunities can we create to engage team leaders in understanding each teaching practice and identifying the practices in action?
>
> 3. What do mathematics teachers on collaborative teams currently understand about the eight NCTM Mathematics Teaching Practices? What opportunities can we create to engage all teachers in understanding each teaching practice and identifying the practices in action?

Figure 9.6: Action-planning discussion tool.

*Visit **go.SolutionTree.com/leadership** for a free reproducible version of this figure.*

We recognize that a shared vision of high-quality instruction is only valuable if all stakeholders consistently monitor it, revisit and revise it over time, and celebrate when they fulfill it. The ultimate goal of focusing on instruction is improved student learning, and as we discussed in chapter 3, it is our responsibility to celebrate the work of the collaborative teams who get the job done. It is also our responsibility to provide descriptive feedback to collaborative teams and individual teachers on their progress with instructional shifts, as well as the evidence they have gathered of student engagement in the Standards for Mathematical Practice. Most districts have a formal evaluation system to let all teachers know their annual progress against expectations. The feedback for formal evaluations is typically not descriptive or tied to the mathematics vision for teaching and learning—it must build a shared vision of instruction. Teachers and collaborative team members need a safe community in which to try new things, make mistakes, and learn *with* their students as they develop their content and pedagogical knowledge. Collaborative teams need feedback that ties into the vision statement to help them support stronger implementation and close the gap between the intended and enacted curriculum.

Let's revisit the vision statement example in figure 9.3 on page 120. We have already developed the big ideas and actions that support this vision; the next step is to deliver feedback to teams as they strive to become role models for collaborative learning.

 The MLT uses the articulated vision statement to create a rubric to monitor and evaluate educators' effectiveness in implementing new curriculum, build students' engagement with the Standards for Mathematical Practice, and focus on NCTM's Mathematics Teaching Practices. A jointly created rubric can be a focus of professional learning and helps site leaders understand what they are looking for when they monitor mathematics instruction. The rubric also supplies collaborative teams with specific feedback to help them grow with the instructional shifts.

When focusing on high-quality instructional practices, district mathematics leaders need to create and monitor structures that ensure *access* to meaningful mathematics. Site leaders and collaborative teams should be able to articulate their *collective response* to students who currently struggle with mathematics or who need enrichment— the last two critical questions of a PLC. NCSM (2014) states, "Raising achievement in mathematics for *every* student and effectively implementing the CCSSM [or new state standards] in *every* classroom requires *a variety of intensification strategies be available to teachers to support the learning needs of struggling students*" (p. 35). In lieu of the words *intervention*, *enrichment*, or *differentiation*, we use the word *intensification* to signify proactive efforts by collaborative teams, site-level leaders, and district leaders to ensure success for *all* students. Mathematics leaders must ensure implementation of the following intensification strategies to support diverse learners.

> ### Effective Leadership Tip
> *As a leader, provide examples of specific, research-affirmed instructional practices to meet the needs of all learners.*

- Make certain that core instruction is high quality and uses research-affirmed instructional practices.
- Consider and employ research-affirmed support structures to assist students as soon as they begin to struggle.
- Use differentiation strategies to grant access to the content instead of diluting or deleting the content.
- Using multiple data points, identify students' needs to create intensification supports and constantly monitor students' progress.
- Ensure access to intensified learning opportunities—match students' needs with levels of intensification; these should be mandatory, not optional (NCSM, 2014; NCTM, 2014).

Structures for intensification should be flexible enough for students to move in and out of supports as needed. Even if students struggle with particular content, that doesn't mean they will *always* need additional supports with other essential learning standards or different units of instruction. With your MLT, answer the questions in figure 9.7 and create action steps for collaborative teams, site-level leaders, and district leaders to ensure access to rich mathematics and proper matriculation through the K–12 program.

To assess your district's current collective response to student learning, answer the following questions.

1. What current structures are in place at each site to support struggling students? How do mathematics leadership teams, at all levels, monitor the implementation of each intensification strategy?

2. What current structures do collaborative teams employ to support diverse learners? Is there an effective level of implementation districtwide?

3. Do collaborative teams have a common understanding of differentiation? What differentiation strategies do they employ to support access to meaningful mathematics?

4. What data do the collaborative teams currently use to assess students' progress on the essential learning standards? Are there other data we should monitor to support intensification strategies?

5. Do our students access rigorous mathematics courses equitably? How do teachers monitor each student's matriculation through the K–12 curricular program? What strategies do they employ to ensure that all students have access to advanced mathematics coursework? What percentage of students access advanced mathematics courses (AP and honors classes, gifted and talented programs, and so on)? Does this percentage represent the district's diversity?

Figure 9.7: District planning tool for collective response.

What other questions might the leaders and the MLT need to answer to clarify which actions are necessary to support *all* learners? When reflecting on current intensification strategies, add specific action steps to the plan in appendix A (page 169) that support a strong partnership among the collaborative team, site-level leaders, and districtwide leaders. The "world's best performing school systems" emphasize high-quality core instruction and value the process of monitoring student learning and supports, consistently evaluating them, and constructing interventions to support individual students before they fall behind. When teachers introduce intensification strategies early and at the individual level, these systems prevent compounding failure for the long haul (Barber & Mourshed, 2007). Visit www.allthingsplc.info for more examples of intervention schedules and support.

Feedback is a critical component of exemplary instruction. Students need feedback during a lesson to promote their continued learning. Collaborative teams and site-level leaders deserve the same during the school year to grow and develop the vision of high-quality instruction. This feedback should be specific for all stakeholders to ensure that they can take action to improve their understanding. For students, this means the feedback targets specific essential learning standards that they need to re-engage with or focuses on their level of proficiency within each standard. For teachers and leaders, the feedback targets implementation of the instructional vision.

Collaborative Team Feedback on During-the-Unit Instruction

Begin by unwrapping your vision statement into observable actions *during* instruction. For example, in the vision statement example in figure 9.3 (page 120), we can identify the following observations during instruction.

- Teachers arrange students' seats to promote rich student-to-student discourse.

- Teachers create access to meaningful mathematics by using high-cognitive-demand tasks.

- Evidence of student thinking is visible throughout the lesson.

- Students audibly provide evidence of their thinking and critique the reasoning of others.

These descriptors become the evidence in the data-gathering tool in figure 9.8. Collaborative teams can use the rubric to provide peers feedback. Site leaders can use the rubric to guide evidence gathering and observation feedback in a mathematics classroom. District leaders can use the collected data and trends across the district to inform next steps and opportunities for continued learning and support with targeted professional development.

Use the Following Scale 1 = No evidence 2 = Little evidence 3 = Some evidence 4 = Strong evidence	Student-to-Student Discourse Look for the following.			
	Teachers arrange students' seats to promote rich student-to-student discourse.	Teachers create access to meaningful mathematics by using high-cognitive-demand tasks.	Evidence of student thinking is visible throughout the lesson.	Students audibly provide evidence of their thinking and critique the reasoning of others.
Identify What Class or Grade Level You Are Observing (No Teacher Names)	Score	Score	Score	Score
Classroom 1				
Classroom 2				
Classroom 3				
Classroom 4				
Total for each indicator				
Comments:				

Figure 9.8: Data-gathering tool example for instructional vision.

Visit **go.SolutionTree.com/leadership** *for a free reproducible version of this figure.*

After observing all teachers within a grade-level or course-alike team, collaborative teams can evaluate the feedback to identify their strengths and challenges. Collaborative teams and site leaders can include specific action steps in their SMART goals to overcome these challenges. This process ensures that teams align their instructional actions to the vision.

District- and site-level leaders should evaluate instructional trends throughout the system. Using figure 9.8 as a template, district and site leaders can create a Google Form and collect evidence from all mathematics collaborative teams in order to guide implementation for all stakeholders.

Move From Vision to Action

The MLT begins with a strong vision for mathematics teaching and learning. To bring the vision to life, begin with transparent articulation of the district vision for high-quality mathematics instruction. Effective mathematics leaders also ensure the vision incorporates research-affirmed teaching practices that meet the needs of all learners. Additionally, they intentionally create multiple opportunities for teachers, teams, site-level leaders, and district-level leaders to align instruction with the district's vision and provide feedback to all stakeholders.

Table 9.1 describes the relationship among district-, site-, and team-level commitments to monitor consistent expectations for exemplary instruction.

Table 9.1: Mathematics Leadership Commitments to Monitor Consistent Expectations for Exemplary Instruction

District's Role	Site-Level Leader's Role	Collaborative Team's Role
Ensure the vision for high-quality mathematics instruction includes research-affirmed teaching practices.	Understand what the teaching practices look like in action from both the teacher and student perspectives.	Team leaders and grade-level leaders work with team members to identify research-affirmed teaching practices that best support student learning.
Provide learning opportunities for site leaders and collaborative teams in research-affirmed mathematics teaching practices and provide feedback on implementation of new strategies.	Provide supportive conditions (for example, time and opportunities to observe each other) for collaborative teams to grow their content and pedagogical knowledge.	Team leaders and grade-level leaders work with team members to collaboratively plan for specific teaching practices that focus on developing the mathematical habits of mind.
Develop a professional learning plan to train site-based administrators to: ♦ Collect evidence of student engagement in the Standards for Mathematical Practice ♦ Collect evidence of teacher engagement in NCTM's Mathematics Teaching Practices ♦ Engage in meaningful instructional conversations Improve the quality of formative feedback teachers receive after classroom visits.	As lifelong learners, site leaders engage in professional learning to improve their facility with effective classroom observation, with instructional conversations, and with providing formative feedback to teachers.	Team members invite site-based leaders into mathematics classrooms to contribute to their professional learning and to provide opportunities to receive instructional feedback.
Provide structures for instructional feedback and data dialogues with instructional data aligned to vision statements.	Review instructional trends and provide specific feedback to collaborative teams regarding instructional data aligned to the vision statements.	Collaborative teams review instructional feedback, provide peer feedback, and have conversations that foster instructional growth.

*Visit **go.SolutionTree.com/leadership** for a free reproducible version of this table.*

Reflection

Review the Key 3 audit statements in figure 9.9 about monitoring consistent expectations for exemplary instruction and reflect upon your current strengths and opportunities to grow.

Key 3: Monitor Consistent Expectations for Exemplary Instruction	Next Steps
Communication in the mathematics classroom is vital to students sharing their understanding of concepts and procedures. Students engage in high levels of discourse every day to develop meaningful understanding of mathematics.	
Differentiation is evident in flexible grouping, lesson design, and mathematical tasks.	
Teachers employ and monitor district-developed and site-based intervention models to ensure all students have access to core instruction and tiered interventions.	
Standards for Mathematical Practices are observable during every classroom walkthrough and students can describe which mathematical practice they are developing.	
Teachers consistently implement the intended curriculum with fidelity. Site and district leaders observe the intended curriculum daily.	
Teachers consistently employ research-informed instructional strategies. Teachers use and connect mathematical representations.	
Teachers design lessons to build procedural fluency from conceptual understanding for application. Teachers support students' productive struggle in learning mathematics.	
District-level leaders, in conjunction with site-level leaders, ensure they provide dedicated time for teachers and intervention program staff to interact, ensuring continuity of instruction.	

Figure 9.9: Key 3—Monitor consistent expectations for exemplary instruction.

*Visit **go.SolutionTree.com/leadership** for a free reproducible version of this figure.*

Once you have added action steps to monitor your vision for teaching and learning and strategies to support exemplary instruction to the template in appendix A (page 169), you are ready to focus on activating the student voice.

Next Steps for Mathematics Leaders With Key 3

The big ideas of Key 3 include *how* to activate the vision and develop systems that support the teaching and learning vision. Effective mathematics leaders consistently provide opportunities for reflective practices and ensure that instructional actions align to the vision. Using figure 9.10, with your MLT, assess the engagement and implementation of practices for developing systems for activating the vision.

Exemplary Evidence of Engagement and Implementation	Strong Evidence of Engagement and Implementation	Partial Evidence of Engagement and Implementation	Limited Evidence of Engagement and Implementation
Teams design and clearly articulate a focused, coherent, and rigorous curriculum that consistently aligns intentions, instruction, and assessments.	Teams design and clearly articulate a focused, coherent, and rigorous curriculum that routinely aligns intentions, instruction, and assessments.	Teams design and articulate a curriculum that sometimes aligns intentions, instruction, and assessments.	Teams design and articulate a curriculum that almost never aligns intentions, instruction, and assessments.
Teachers consistently design mathematics classroom instruction to engage all students in specific learning behaviors of mathematically proficient students and they can articulate which behaviors are present in the lesson.	Teachers routinely design mathematics classroom instruction to engage all students in specific learning behaviors of mathematically proficient students.	Teachers sometimes design mathematics classroom instruction to engage all students in specific learning behaviors of mathematically proficient students.	Teachers do not design mathematics classroom instruction to engage all students in specific learning behaviors of mathematically proficient students.
Teachers consistently design mathematics classroom instruction to leverage NCTM's Mathematics Teaching Practices.	Teachers routinely design mathematics classroom instruction to leverage NCTM's Mathematics Teaching Practices.	Teachers sometimes design mathematics classroom instruction to leverage NCTM's Mathematics Teaching Practices.	Teachers do not design mathematics classroom instruction to leverage NCTM's Mathematics Teaching Practices.
Collaborative teams consistently use high-leverage team actions to strengthen before-, during-, and after-the-unit activities.	Collaborative teams routinely use high-leverage team actions to strengthen before-, during-, and after-the-unit activities.	Collaborative teams sometimes use high-leverage team actions to strengthen before-, during-, and after-the-unit activities.	Collaborative teams do not use high-leverage team actions to strengthen before-, during-, and after-the-unit activities.

Exemplary Evidence of Engagement and Implementation	Strong Evidence of Engagement and Implementation	Partial Evidence of Engagement and Implementation	Limited Evidence of Engagement and Implementation
During instructional conversations prior to instruction, teachers can clearly articulate how they will develop the intended student learning behavior using specific NCTM Mathematics Teaching Practices and justify the selection of each.	During instructional conversations prior to instruction, teachers can usually articulate how they will develop the intended student learning behavior using specific NCTM Mathematics Teaching Practices and justify the selection of each.	During instructional conversations prior to instruction, teachers can sometimes articulate how they will develop the intended student learning behavior using specific NCTM Mathematics Teaching Practices.	During instructional conversations prior to instruction, teachers cannot clearly articulate how they will develop the intended student learning behavior using specific NCTM Mathematics Teaching Practices.

Figure 9.10: Reflection tool for Key 3.

*Visit **go.SolutionTree.com/leadership** for a free reproducible version of this figure.*

The chapters in part III guide you through the design of systematic reflective practices and processes to ensure stakeholder actions align with the teaching and learning vision. Creating structures to support activating the vision is vital for ongoing reflection and subsequent adjustments. Collaborative team structures must support strong engagement in high-quality, research-affirmed actions that focus on answering the four critical questions of a professional learning community (DuFour et al., 2016). Curriculum structures must focus on creating a guaranteed and viable curriculum that is visible to all stakeholders. This framework will also promote continual reflection and accountability measures, which close the gap between the intended and enacted curriculum. Lastly, assessment structures will engage all stakeholders in a culture focused on mathematical thinking and understanding. In this culture, all stakeholders build strong relationships with students through meaningful mathematics assessment processes supported with feedback and action.

Structures supporting reflection, feedback, and action promote intentional teacher planning and purposeful response to stakeholder needs. In Key 4, you will learn how to engage students, parents, and community members as advocates for your mathematics teaching and learning vision.

Key 4 Overview:

Empower the Vision of Family and Community Engagement

Simply asking students what they think does very little for creating meaningful change, and it does very little to support the attainment of their aspirations. The real challenge lies in listening carefully to what they are telling us, *reflecting upon it, learning from it, and leading change with students by our sides. Listen, learn, and lead. Those are my new favorite words.*

—Russell J. Quaglia

What does it mean to empower students, families, and community members as true partners in education? In Key 4, we explore strategies to amplify your students' voices, empower families with the knowledge to guide their children toward rigorous coursework, and enlist the talents of community and business leaders.

The big ideas and essential understandings of Key 4 prepare mathematics leaders to engage in the following leadership actions.

- ◆ Empower students as equal partners who serve as catalysts for the continual improvement of classroom instruction and mathematics program development.

- ◆ Increase the role of families as advocates for equity, access, and excellence for school and district programming.

- ◆ Leverage the strengths of community partners to broaden opportunities for students to become stewards of their communities.

10 | Activate the Student Voice to Check Alignment Between Vision and Reality

A student is not a container you have to fill but a torch you have to light up.

—Albert Einstein

In this chapter, you will learn how to leverage your most precious asset—students—to improve the quality of your mathematics program. First, you will explore strategies for activating students as consultants by partnering with them to shine a light on the current state of mathematics instruction. Then, you will learn how to engage students as equal partners in the design of professional learning and curricular resources. Finally, you will explore how to engage students as advocates who influence culture, practice, and even policy.

How would you describe the level of student engagement in your school or district? How would members of your MLT or leadership community describe their engagement? Eric Toshalis and Michael J. Nakkula (2012) offer the tool in figure 10.1 (page 134) as common language describing student involvement in educational decision making.

The tool describes, from left to right, the release of responsibility from adults to students in day-to-day routines. Take a few minutes to think about how students are engaged in your district. What do you notice? Do you provide a wide range of opportunities across the entire continuum or are most of the student activities described by the left side of the tool? As you read, consider how each example in this chapter might be classified using this tool.

Think about the students sitting in mathematics classrooms across your school or district when you consider the following questions.

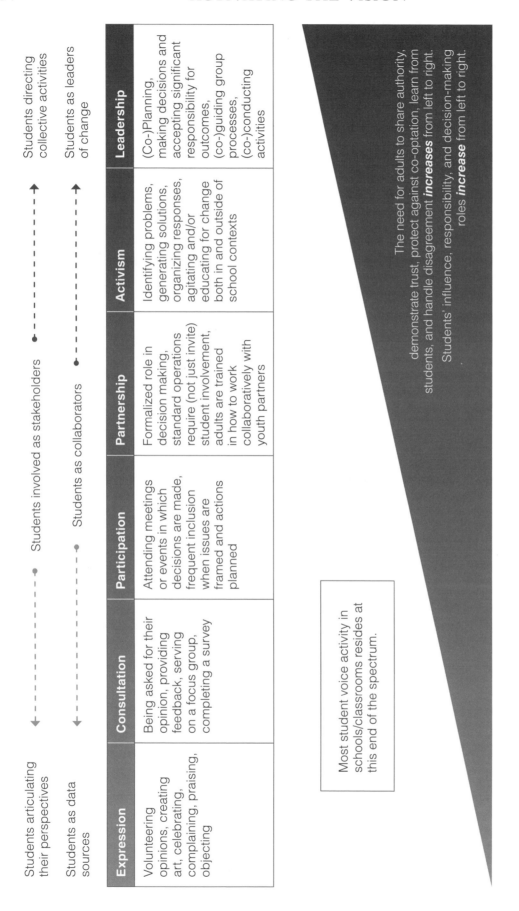

Expression	Consultation	Participation	Partnership	Activism	Leadership
Volunteering opinions, creating art, celebrating, complaining, praising, objecting	Being asked for their opinion, providing feedback, serving on a focus group, completing a survey	Attending meetings or events in which decisions are made, frequent inclusion when issues are framed and actions planned	Formalized role in decision making, standard operations require (not just invite) student involvement, adults are trained in how to work collaboratively with youth partners	Identifying problems, generating solutions, organizing responses, agitating and/or educating for change both in and outside of school contexts	(Co-)Planning, making decisions and accepting significant responsibility for outcomes, (co-)guiding group processes, (co-)conducting activities

Students articulating their perspectives — — — — — • Students involved as stakeholders — — — — — • Students directing collective activities

Students as data sources — — — — — • Students as collaborators — — — — — • Students as leaders of change

Most student voice activity in schools/classrooms resides at this end of the spectrum.

The need for adults to share authority, demonstrate trust, protect against co-optation, learn from students, and handle disagreement *increases* from left to right. Students' influence, responsibility, and decision-making roles *increase* from left to right.

Source: Toshalis & Nakkula, 2012, p. 24. Used with permission.

Figure 10.1: The spectrum of student voice–oriented activity.

♦ How do students engage in mathematics learning?

♦ How many students succeed? What evidence supports this measure?

♦ How many students seem genuinely excited to sit in their mathematics classroom?

♦ In which ways do your students directly contribute to the continual improvement of mathematics instruction in your district?

Did the last seem out of place? When you pose that question to large groups of leaders, some will respond, "We don't want our students running the school! After all, we are the ones with the degrees in education." These responses reflect the long-standing hierarchical culture of education systems. Think about it. We leave our students, the central figures in the school district, out of the decision-making process when it comes to instructional improvement. What other business functions in this manner? Fast-food companies sometimes spend millions of dollars on market research before launching new products or revamping existing ones (Zikmund & Babin, 2010). And yet, educators often fail to enlist a single student voice for feedback on the topic that matters most: the quality and effectiveness of the daily classroom learning experience.

The issue is not that students are a complete afterthought in the school community. In data collected from interviews of two hundred high school students from a school district in the mid-Atlantic region of the United States, students reported that they believed their voices mattered, in rank order of frequency of response (Barnes, Wray, & Novak, 2012), for:

1. Determining high school dance themes

2. Determining the themes for spirit weeks and pep rallies

3. Providing feedback, as part of the principal's student leadership team, about possible threats of bullying or cyberbullying

4. Electing officers for the Student Government Association

5. Competing against other district schools in social media competitions designed to build school pride

Of the top five answers, only the action in the third answer might impact mathematics instruction, and only in an indirect manner. The truth is that students receive a great deal of autonomy with noninstructional school functions. But what would happen if we asked two hundred students in the school district to provide specific, formative feedback to their teachers about the effectiveness of mathematics instruction? What if students in each school across the district participated regularly in the development of curricular resources and common assessments? What if students played a prominent role in the professional learning plan? What if we empowered students as equal partners in mathematics education and as advocates for improved quality of mathematics instruction? The answers to these questions reveal a great deal about leadership and the real potential for the mathematics program's growth. If a world-class mathematics program is the goal, then mathematics leaders need to involve students in meaningful ways. Students must win entrance to those sacred spaces in the mathematics program: the planning rooms, the training rooms, and the curriculum production rooms. If you have been following the recommendations in this book, you have already seen the power of student participation in your MLT. Your challenge now is to expand student influence by amplifying their voices in your district.

A Word About Readiness

Inviting students to become equal partners in the program improvement plans is a worthwhile pursuit. But as great as it sounds in this book, it is much harder to actually achieve. In order to shift perceptions about students' roles, mathematics program leaders need to work diligently to create a state of readiness. This level of student engagement is not the norm, and leaders will have to prepare students, staff, and school and district leaders for the journey ahead.

To begin, mathematics leaders communicate their intentions to students and families. Take time to craft a message to share with all stakeholders. This message can appear on the district or school website, go out in the school newsletter, or go directly to families via mail or email. Figure 10.2 provides a short example.

To our amazing students and their families:

As the mathematics leader, I am charged with working with your teachers to create the best mathematics learning experience possible. I believe that we can create even better mathematics classrooms if we listen and learn from you, our students. I am writing to ask you to consider being part of any of these exciting new experiences:

♦ Interviewing students

♦ Training teachers

♦ Developing classroom resources and assessments

For each of these experiences, you will be working closely with teachers and leaders to make our mathematics classrooms more exciting and effective. Thank you for considering this invitation. Visit our website to sign up. Hope to see you soon.

Figure 10.2: Message example to students and families.

Be sure to target all students and every student group. Leaders should strive for a demographic balance on the student team, and some students for whom the current mathematics program is not working and some for whom it is working well. The latter may be a bit trickier. Disengaged students tend to resist invitations to participate in these types of endeavors. Mathematics leaders must appeal to them with transparency and humility. Saying, "I am committed to making sure that your mathematics experience improves and I need your help to make this happen," communicates with sincerity that you honor students' reality, take ownership of their experience, and value their perspective in the improvement process.

Preparing staff for increased student involvement can sometimes be a challenge. Mathematics leaders serve amazing teachers who work hard every day to deliver engaging lessons to students. Openly inviting students to participate in a program improvement process could send the message to these teachers that leaders do not value their input. Communication is the key to establishing readiness with staff. First state your purpose—why student voices? Collaborative teams and teachers need to understand how engaging students supports creating a culture of continual improvement. Student engagement, at this level, provides all educators with previously unavailable insights. Further, mathematics leaders build a student community whose members understand that adults value them as partners in mathematics education. Please note that this initiative is not about letting students make all of the important decisions. It is about engaging students, with their teachers, to learn from each other for a better classroom experience for all.

Be sure to involve teachers in the planning process. Teachers can help develop student interview questions so that they can gather the data that matter to them most. As the program leader, be sure to have an open-door policy for teachers so that they can communicate any concerns moving forward. After all, these processes will leave some teachers vulnerable. Students may provide feedback on specific lessons that disengages teachers if you do not establish clear protocols first. Ensure that teacher disillusionment does not happen through thoughtful communication, staff engagement at all levels of planning, and a nurturing environment that honors staff and students alike.

Students as Catalysts for Improving Mathematics Instruction

In mathematics classrooms across the United States, the focus of classroom observation is changing from what the teacher is doing to what the students are doing. The shift from collecting evidence of teacher actions to collecting evidence of student actions has increased attention on mathematics classrooms since the emergence of the Standards for Mathematical Practice (NGA & CCSSO, 2010). These mathematics learning behaviors have clarified, for observers, exactly what mathematics students should be doing in the classroom. The attention to student learning behaviors and student engagement is not limited to mathematics classrooms. In her popular framework for instructional improvement, Charlotte Danielson (2007) reserves *distinguished practice* for any subject-area teacher who is able to create a culture that empowers students as equal learning partners. With an unprecedented focus on student actions, the question becomes, What might students have to say about efforts to improve mathematics classrooms? The easiest way to find out is simply to ask the students themselves. Interviewing students about classroom instruction is an essential leadership process, providing data that inform the teaching and learning quality, the classroom learning environment, and issues of equity and access. If you haven't interviewed students about their instructional experience, the process will forever change the way you think about mathematics leadership. Incorporate five key actions to conduct effective student interviews.

1. Develop a purpose for a specific round of student interviews.

2. Select a target group of students to interview.

3. Write open-ended questions that draw out the student experiences.

4. Recruit an interview team.

5. Listen carefully and without judgment when interviewing.

The selection of students to interview depends entirely on the purpose of the interviews. If you intend to work with a middle school mathematics department to learn how to engage more students in productive classroom discourse, then you will want to select students who represent each grade level, every course, and every teacher. When selecting students, it is important to determine the size of the group that you want to interview. Interviewing individual students may be too time consuming, and interviewing a whole class at one time can prevent all student voices from contributing in meaningful ways. Instead, consider interviewing between six and ten students at a time. Another factor is the duration of the interview. Be sure to provide students with enough time to fully respond to the questions. For example, if you are going to ask a group of ten students to respond to three questions, then you are probably going to want to schedule at least forty-five minutes for the interviews.

The primary job of the interviewer is to get students talking about a particular area of focus and then let the conversation unfold in an authentic way. The best way to do this is to create engaging and open-ended questions.

An open-ended question has multiple entry points and provides students with some flexibility in telling their stories. Avoid creating questions that they can answer with just a few words. For example, asking students, "Do you like mathematics class?" could be a question of interest but may not provide as much meaningful data as asking students, "Describe a time that you enjoyed learning something new in any part of your life. Why did you enjoy that experience so much?" Remember, this process is all about permitting the students to tell their stories. Figure 10.3 provides interview question examples for a variety of stated purposes.

Purpose: To learn about student learning
- ◆ "Describe a time that you enjoyed learning something new in any part of your life. Why did you enjoy that experience so much?"
- ◆ "Tell me about your mathematics learning experiences. Compare your experiences in elementary school, middle school, and high school."
- ◆ "If you could give your mathematics teacher one piece of advice to improve the effectiveness of your learning, what would it be?"
- ◆ "Describe how you learn best."

Purpose: To learn about mindsets, equity, and access
- ◆ "Do you believe that all students can become good at mathematics? Justify your answer."
- ◆ "In what ways have you been encouraged or discouraged from taking advanced mathematics courses throughout your time in school?"

Purpose: To learn about students' hope, well-being, and engagement
- ◆ "Tell me about a time when a teacher made you feel good about your ability in mathematics."
- ◆ "Tell me about a time when a teacher made you feel bad about yourself in mathematics."

Figure 10.3: Interview question examples.

While you should appreciate open sharing and candor during these interviews, as the facilitator, it is wise to establish a few ground rules for student responses. Here is a list of norms to consider for student interviews.

- ◆ Please respect confidentiality throughout this process. It is not appropriate for anyone in this room to share information or stories outside of this room. We will anonymously analyze your responses after we have collected all of the student interview data from today.

- ◆ When responding, please refrain from using a specific teacher's name.

- ◆ When responding, remember that all of your peers have a story that is important to them. Refrain from judgment and honor your peers' perspectives.

- ◆ Please be respectful and try not to interrupt when others speak. You will have plenty of time to share your thoughts and ideas.

During the interviews, be sure to gently remind students of the norms if they unintentionally violate a particular agreement.

In order to capture as many data points as possible, we recommend that two educators work collaboratively to interview the students. One educator, preferably a mathematics leader, asks the questions while the other captures student quotations and summaries of anecdotes. If a school staff member is part of the team, take care to ensure that none of the students being interviewed is in his or her classes, which would mean the members of the interview team will influence student participation. For example, students are much less likely to engage in the process if they believe that the teacher joining the interview team will violate the confidentiality norm. School administrators or guidance counselors are excellent candidates as members of the interview team because students tend to trust each as a confidant.

The important leadership work begins once all of the interviews are complete and the interviewers have collected and organized the data. In this instance, *data* describes each quote, anecdote, or summarized statement. In some instances, several students will have agreed that a particular student response also reflects their own beliefs. In these cases, be sure to indicate that. For example, a student may say, "My geometry teacher always lets us work in teams to solve difficult problems. I really like that." Several other students might agree that they like to work in groups. Be sure to capture the number of students who agree with that idea in your notes. Work with your interview partner to verify that each data point is accurate and relevant. If you capture statements that you cannot associate with a specific question, you can place them in a separate section titled Additional Comments. Figure 10.4 provides you with actual student data examples that we have sorted by question (Barnes et al., 2012).

Question: Describe a time that you enjoyed learning something new in any part of your life. Why did you enjoy that experience so much?

- "I learned how to play the guitar when I was 13. It was so cool. I liked it because I could use YouTube to learn new songs."
- "I remember learning about factoring. I like it because it was hard and because I was good at it. My teacher brought in these tiles that made it really make sense at first. I like being good at things."
- "In elementary school, I learned how to speak Spanish. My school started teaching Spanish when I was in third grade. I felt good because I could speak another language and my parents could not."

Question: If you could give your mathematics teacher one piece of advice to improve the effectiveness of your learning, what would it be?

- "We need to practice real-life problems."
- "We want to work in groups."
- "We do not want to feel intimidated."
- "We would be able to download digital textbooks to our phones."

Purpose: Hope, well-being, and engagement

- "Mrs. Babbich is the best. She learns everyone's name and asks about our families and friends. I love going to her class."
- "I don't think my teacher cares one way or another about me. She probably doesn't hate me . . . she just doesn't care."
- "One of my mathematics teachers actually tries different techniques. She works hard to connect to the way I learn best. My other teacher does not do this at all. If I don't conform to her style, I'm sunk."
- "My teacher said that not everyone was born to do mathematics."
- "In elementary and middle school you get blocked in to a track. Once you are there you are screwed. I took a test in elementary when you were supposed to put a smiley face by problems you could not do. I misunderstood directions and put smiley faces by each problem. As a result I was put in low-level mathematics and just could not get out."
- "I can tell in the first two weeks whether or not I am going to pass a class. If the teacher cares about me, I am going to pass, usually with a B or C. If the teacher doesn't like me, I'm going to fail. I don't have time for people that don't have time for me."

Source: Barnes et al., 2012.

Figure 10.4: Sorted data table examples.

A Professional Learning Activity to Process the Data

The MLT and mathematics leaders gain a great deal of meaningful data from interviews. The question is, What are you going to do with the data? Some of the data points give rise to celebration. Others may bring team members to tears. When working with schools, it is important to engage teachers and leaders in a professional learning activity focused on analyzing, synthesizing, and responding to the student data. As we mentioned before, mathematics leaders should ensure that they have created a state of *readiness* because these data are very personal in nature. It would be natural for staff to feel defensive and pull away from the whole process. Work with the site-based administrators to design a course of action that best matches the readiness of the team.

Before engaging staff in the professional learning activity, take some time to prepare the data. You could transfer each data point onto an index card, or organize the data into a chart listing positive data in one column and constructive data in another column. Whatever the representation, we recommend that leaders strategically select a small sample of data to begin the process. Here is an example of how you might facilitate professional learning focused on just one of the questions.

- Begin by transferring each data point from one interview question onto index cards (one per card).

- Develop and review norms with staff.

- Provide a set of index cards to each group of three staff members.

- Instruct staff members to organize the cards into three groups: (1) positive comments, (2) constructive comments, and (3) negative comments.

- Facilitate a discussion focused on these questions after sorting the cards.

  ◇ When looking at the data, what brings you the greatest sense of pride?

  ◇ What concerns you?

  ◇ What frustrates you?

  ◇ What surprises you?

- Ask groups of three staff members to identify trends that emerge from the data.

- Facilitate a discussion about the trends each group identified.

- Reach group consensus on which trends they would like to gather more data for, develop and take immediate action on, and put aside for now.

- Summarize the process by reviewing common agreements, actions, and next steps.

Empowering students as catalysts for instructional improvement begins with listening carefully to their stories and experiences. It continues with exploring strategies for increasing the frequency and quality of feedback that students provide to their teachers. Many teachers use student surveys to gather information about their students' experiences in the classroom. The problem is that teachers administer these surveys at the end of the semester or, more typically, at the end of the school year. For feedback to be meaningful, it must be *FAST*: fair, accurate, specific, and timely (Briars et al., 2012; Reeves, 2011). This is true for teacher-to-student feedback *and* student-to-teacher feedback. Designing a real-time system for collecting student feedback about daily instruction has the potential to transform a teacher's practice. To achieve this, a teacher or collaborative team could use an online survey tool, such as Google Forms, to gather and review feedback to inform:

- The effectiveness of specific learning tasks

- The quality of student-to-student discourse

- The clarity of content development

- Student interest

- The effectiveness of instructional strategies

Reviewing these data throughout the school year provides insights for teachers and teams to consider when planning lesson experiences and assessments. The process of leading students and teachers to a place where formative feedback about mathematics instruction and student learning flows freely between students and teachers is a significant step forward in learning for any district mathematics program.

The Mathematics Student as Professional Developer

Consider the following story. As you read, think about how your district uses students' feedback to improve the quality of mathematics instruction.

Scenario

It is August and the new mathematics teachers are reporting to a weeklong series of trainings designed as a district orientation. The event kicks off with a short greeting from the superintendent in the auditorium followed by a review of the week's schedule. During the week, new teachers take part in a number of procedural activities like picking up their ID badges, learning how to use the email system, and learning about the district's mentoring and support systems. But before they do any of those things, they report to the mathematics leader for new teacher induction. The first two days are reserved for new teachers to meet with curriculum staff to learn about the vision for mathematics teaching and learning, understand how to access curricular resources, learn about local assessment systems, and receive differentiated professional learning on topics that interest them. This is an important moment in the life cycle of the new teachers because it is the mathematics leader's first chance to make an impression. This is the one moment in time when these new mathematics teachers will be free of opinions that will eventually form based on school culture, the demands of students and parents, and their heavy workload. New teachers burst from the auditorium, eager to meet their curriculum supervisors and more eager to learn how they can access district curricular materials to plan lessons for their students. Outside the auditorium, the superintendent shakes hands with new staff. One particularly well-dressed man approaches the superintendent. She greets him with a couple of questions: "What will you be teaching for us this year? Which school is lucky enough to have you on staff?" The man replies, "Oh, I'm not a new teacher, I'm a student. I was just coming to ask you if you knew where the new mathematics teachers were scheduled to meet. You see, I'm here to train the teachers."

Students in your school or district, as the primary consumers of mathematics instruction, have a great deal of knowledge and experience that will grow your mathematics program. As an effective district mathematics leader, it is important to provide opportunities for students to play an integral role in the professional learning plan. Professional learning is designed to increase a mathematics teacher's capacity to provide an exemplary learning experience for students. But, traditionally, we leave students out of this process. Instead of sharing their experiences directly with staff, the student voice manifests itself during professional learning sessions through storytelling. Teacher participants take responsibility for communicating what students want, what they need, and how they prefer to work in classrooms. This process, like the children's game Telephone, is leaky. Messages passed from one source to another change slightly until the message, after being shared via many teachers, no longer resembles the original message. The students' actual wants, needs, and preferences may take new shapes when teachers communicate them secondhand. Student panels, learning labs, and professional learning roles are a few ways that students can become active members of your professional development team. Let's explore each of these opportunities.

Students are willing to share their stories. Including student panels as part of professional development sessions is an excellent way to provide insights to teachers. Consider providing mathematics teachers with access to students' perspectives throughout the school year. Student panels can enhance new teacher orientation, professional conference sessions, or lesson study reflections. Be sure to invite students with a variety of perspectives to join the panel. Here are some examples of student panel questions.

- If you could design the perfect mathematics classroom experience, one that results in you learning the most, what would it look like? What is your teacher doing? What are you doing?

- How much time do you typically spend completing mathematics homework? What are your feelings about the quantity and quality of the assigned homework? How does this compare to the quantity and quality of your homework in other classes?

- What are some tips you might give to new mathematics teachers? What motivates you to engage in a lesson? What teacher actions are likely to disengage you from the lesson?

Sometimes referred to as *fishbowl lessons*, learning labs are learning experiences that educators or leaders called *process observers* observe. In a learning lab, a guest teacher engages invited students in a small portion of a mathematics lesson. The teacher focuses on an instructional shift or goal and the observers treat it as a live-action research process. A lab could focus on engaging groups of students in a worthwhile mathematical task, productive mathematical discourse, or the Standards for Mathematical Practice. Prior to the lesson, facilitate a meeting between the process observers and the guest teacher. The guest teacher should describe the focus for the lesson and provide any insights. While this lesson preparation takes place, the invited students receive their own briefing. Students should understand the focus of the lesson and receive instructions about how they will work, including encouragement to ignore the adults sitting around the room. During the lesson, process observers should sit silently, taking notes and jotting down questions that they intend to ask. At the conclusion of the lesson, which is usually twenty-five to thirty minutes in length, there are three rounds of summary activities. During the first round, process observers ask students about their learning experience. For example, one observing teacher might ask, "During the lesson, I noticed that you were struggling to model the equation using the cups-and-counters model. What were you thinking at that time? What happened to help you begin to understand?" This grain size of questioning elicits specific student feedback that provides great insight into how students were actually learning—in this case, the specific learning event that triggered understanding. This is very useful information for teachers. During the second round of reflection, process observers ask the teacher specific questions about the lesson. Students may also chime in with feedback based on the teacher's responses. For example, if a process observer asks, "Why did you use cups-and-counters to model equation solving?" and the teacher responds, "I often use concrete models to introduce abstract concepts. In this case, I wanted to emphasize equality," a student may jump in by saying, "Using models helps me understand *why* the mathematics works." Round three is for students. During round three of the summary, students ask questions of the guest teacher or the process observers. Students may be curious about how teachers plan for exemplary mathematics teaching and learning. For example, a student might ask, "How did you think to use rice as a tool to get us to compare the volumes of different solids? That really helped me understand the difference between area and volume." Learning labs are an exceptional way to engage teachers and students in a clinical and reflective process about teaching and learning.

Mathematics leaders grow students as professional developers over time. Eventually, students will be ready to serve as co-presenters or even lead presenters for professional learning opportunities. For example, a teacher and student could present a session to teachers to engage them in completing a task. The teacher might talk through key points related to NCTM's Mathematics Teaching Practices while the student highlights mathematics process standards. Consider using student-led sessions as a strategy for attracting students to professional development workshops. Why should professional conferences focus on the instructor? Your students would benefit from learning about learning just as much. In fact, consider hosting at least one jointly sponsored professional development workshop focused on providing learning to both teachers and students.

Students have a unique perspective on mathematics teaching and learning in your school or district. Effective mathematics leaders work to engage the student voice as an important asset to a professional development program.

 # The Mathematics Student as Curriculum Developer

Consider the following story. As you read the story, think about how your district uses the voices of students to improve the quality of mathematics instruction.

Scenario

A mathematics leader works with teachers to design a new statistics course. Teachers clamor for a non-AP statistics course to engage students in this mathematics discipline with hopes that many of these students would enroll in AP statistics the following semester. During the process, the district mathematics leader struggles with the notion of churning out just one more typical mathematics course, so his team decides to try something new. The next planning meeting takes place two weeks later. When the planning team reconvenes, a group of six students is present. Within two hours of focused discussion, the new statistics course is transformed. The student members of the planning team challenged the district to do the following.

- *Develop an application-based statistics course. They insist that the course focus on students exploring their world through the use of statistics.*

- *Develop a course focused on student teams researching a question of interest. Further, student teams could be formed with students from various schools across the district. For example, if four students, each from different schools, wanted to study the extent of performance-enhancing drug use for local high school athletes, they should be permitted to do so.*

- *Develop flipped models for learning content. Student teams would reserve class time to engage in differentiated experiences including designing research questions, developing data collection tools, collecting and analyzing data, reaching out to community partners to strengthen their research, and, almost as an afterthought, soliciting teacher support with statistics content.*

When the summer curriculum workshops begin, these six students join the curriculum development teams, churning out resources for teachers and students alike. The course is piloted in a few high schools the following fall.

This story highlights just one way that students can enhance the curriculum development process. Students provide meaningful feedback to curriculum and assessment developers, feedback that can increase the quality of course design, classroom resource design, or the design of assessments.

Students can be active members of the curriculum development team by becoming product testers, production staff, and authors, to name a few. Let's examine each role.

This student role is probably the easiest to implement. During curriculum and assessment development workshops, enlist a cadre of students to test out the developed resources. For example, if a team of teachers designs a worthwhile mathematical task focused on building conceptual understanding for solving systems of linear equations, a team of students can actually engage in the task. The teachers who designed the task could observe students working on the task long before a teacher uses it in full classes. Item writers observing students, coupled with feedback from the students themselves, could help the teachers clarify directions, strengthen the sequence of questions, or update the problem context to better reflect student interest. As an added bonus, the writing team collects student work samples that will become a valuable part of the task's answer key. This process is effective for lesson activities and assessment items alike. If you want to upgrade the process, record a video of students providing insights to teachers about the problem or task. This will be invaluable during instructional planning sessions.

Students are some of the most technologically savvy members of your mathematics community. During the curriculum development process, enlist students to create graphics, research online resources, or look into an app to support the learning experience. Students can also work with teachers to produce videos or audio clips supporting the implementation of a curricular resource. For example, a student may star in a video designed to show teachers how to use fraction strips and number lines to build conceptual understanding of division of fractions. Or, a student may direct a video of a teacher explaining big ideas for implementing a written lesson. Engaging students as production assistants is a great way to increase the productivity of the whole team. Nothing bogs down a curriculum-writing workshop faster than a team of teachers spending three hours trying to create an online graphic. Give that task to a student instead.

In some cases, student content knowledge exceeds the content knowledge of the teachers assigned to develop curricular resources. For example, second-year calculus students may sign up to take part in the curriculum development process. Consider involving students as members of a curriculum workshop team. Students have great ideas and experience with mathematics content.

There are limited possibilities for students to play a major role in improving the design and implementation of curricular resources. Mathematics leaders will have to invest some additional time and energy to build a culture of inclusion. But, once that work is complete, we will have a never-ending pipeline of students working to strengthen our curriculum design processes.

The Mathematics Student as Advocate

The following scenario underscores the power of the student voice to influence policy and practice. In fact, these voices have great potential to cut through some of the red tape of education bureaucracy and speedily resolve dilemmas if mathematics leaders, collaborative teams, and teachers invite them into discussions. In addition to encouraging students' participation in committees, advisory groups, or the MLT, mathematics leaders, collaborative teams, and teachers should leverage the student voice as a catalyst for change.

> ### *Scenario*
>
> *A school district enlists a team of stakeholders to revise its high school graduation policy. The team includes central office curriculum staff, school administrators, school counselors, parents, community members, representatives from local institutions of higher education, and two students. The central point of contention is the issue of whether to award an actual high school credit to middle school students taking high school mathematics courses. In the current state, an eighth-grade student successfully completing the high school algebra 1 course gets credit for taking the course, but does not receive one of the twenty-four high school credits needed to move a step closer to graduation. The debate rages on with proponents of each side offering doomsday scenarios to persuade others to come to their side. After three hours of rich debate, one of the students raises his hand and says, "We'd like to speak now." The adults in the room are astonished—not by the fact that the students want to participate in the discussion, but instead because, over the past three hours, no one has even considered inviting the students into the discussion. The student follows his request with, "We have been talking about this. We do not think it is fair for students to complete a high school course and not get credit. We learn the same lessons, work on the same problems, and take the same final exam. But we do not get high school credit. It just doesn't make sense. It's like we are being punished for wanting to accelerate in our mathematics coursework." With his fellow student nodding in assent, the debate is effectively over. After a couple of clarifying questions, the room falls silent, the team members vote, and middle school students are set to receive high school credit when taking high school courses in middle school.*

Students' collective stories represent the purest form of performance assessment data available to mathematics leaders. As a program leader, your responsibility is to partner with students as advocates for your vision of exemplary mathematics teaching and learning. For example, consider asking student mentors to encourage students in lower grades to work toward advanced mathematics coursework. This is not a new idea. Encourage mentors to insist that those they coach engage in the mathematics program as professional developers or as members of curriculum workshop teams. Student mentors provide an important service to students in lower grades.

Amplifying the student's voice as a catalyst for change is an important leadership action. Effective mathematics leaders invite students into new spaces to spark innovation and growth. A few years after they make the shift to include students, mathematics leaders will not believe that they ever led without allowing students' perspectives to influence every part of the mathematics program.

Move From Vision to Action

Effective mathematics leaders work to amplify the student voice as a catalyst for improvement of mathematics instruction. To achieve the vision, leaders engage students as members of the professional development team of trainers, as valued members of the curriculum development workshop teams, and as advocates for the shared vision of exemplary mathematics teaching and learning. Table 10.1 (page 146) describes the relationship among district-, site-, and team-level roles in activating the student voice to check alignment between vision and reality.

Table 10.1: Mathematics Leadership Commitments to Activate the Student Voice to Check Alignment Between Vision and Reality

District's Role	Site-Level Leader's Role	Collaborative Team's Role
Collaborate with site-based staff to develop a state of readiness to receive feedback from students to inform instructional improvement.	Collaborate with teachers delivering mathematics instruction to address staff concerns about elevating student perspectives related to mathematics instruction.	Engage in discussions to identify the various ways that team members might use the student voice to improve their professional practice.
Develop structures for conducting student interviews to improve the classroom learning environment and the quality of mathematics instruction.	Collaborate with teachers delivering mathematics instruction to ascertain what information teachers wish to collect from students. After supporting the student interview process, facilitate the collaborative analysis and synthesis of student interview data. Develop strategic plans to address student concerns if necessary.	Collaboratively analyze and synthesize student interview data. Implement strategies to address student concerns if necessary.
Develop structures for engaging students as professional developers.	Empower students as equal partners in the mathematics teaching and learning community.	Empower students as equal partners in the classroom.
Develop structures for engaging students as curriculum developers.	Recruit students to be part of curriculum workshop teams.	Recruit students to be part of the school improvement planning team.
Provide students with the knowledge and resources to advocate for effective mathematics programming.	Listen carefully to student feedback and consider appropriate actions for growth.	Develop formative feedback tools to gather information about the student learning experience. Take action on student feedback that informs instructional practice.

*Visit **go.SolutionTree.com/leadership** for a free reproducible version of this table.*

Reflection

Review the Key 4 audit statement regarding how to activate the student voice in figure 10.5, and with your MLT, reflect on your current strengths and opportunities to grow. Describe specific action steps to support this specific Key 4 statement.

Key 4: Activate the Student Voice to Check Alignment Between Vision and Reality	Next Steps
The student voice is prevalent and honored throughout the mathematics program. Leaders make regular efforts to gather insights from students through interviews or surveys. The student voice serves as a catalyst for program improvement.	

Figure 10.5: Key 4—Activate the student voice to check alignment between vision and reality.

*Visit **go.SolutionTree.com/leadership** for a free reproducible version of this figure.*

Students, as the primary stakeholders in the mathematics community, have a unique perspective on mathematics teaching and learning. Leveraging those perspectives will provide teachers and leaders with insights to guide more effective instructional planning. But students need the support of their families and guardians to ensure that they successfully navigate the instructional program. In chapter 11, we share strategies for engaging families as advocates for their children and for greater equity and access in your mathematics program.

11 | Empower Families as Informed Advocates

A child educated only at school is an uneducated child.

—George Santayana

When considering the growth of the mathematics program, remember to include families, another stakeholder group that leaders have traditionally marginalized in education systems. Educators certainly recognize the value of families as clients and often endeavor to engage families as equal partners in education in their mission statements. However, in reality, we often relegate families to the role of silent partners.

Effective mathematics leaders question how they will engage and empower families as advocates who support the vision for exemplary mathematics teaching and learning. When responding to this question, it is important to consider where the involvement of parents can be most effective in both the short and long term. To engage families in new ways, which parts of the mathematics program make the most sense? In this chapter, we explore how mathematics leaders can involve families by:

- Building knowledge of exemplary mathematics teaching and learning so that parents can support that learning at home

- Strengthening families' capacity to serve as advocates for issues of equity and access to ensure that their children graduate from high school ready for success

- Empowering families as active members of their children's school improvement planning team

- Teaching families how to serve as effective members of policy or advisory committees

- Recruiting families as champions ready to celebrate the great works of students, teachers, and school staff

How Will Families Support the Vision for Exemplary Mathematics Teaching and Learning?

Mathematics educators have been researching strategies for teaching mathematics more effectively since 1989, when NCTM encouraged them to adopt a standards-based approach to mathematics teaching and learning. As part of that movement, NCTM urged teachers to move away from a singular focus on traditional "skill and drill" and memorization strategies. Instead, teachers should work to strengthen a student's capacity to reason, problem solve, and communicate effectively (NCTM, 1989). This movement would evolve as new research emerged and as federal policy began to reshape our schools and school systems. In 2010, the Common Core State Standards for mathematics (NGA & CCSSO, 2010) heightened the focus of families and community stakeholders on mathematics classroom instruction. The debate about *what* to teach and *how* teachers should teach mathematics has been the subject of public scrutiny for a generation. The journey toward engaging families in support of the vision for exemplary mathematics teaching and learning begins by building a common understanding of what exemplary mathematics teaching and learning should look like. Using the phrase *should look like* is intentional. As leaders begin to educate parents and community members, they will be empowered to serve as advocates for their children. They will come to expect that the intended classroom standards for effective teaching should be the reality for their children.

> ### *Effective Leadership Tip*
>
> *Your first step in building a common understanding of exemplary mathematics teaching and learning is to make expectations clearly visible in your school or district.*

The first step in building a common understanding of exemplary mathematics teaching and learning is to make expectations clearly visible in your school or district. For example, leaders can publicize research-affirmed teaching and learning standards, such as NCTM's (2014) Mathematics Teaching Practices and the Standards for Mathematical Practice (NGA & CCSSO, 2010), on the school website or in the newsletter and other office publications. Work to develop an effective plan for marketing and branding these expected teacher and student behaviors. One example from which you can build is the Howard County Public School System's Family Mathematics Support Center (Howard County Public Schools Office of Secondary Mathematics, 2015/2016), an open-sourced website at http://hcpssfamilymath.weebly.com focused on clearly articulating standards for exemplary teaching and learning.

Developing a brand for exemplary mathematics teaching and learning in print will only take you so far. It is essential to design face-to-face events to engage families and community members in discussions about mathematics teaching and learning. For example, consider the following possibilities for face-to-face interactions with families and community members.

- Host a family mathematics gathering designed to engage families in mathematics learning, current policy, mathematics programming, and steps to ensure that their children graduate ready for college mathematics. Include sessions that present families with alternative approaches for learning mathematics.

- Provide parents with authentic learning experiences to grow their understanding of the instructional shifts. Recruit exceptional teachers to explain why it is important to develop conceptual understanding of mathematics for procedural fluency.

Face-to-face mathematics events, held once or twice per school year, are an excellent way to build a family's understanding of your vision for exemplary mathematics teaching and learning.

Armed with knowledge of the mathematics program's vision for exemplary mathematics teaching and learning, parents will use this new lens to reconcile the intended learning experience with what their children actually experience. Of course you strive for complete alignment between expectations and delivery. But if there is misalignment, parents need to know how to proceed. As a mathematics program leader, your responsibility is to provide parents with talking points to support their instructional conversations with staff. Here are a few questions that could be useful for families during instructional conversations with school or district leaders.

- What are some strategies you are using to help my child develop a deep, conceptual understanding of mathematics content?

- What is your plan for developing my child's understanding of, and facility with, the Standards for Mathematical Practice?

- How might I support the development of the Standards for Mathematical Practice at home?

The mathematics program leader's job is to prepare families with the knowledge to support the vision for mathematics teaching and learning. Providing opportunities for parents to engage in mathematics in person, online resources for them to access, and questions to deepen the quality of instructional conversations with staff is a great first step in increasing family engagement.

How Will Families Support Your Vision for Equity and Access?

Families often ask, "Will my child be ready to succeed in the real world based on school experiences?" Mathematics leaders, site leaders, and collaborative teams work collectively and share responsibility to help all families understand how to advocate for their children to ensure that they achieve the goal of college readiness in mathematics. Some possible actions to empower families as advocates in this work include the following.

- **Build a common understanding of the term *college readiness* in mathematics:** Exactly which course profile and standardized test profile increase the likelihood of a student graduating ready for college in mathematics? Explore this question with parents as early as third grade. Invite representatives from local institutions of higher education to the district to work with parents to highlight admission requirements. If the local university is focused on admitting students who have completed AP calculus AB and earned a 600 on the mathematics SAT, families should know that information as early in the process as possible.

- **Build a strong understanding of the mathematics program's course pathways:** In all likelihood, your mathematics program offers a variety of pathways. It is your responsibility to highlight the destination courses likely to indicate college readiness (such as precalculus, college algebra, calculus, statistics, and so on). Further, you must help families chart a course from the student's current mathematics course to the desired destination courses. As a mathematics leader, you must communicate the various entry points that permit students to accelerate to a college readiness pathway. For example, a student who is on a pathway to complete algebra 2 (or integrated mathematics 3) in grade 12 is less likely to graduate ready for college than the student enrolled in precalculus or a college-level mathematics course. Families need to know how to advocate for their students as they work toward an advanced mathematics course. Develop clear mathematics progressions so that families can easily chart a course from their child's current grade level through grade 12. For example, a family with a third-grade student might work with a guidance counselor to adjust the current sequence to ensure that the student reaches algebra 1 or integrated mathematics 1 by the end of middle school.

- **Work with families to understand student achievement data:** Mathematics leaders need families to move beyond the scope of their own child, and support equitable learning for all children. When you publish student achievement data in your district, engage families in data discussions to talk about existing gaps in achievement among student groups. Empowering families in this manner builds greater ownership in the community. It will be difficult to reach every family by yourself. You may need to enlist the help of more reachable families to engage those with more reluctance to engage.

- **Empower families to improve existing practices:** There are a number of practices within school districts that widen achievement gaps. For example, there may be a number of clear and absolute prerequisites listed in your course catalog. While these prerequisites make it easy for educators to build school schedules and academic support, they also prevent students from accelerating. Enlisting the support of families as problem solvers may produce solutions to long-standing institutional issues such as these. Invite families to participate on policy committees, advisory boards, their school's school improvement planning team, or your MLT. Encourage family members to question everything in an effort to shape a better future for all children.

Table 11.1 describes the roles of mathematics leaders working together to empower families as advocates who strengthen your mathematics program.

Table 11.1: Empowering Families—Summary of Leadership Actions

	Mathematics Leaders	Site Leaders	Collaborative Teams
Build a common understanding of the term *college readiness* in mathematics.	Design learning experiences for families to define *college readiness*.	Connect families with resources to deepen their understanding of *college readiness*.	Ensure that students receive instruction leading to *college readiness*.
Build a strong understanding of the mathematics program's course pathways.	Develop resources that clearly articulate college readiness course pathways.	Ensure that families and students receive guidance for accessing rigorous college readiness pathways.	Design and implement rigorous first instruction and differentiated interventions to ensure all students have access to rigorous course pathways.

	Mathematics Leaders	Site Leaders	Collaborative Teams
Work with families to understand student achievement data.	Develop resources to help parents make sense of data reports.	Ensure that families receive guidance for making sense of student achievement data.	Work with students to routinely analyze data and set learning goals.
Empower families to improve existing practices.	Design learning experiences for families to clearly define anticipated student learning behaviors and intended teaching practices.	Invite families into the classroom to observe exemplary mathematics teaching and learning.	Design and implement learning experiences that engage students in intended learning behaviors by leveraging the NCTM (2014) Mathematics Teaching Practices.

Families have the potential to advocate for the mathematics vision of equity and access. Work to engage families so they champion their own children first and then they fight to ensure that all of the children in your mathematics program receive the same support.

Families Support Intentional Celebration

Other than the students and mathematics teachers in your district, no one is likely to have more information about daily mathematics instruction than family members. Consequently, you will want to engage students and family members in the culture of intentional celebration. You can suggest that families take a number of actions when they experience something positive in the mathematics community. They include the following.

- Write a thank-you note to the teacher reinforcing a moment that inspired student learning, strengthened a student's feeling of self-worth, or generated genuine appreciation. Of course, a thank-you email works just as well—bonus points for copying the teacher's administrators or curriculum supervisor.

- Post a message through social media. Respecting student privacy laws, students and families can celebrate the efforts of the teacher or class via social media. Of course, anyone can use this tool for the exact opposite purpose, so be sure to nurture the culture of celebration and provide guidelines for when to make news public, and how to address concerns in private.

In each and every school, there are dozens, maybe hundreds, of moments worth celebrating. Engage students, staff, and families in the spirit of authentic and meaningful celebration. Everyone works hard to help students learn mathematics. Be sure that everyone knows how much stakeholders appreciate his or her efforts.

As the mathematics program leader, work hard to develop a culture that welcomes families as advocates for the vision of exemplary mathematics teaching and learning. Find new opportunities to engage families in your program and search to expand those spaces each year. As was the case with your work to amplify the student voice, in a few years, you will not be able to imagine a time when families were marginalized in your mathematics community.

Move From Vision to Action

Effective mathematics leaders work to empower families as equal partners in mathematics education. Engaging families as advocates for exemplary teaching and learning, as well as equity and access, in mathematics education accelerates attainment of the vision. These partners in education also contribute to the culture of intentional celebration. Table 11.2 describes the relationship among district-, site-, and team-level roles to empower families as informed advocates.

Table 11.2: Mathematics Leadership Commitments to Empower Families as Informed Advocates

District's Role	Site-Level Leader's Role	Collaborative Team's Role
Develop parent-training workshops to clearly communicate mathematics pathways, college readiness expectations, and strategies to advocate equity and access in mathematics programming.	Empower families as equal partners in the mathematics teaching and learning community.	Clearly communicate mathematics pathways, college readiness expectations, and strategies for advocating for equity and access in mathematics programming to students and families.
Develop resources to assist families with supporting mathematics learning at home.	Recruit families to be part of the school improvement planning team.	Invite parents into the classroom to observe mathematics teaching and learning.

*Visit **go.SolutionTree.com/leadership** for a free reproducible version of this table.*

Reflection

Review the Key 4 audit statements about how to empower families as informed advocates in figure 11.1, and with your MLT, reflect on your current strengths and opportunities to grow. Describe specific action steps to support these specific Key 4 statements.

Key 4: Empower Families as Informed Advocates	Next Steps
Educators honor the parent or guardian voice throughout the mathematics program. District and site-based leaders make regular efforts to develop parents as advocates and to ensure that parents participate in professional development, curriculum development, and advisory groups.	
District- and site-level leadership teams have a well-defined process for gathering and responding to feedback on practices for involving parents and families in student achievement.	

Key 4: Empower Families as Informed Advocates	Next Steps
District- and site-level leadership teams have a systematic process for analyzing the data and the reasons for the noninvolvement of identified parents and families in student achievement.	
The site-level MLT has a process to inform parents and families about school programs and student progress. The process fosters two-way communication and ensures participation is representative of the school community.	

Figure 11.1: Key 4—Empower families as informed advocates.

*Visit **go.SolutionTree.com/leadership** for a free reproducible version of this figure.*

The mathematics program is strengthened by the active involvement of families and guardians. Advocating for their children as they navigate the mathematics program ensures that students receive the highest quality education. In chapter 12, we explore how to leverage the assets of community and business leaders. Empowering these leaders opens the doors of opportunity for your students as they transition from high school to college or careers.

12

Build and Engage a Strong Network of Partnerships

It takes a village to raise a child.

—African proverb

Education, at its root, is designed to produce graduates with the capacity to thrive in their communities. Effective school systems improve society in a number of ways. For example, the local economy grows because educated citizens earn more money, pay more taxes, and spend more money to support local businesses. Community partners and local business owners, therefore, have a vested interest in the school system. The question that mathematics leaders have to answer is, How will we leverage the resources available from community leaders and business owners to support our vision for exemplary mathematics teaching and learning?

In this chapter, we explore strategies that engage your network of community stakeholders as equal partners in mathematics education by:

- Developing and nurturing a variety of internships and externships that engage students in their intended field of study

- Leveraging the resources of community partners to support extracurricular opportunities in science, technology, engineering, and mathematics (STEM) or even these disciplines and the arts (STEAM)

- Training community professionals as mentors and tutors supporting student achievement and engagement

- Empowering community leaders to host events promoting mathematics and STEM professions

- Exploring innovative systems for pairing community leaders with students to improve the conditions of the community

The mathematics leader's role is to strengthen partnerships over time. By broadening the network of partnership opportunities, mathematics leaders ensure that

157

students not only graduate ready for success but also enter the next level with practical, real-world experiences and a professional network to leverage when they begin their full-time careers.

Develop and Nurture a Variety of Internships and Externships

When working to develop strong networks of engaged community partners, mathematics leaders need to be sure that both the school system and the community partner value a partner initiative. Most community organizations support some level of volunteerism as part of their organizational structure, but we want to elevate these partnerships above the status of merely giving back to the community. Students need to engage in real-life experiences that advance their interest in a particular field of study. Reach out to others to provide this experience. Partner with the career and technology education (CTE) program leaders to generate leads for potential partners. The CTE staff should have strong community partnerships and very likely an existing system of internships.

> **Effective Leadership Tip**
>
> *Partner with career and technology education (CTE) program leaders to generate leads for potential partners.*

Working with CTE staff and the leaders from organizations and businesses in the STEM fields, develop a comprehensive list of internships available to mathematics students. With the support of collaborative teams and site-level leaders, broadly promote these opportunities through the school district's website, newsletters, and social media. When planning the internships, be sure to include:

- A reflective component

- An opportunity for students to summarize their experience in a publication or presentation (for example, a portfolio presentation)

- A plan for celebrating their successes, which could include hosting an event showcasing the experiences of interns

- A marketing and recruitment component, such as inviting potential business partners, families, and potential student interns to this celebration

In time, the STEM internship program will grow, producing interns who return from their college experience as business leaders. These former interns become natural partners who want to provide students with the same rich opportunities they had. Mathematics leaders should be aware of one inevitable phenomenon: STEM professionals hire and recruit the very best candidates as future employees. It is our responsibility to ensure that all students, not just the most successful, have the opportunity to participate in the internship programs. It is best to be open with community partners about this charge right up front. The internship program will not reach its full potential unless all members of the community have equal opportunities to participate.

Externships, like internships, provide opportunities for members of the mathematics community to learn more about a field of study or program of interest. One strategy for increasing the capacity of the community members is to set up a variety of externships for staff members. For example, a group of interested teachers may decide to work with a local marketing firm, collecting and analyzing data as part of market research. The marketing firm receives some temporary human resources while the teachers engage in a real-world application of statistics. The lessons they learn in the field enhance the learning experience of their students in the statistics classroom. At the very least, when students ask the teacher, When am I going to use this when I grow up? the teachers can respond with personal examples from their externship. In addition to providing teachers and collaborative teams with these rich experiences, consider hosting interns as assets at the site or district level. College professors looking to engage in meaningful research during a sabbatical can provide some useful feedback about the growth of the mathematics program. Work with community partners to set up job-shadowing days. These opportunities enhance the perspective of school system staff and community partners alike.

Leverage Resources From Community Partners

Some community partners will not have the time or human resources to participate fully in internship or externship programs but will still want to find some way to support students and promote STEM education. Engage these partners by finding ways for them to sponsor a STEM function. For example, recruit a community partner to financially support the transportation costs associated with managing a mathematics competition. If the costs are prohibitive, then recruit two or three businesses to share the cost of running the league. Be sure to provide various levels of partnership. Lower levels of contribution may be able to support after-school tutoring programs at an elementary school. Higher levels may be able to fully support a school's robotics team. Local business partners often want to help. We just have to show them the way.

Some community partners want to engage at a personal level. They may have benefited from a program such as Big Brothers Big Sisters of America when growing up, and they want to provide that level of mentorship to a student in your school or district. As part of the vision of engaging community members, work to recruit and enlist STEM professionals as mentors for students. This is a great way for community members to support and enrich the lives of students. Be sure to work with school systems to ensure that community partners go through the proper procedures to be certified to work with your students. For example, outside mentors may have to be fingerprinted or take part in a background check. A professional mentor could be the one person who leads an otherwise wayward student toward college and a career as a STEM professional.

All students should feel empowered to contribute in authentic and meaningful ways to the growth of their communities. Students should graduate with the understanding that other adults now expect them to actively engage in these efforts. One innovative idea for developing this culture of service is to work with community partners to create community challenges. *Community challenges* engage students, families, and community partners in the work of improving the community. Consider this scenario of how a community challenge could support community growth.

Scenario

The manager of the local soup kitchen realizes that she is not able to serve lunch to all of the people who show up hungry. The lines are just too long and some people grow frustrated and leave. The manager puts out a call for help on the local community challenge board. She writes, "We are struggling to serve lunch to all of our citizens in a timely fashion. Some people are frustrated and leave hungry. My challenge: to see if there are ways to become more efficient in serving lunch to our community. Who will take this challenge?" Within two hours, a team of students with one lead parent writes back, "We will take the challenge." The team shows up to observe the lunch shift on two different days. They watch the food preparation process, see the distribution of food, interview people waiting in line for lunch, and collect data on the length of time it takes to serve each person. During their observations, they record, "A person approaches the counter and is greeted with a smile. The employee asks the customer what kind of sandwich, side dish, and drink the customer would like to eat. There are limited choices. Once the order is taken, the employee assembles the brown-bag lunch and hands the lunch to the customer at the end of the line. A team of four employees engages in this process. It takes an average of one minute and thirty seconds to feed each customer." The team considers the situation and provides the following recommendation to the manager: "Consider using one employee to walk down the lunch line to gather the orders from the customers (ten people at a time). Return to the main counter and report the information to the staff using a ticket system. Create a two-person assembly line to bag the lunches and the other team member can serve the lunches to the customers with a smile." The manager takes the recommendation of the team and cuts the service time down to forty seconds per customer within the span of two weeks. This is enough time saved to serve 200 percent more people for lunch each day.

In the preceding scenario, we provide you with a vision for how you might engage your mathematics community in efforts to support the community. Mathematics leaders at all levels are responsible for bringing the community into the school setting to enhance the learning of students *and* bring the students into the community to enhance overall quality of life.

Celebrate and Honor Community Partners

Developing strong network community partnerships takes time, energy, and passion. In time, mathematics leaders can engage students in a variety of authentic and exciting community experiences that make them better students and citizens. Success in this space requires coordination and a large group of volunteers. Start out small and grow your program steadily over time. Then your partnerships will endure over time. Another key ingredient to maintaining partnerships is to take the time to formally celebrate and honor community partners. In addition to securing letters and certificates of appreciation signed by the superintendent, write a personal thank-you note from your mathematics community. Include anecdotes or stories from those positively affected by the partnerships. Host an event to bring partners together to celebrate successes and to share new ideas. Be sure to visit each partner to shake hands and deliver a personal message of appreciation.

Engaging a strong network of community and business leaders as partners in supporting your vision for exemplary mathematics teaching and learning is an essential step. Your efforts will provide students with real-world work experiences, bring financial resources into the school or district to support clubs and programs, and strengthen your students' roles as active citizens in their communities.

Move From Vision to Action

Effective mathematics leaders work to empower a strong network of community and business leaders as equal partners in mathematics education. Creating internship and externship programs provides community partners with authentic and exciting work experiences that enhance their mathematics learning experience. Securing financial resources to support student engagement in STEM clubs and competitions builds student interest and could increase the number of students participating in advanced coursework. Building a network of community partners brings the classroom into the community and the community into the classroom. Table 12.1 describes the relationship among district-, site-, and team-level roles in building and engaging a strong network of partnerships.

Table 12.1: Mathematics Leadership Commitments to Build and Engage a Strong Network of Partnerships

District's Role	Site-Level Leader's Role	Collaborative Team's Role
Enlist community leaders and business partners as active members of the mathematics community.	Engage community partners in school planning processes to ensure that students have access to community resources and enrichment experiences.	Design and teach lessons that focus on the applications of mathematics in the community to build student interest and engagement.
Work with community leaders and business partners to collaboratively design programs to engage students in internships and community enrichment experiences.	Select and manage community programs that provide students with opportunities to participate in internships and community enrichment experiences.	Actively recruit students to participate in community and business initiatives.

*Visit **go.SolutionTree.com/leadership** for a free reproducible version of this table.*

Reflection

Review the Key 4 audit statements in figure 12.1, and with the MLT, reflect on the current strengths and opportunities to grow. Describe specific action steps to support these specific Key 4 statements.

Key 4: Build and Engage a Strong Network of Partnerships	Next Steps
Educators honor the community voice throughout the mathematics program. District and site-based leaders make regular efforts to activate community stakeholders to promote the love of mathematics (for example, through hosting community fairs, developing student intern programs, and serving as mentors and role models).	
Additional staff (such as counselors, support staff, para-educators, intervention specialists, and administration) take ownership of and establish collective capacity for ensuring improved student achievement.	
The site-level leadership team collects data on the school climate and takes steps to make it welcoming and inviting for all visitors.	

Figure 12.1: Key 4—Build and engage a strong network of partnerships.

*Visit **go.SolutionTree.com/leadership** for a free reproducible version of this figure.*

The fundamental purpose of education systems is to prepare students to be productive and successful adults. Providing students with opportunities to gain valuable experience in their communities prior to graduation opens their minds to a world of expanding possibilities. By gaining practical experience and building a network of community support, mathematics leaders provide students with a head start on the attainment of their dreams.

Next Steps for Mathematics Leaders With Key 4

The big ideas of Key 4 include *how* to amplify the student's voice, empowering families with the knowledge to guide their children toward rigorous coursework, and enlisting the talents of community and business leaders. Using figure 12.2 with your MLT, reflect on the level of engagement and implementation necessary for Key 4, empowering the vision of family and community engagement.

Exemplary Evidence of Engagement and Implementation	Strong Evidence of Engagement and Implementation	Partial Evidence of Engagement and Implementation	Limited Evidence of Engagement and Implementation
Educators activate students as leaders in the mathematics community by taking actions that improve mathematics instruction, professional learning, district policy, and curriculum development.	Educators activate students as partners in the mathematics community by informing processes that improve mathematics instruction, professional learning, district policy, and curriculum development.	Educators activate students as consultants in the mathematics community by providing insights on processes that result in some improvements in mathematics instruction.	Students are not active members of the mathematics community.
Educators activate families as leaders in the mathematics community by taking actions that improve mathematics instruction, professional learning, district policy, and curriculum development.	Educators activate families as partners in the mathematics community by informing processes that improve mathematics instruction, professional learning, district policy, and curriculum development.	Educators activate families as consultants in the mathematics community by providing insights on processes that result in some improvements in mathematics instruction.	Families are not active members of the mathematics community.
Educators activate community members as leaders in the mathematics community by taking actions that improve mathematics instruction, professional learning, district policy, and curriculum development.	Educators activate community members as partners in the mathematics community by informing processes that improve mathematics instruction, professional learning, district policy, and curriculum development.	Educators activate community members as consultants in the mathematics community by providing insights on processes that result in some improvements in mathematics instruction.	Community members are not active members of the mathematics community.
All students, families, and community members are educated advocates for equity and access in mathematics education.	Most students, families, and community members are educated advocates for equity and access in mathematics education.	Some students, families, and community members are advocates for equity and access in mathematics education.	Few students, families, and community members are advocates for equity and access in mathematics education.

Figure 12.2: Reflection tool for Key 4.

*Visit **go.SolutionTree.com/leadership** for a free reproducible version of this figure.*

The mathematics leaders' action in Key 4 helps leverage the skills and talents of students, families, and community members. Traditionally, these stakeholders have participated on the outer edges of schools and school systems, perhaps providing insight as consultants, but rarely as partners shaping practice or improving instruction.

The four keys to effective mathematics leadership and the supporting leadership actions provide a road map for mathematics leaders. In the epilogue, you will see how these keys work together to support your leadership.

Epilogue
Move Your Vision to Action

Creating a highly successful mathematics program requires the thoughtful planning and skillful actions of an effective mathematics leader. A skilled leader engages stakeholders in the pursuit of a common vision for exemplary mathematics teaching and learning. An elite mathematics leader understands the importance of systematically building capacity and the fact that this process takes time, patience, careful monitoring, and continual nurturing.

In Key 1, you learned how to develop and nurture a highly functioning collaborative team that takes stock of your current program realities and then develops a vision for a better future in student learning. You learned how to leverage the talents of the MLT to design a strategic plan with regularly monitored performance measures. You learned the importance of intentional and thoughtful celebration.

In Key 2, you explored strategies for building the capacity of all stakeholders to deliver on these clarified expectations. You considered professional learning experiences designed to strengthen teachers' content knowledge and improve their facility with each of NCTM's (2014) Mathematics Teaching Practices. You learned how to add value and sustainability to your program by developing professional learning experiences that enlist site-based mathematics leaders, site-based administrators, and district-level leaders to your cause.

In Key 3, you learned how to leverage your collaborative culture to improve classroom instruction. In collaboration with site-based leaders, you learned the value of creating collaborative teams working in a PLC culture. Further, you explored the research-informed actions of teams planning for exemplary mathematics teaching and learning, including focused team planning for the creation of common assessment instruments, common scoring routines, and consistency of quality feedback to students, among other actions. You learned the purpose behind a balanced assessment model and actions to build assessment literacy. You learned the importance of establishing clear expectations for the classroom actions of teachers (NCTM's [2014] Mathematics Teaching Practices) and the resultant behaviors of students (Standards for Mathematical Practice [NGA & CCSSO, 2010]).

In Key 4, you explored strategies for empowering students, families, and community leaders as equal partners in mathematics education. You learned how activating and amplifying the student voice serves as a catalyst for instructional growth, how empowering families as advocates strengthens your district's pursuit of equity and access, and how engagement of community leaders brings the real world into your schools.

As you can see, while reading this book, you have explored a number of strategies for creating the structures necessary to improve student learning experiences and achievements. But possessing knowledge of what you must do and actually summoning the discipline to engage in these actions are two entirely different things. Increase your chance of sustained success by strategically building your program a few components at a time. Think of your vision in terms of years and plan with this in mind: one year from now, we can accomplish _____, or five years from now we can accomplish _____. Figure E.1 provides you with a tool to help prioritize your work. Examine each element of your program and determine, based on your rating, which elements to overhaul, which elements to fine-tune, and which elements to lightly monitor. We did not design this tool for one-time use. Instead, use the tool to evaluate your program regularly, twice per year.

Assessing Your Next Steps for Moving Your Vision Into Action

Rate your mathematics program on a scale of 1 (low) to 10 (high) for your current reality of the four keys and your commitments to support each key.

Key 1: Establish a Clear Vision for Mathematics Teaching and Learning

Using the mathematics program audit, take stock of your mathematics program's health.

Rating: _____   Evidence: _____

Next steps:

Develop a collaborative vision for an exemplary mathematics program.

Rating: _____   Evidence: _____

Next steps:

Establish measures of success.

Rating: _____   Evidence: _____

Next steps:

Key 2: Support Visionary Professional Learning for Teachers and Teacher Leaders

Engage teachers in worthwhile and differentiated professional learning.

Rating: _____   Evidence: _____

Next steps:

Develop highly skilled and highly effective mathematics leaders.

Rating: _____   Evidence: _____

Next steps:

Build capacity of site-based administrators and district leaders.

Rating: _____   Evidence: _____

Next steps:

Key 3: Develop Systems for Activating the Vision

Leverage collaborative team actions.

Rating: _____   Evidence: _____

Next steps:

Create and implement well-designed and articulated curriculum and assessments.

Rating: _____   Evidence: _____

Next steps:

Monitor consistent expectations for exemplary instruction.

Rating: _____   Evidence: _____

Next steps:

continued on next page ⇨

Figure E.1: Tool for assessing your mathematics program's key priorities.

Key 4: Empower the Vision of Family and Community Engagement

Activate the student voice to check alignment between vision and reality.

Rating: _____   Evidence: _____

Next steps:

Empower families as informed advocates.

Rating: _____   Evidence: _____

Next steps:

Build and engage a strong network of partnerships.

Rating: _____   Evidence: _____

Next steps:

Visit **go.SolutionTree.com/leadership** *for a free reproducible version of this figure.*

As daunting as your leadership task may seem, be comforted by the fact that you are not alone in your journey. A network of teachers and leaders focused on continual improvement and increased student learning exists all around you. Associations like NCSM and NCTM provide resources and learning experiences that will connect you to others engaged in similar work. Join these associations and become an actively engaged member of the larger mathematics education community. When you find yourself stumped by a problem in your district, you will undoubtedly find someone in the community who has experienced the same challenge and might even have a solution for you to consider.

Now it is time for you to begin applying what you have learned. Research and reading strengthen the work of an effective mathematics leader, and application of the learning begins with the teachers, leaders, and students you serve. Be steadfast in your commitment to develop the best possible mathematics learning experience for students. Be resolute in your commitment to develop the best staff of mathematics teachers in the world. Be determined in your commitment to engage stakeholders in a collaborative process for program improvement. And, be disciplined as you lead all of this important work. Are you ready? Then *go!*

Appendix A
Reproducibles

Action Plan

Use the following action plan to outline your team's vision for teaching and learning mathematics.

District: _____

Mathematics Leadership Team: _____

_____

_____

Goals: _____

The Mathematics Leadership Key or Characteristic We Are Developing	Strategy or Action Steps	Person or Group Responsible for Monitoring and Completing the Action Step	Target Date or Timeline	Evidence of Effectiveness

Planning Template for Change

Instructional Vision	
Step Considerations	**Plan for Professional Learning**
Phase 1: Preparation ♦ Define key terms. ♦ Develop common understanding. ♦ Create measurable targets. ♦ Research. **Questions to Address** ♦ How does this new learning connect to what we already have been learning? ♦ Do we have a shared understanding?	
Phase 2: Incubation ♦ Compare various understandings of the topic. ♦ Develop common understanding. ♦ Analyze measurable targets. ♦ Research and discuss. **Questions to Address** ♦ What better ideas and practices can we generate? ♦ How will our team integrate this new learning?	
Phase 3: Insight ♦ Analyze various aspects of the topic. ♦ Deploy the new initiatives or change. ♦ Collect data and explore how to read them. ♦ Start to use new practices. **Question to Address** ♦ How might we support implementation?	
Phase 4: Evaluation ♦ Analyze the various stages of the new initiative or change. ♦ Collect data and explore how to analyze and use them to change practice. ♦ Use new practices. ♦ Create feedback loops to analyze implementation, measure targets, and make changes to fit individual needs. **Questions to Address** ♦ How well is this connected to successful outcomes? ♦ How well is it working?	

page 1 of 2

Instructional Vision	
Step Considerations	**Plan for Professional Learning**
Phase 5: Elaboration ◆ Engage in predictive and reactive data analysis. ◆ Create feedback loops. ◆ Use technology at a mastery level. **Questions to Address** ◆ How might the idea connect to other applications? ◆ Can we use it in other capacities?	

Sources: Adapted from Armstrong, A. (2014). Professional learning as a creative process: A new learning map for differentiation. Tools for Learning Schools, 17(3), 1–3; *Csikszentmihalyi, M. (1996).* Creativity: Flow and the psychology of discovery and invention. *New York: HarperCollins.*

Framework for Connecting the Student and Teaching Practices

Standards for Mathematical Practice (SMP)		Teacher Action Connections
SMP1	Make sense of problems and persevere in solving them.	Mathematics lessons align to the essential learning standards and teachers clearly communicate them to students (MTP1). Lessons include complex tasks (MTP2), opportunities for visible thinking (MTP8 and MTP4), and intentional questioning (MTP5) to promote deeper mathematical thinking (MTP6). Teachers design lessons from the student's perspective to provide multiple opportunities to make sense of the mathematics (MTP7).
SMP2	Reason abstractly and quantitatively.	
SMP3	Construct viable arguments and critique the reasoning of others.	
SMP4	Model with mathematics.	To build SMP1, teachers focus on MTP7 and MTP2.
SMP5	Use appropriate tools strategically.	To build SMP2, teachers focus on MTP2 and MTP3. To build SMP3, teachers focus on MTP4 and MTP5.
SMP6	Attend to precision.	To build SMP4, teachers focus on MTP3 and MTP8. To build SMP5, teachers focus on MTP2 and MTP3.
SMP7	Look for and make use of structure.	To build SMP6, teachers focus on MTP4 and MTP2.
SMP8	Look for and express regularity in repeated reasoning.	To build SMP7 and SMP8, teachers focus on tasks (MTP2).

Mathematics Teaching Practices (MTP)	
MTP1	Establish mathematics goals to focus learning.
MTP2	Implement tasks that promote reasoning and problem solving.
MTP3	Use and connect mathematical representations.
MTP4	Facilitate meaningful mathematical discourse.
MTP5	Pose purposeful questions.
MTP6	Build procedural fluency from conceptual understanding.
MTP7	Support productive struggle in learning mathematics.
MTP8	Elicit and use evidence of student thinking.

Mathematics Leadership Commitments for Taking Stock of Your Mathematics Program's Health

District's Role	Site-Level Leader's Role	Collaborative Team's Role
Form a mathematics leadership team (MLT) with stakeholders representing all student groups and the community.	Form a site-level MLT responsible for representing the school's voice in the mathematics program.	Apprise all team members of district mathematics leadership actions and initiatives and provide feedback to the site-level MLT.
Facilitate analysis and revision of the mathematics program audit.	Facilitate analysis and revision of the mathematics program audit for site-based staff.	Submit team recommendations for revisions for the mathematics program audit to the lead facilitator of the MLT.
Charge MLT members to collect data using the mathematics program audit.	Gather site-level data to include in the mathematics program audit.	Provide evidence and artifacts to support the mathematics program audit data collection process.

Mathematics Leadership Commitments for Developing a Collaborative Vision for an Exemplary Mathematics Program

District's Role	Site-Level Leader's Role	Collaborative Team's Role
Lead the collaborative development of a vision for exemplary mathematics teaching and learning.	Site leaders engage in drafting the vision for high-quality mathematics instruction.	All staff members review the vision for exemplary mathematics teaching and learning and ask clarifying questions.
With support of the mathematics leadership team, provide learning opportunities for all stakeholders to teach the vision for high-quality instruction.	Site leaders teach the vision to all staff responsible for teaching mathematics. Throughout the process, leaders develop a professional learning plan to ensure all stakeholders have the skills and knowledge necessary to achieve the vision.	School mathematics educators assess their current state of mathematics teaching and learning to determine how well current practice aligns to the new vision.
Lead the development of a strategic plan guided by SMART goals.	School leaders infuse district mathematics SMART goal plans into the school improvement plan to ensure alignment to the vision.	School mathematics educators enact strategies outlined in the school improvement plan and regularly review data to monitor progress toward the attainment of SMART goals.

Mathematics Leadership Commitments to Establish Measures of Success

District's Role	Site-Level Leader's Role	Collaborative Team's Role
Lead the development and articulation of performance measures that mark progress toward realizing the vision for exemplary mathematics teaching and learning.	Facilitate data discussions to monitor performance measures and to inform instructional design.	Routinely collect data and monitor progress toward stated goals.
Nurture a culture of celebration, in which all teachers and leaders receive meaningful praise for their work weekly.	Celebrate the efforts of teachers and leaders working hard to improve the mathematics learning experience for students.	Celebrate the efforts of colleagues working hard to improve the mathematics learning experience for students.

Mathematics Leadership Commitments to Engage Teachers in Worthwhile and Differentiated Professional Learning

District's Role	Site-Level Leader's Role	Collaborative Team's Role
Establish multiple systems to support collaboration as a vital element of continual professional learning.	Monitor and provide feedback to grade-level or course-based collaborative teams to support continual learning.	Value collaboration as a means for continual learning.
Work with the district mathematics leadership team to align professional learning opportunities to the district vision.	Ensure collaborative teams and site leaders engage in opportunities for professional learning that support alignment with district vision.	Grade- and course-level team leaders work with team members to evaluate current learning opportunities and align teams' action steps and professional learning to support the district vision.
Create a systemic plan for professional learning that attends to progression of learning and focuses on building the capacity of all stakeholders.	Ensure collaborative teams engage in professional learning and provide systemic support for learning progressions to build team capacity.	Evaluate and reflect on grade- and course-level teams' progress in professional learning and request additional support when needed.
Provide high-quality professional learning and consistently evaluate, revise, and revisit it when needed.	Attend high-quality professional learning and consistently provide feedback to adapt or revise the professional learning plan when needed.	Engage in high-quality professional learning with the collaborative team and consistently provide feedback to adapt or revise the professional learning plan when needed.

Mathematics Leadership Commitments to Develop Highly Skilled and Highly Effective Mathematics Leaders

District's Role	Site-Level Leader's Role	Collaborative Team's Role
Include in the district professional learning plan a variety of capacity-building learning opportunities for teacher leaders that support the professional learning community process.	Identify potential teacher leaders and build capacity by supporting engagement with shared leadership opportunities.	Share team responsibilities and work cohesively to equally support the team members and the team leaders.
Create a systemic model that incorporates shared leadership across multiple layers in the district.	Support mathematics teachers' participation in all aspects of the systemic shared leadership model to represent site voices.	Ensure that the team's voice is present in all layers of the shared leadership model.
Prioritize open communication by providing multiple engagement opportunities for all stakeholders.	Regularly schedule meetings with team leaders, coaches, and teacher leaders to discuss current strengths and challenges.	Consistently evaluate current progress and share results with other stakeholders to build shared knowledge.

Mathematics Leadership Commitments to Build the Capacity of Site-Based Administrators and District Leaders

District's Role	Site-Level Leader's Role	Collaborative Team's Role
Develop a professional learning plan to train site-based administrators to do the following. ◆ Collect evidence of student engagement in the Standards for Mathematical Practice. ◆ Collect evidence of teacher engagement in the Mathematics Teaching Practices. ◆ Engage in meaningful instructional conversations. ◆ Improve the quality of formative feedback provided to teachers after classroom visits.	Engage in professional learning to observe classrooms effectively, improve instructional conversations, and provide formative feedback to teachers.	Routinely invite site-based leaders into mathematics classrooms to contribute to their professional learning and to provide opportunities for teachers and site-based leaders to receive instructional feedback.
Develop a professional learning plan to train district leaders to do the following. ◆ Advocate for exemplary mathematics teaching and learning. ◆ Make informed decisions about allocation of funds to support mathematics programming. ◆ Ensure that recruited teacher candidates hold beliefs aligned to the district vision for exemplary mathematics teaching and learning.	Develop an understanding of the big ideas of the professional learning plan in order to do the following. ◆ Advocate for exemplary mathematics teaching and learning. ◆ Encourage decisions regarding allocation of funds to support mathematics programming. ◆ Ensure that potential teacher candidates' beliefs align to the district and site vision for exemplary mathematics teaching and learning.	Routinely invite district-level leaders into mathematics classrooms to contribute to their professional learning and to provide opportunities for teachers and site-based leaders to receive instructional feedback.

Mathematics Leadership Commitments to Leverage Team Actions

District's Role	Site-Level Leader's Role	Collaborative Team's Role
Provide opportunities for all grade-level or course-based collaborative teams in every school to understand and practice the high-leverage team actions.	Monitor and provide feedback to grade-level or course-based collaborative teams to ensure they practice the high-leverage team actions.	Work with team members to practice research-affirmed, high-leverage team actions to answer the four critical questions of a professional learning community.
District mathematics leaders work with the mathematics leadership team and site leaders to understand how collaborative teams grow and evolve from cooperation, to coordination, to highly effective collaborative teams.	Understand the seven stages of collaborative teams and provide resources (such as time, tools, resources, and guidance) to move each grade-level or course-based team forward through the stages.	Reflect with team members on their current collaborative team stage and identify specific action steps to move forward.
Create systems that provide ongoing feedback to site leaders and grade-level or course-based team leaders on each collaborative team's stage and progress.	Use systematic structures that provide feedback to each grade-level or course-based collaborative team to promote their collaborative growth and understanding of highly effective NCTM Mathematics Teaching Practices.	Work collaboratively together with team members to evaluate feedback and ensure SMART goal action steps support opportunities for personal growth and improvement.
Develop several scheduling models for schools to support the infusion of collaborative planning time into the schedule.	Site-based leaders review district scheduling models to determine which model will be adopted to ensure the inclusion of collaborative planning time.	Create an agenda for collaborative team time to intentionally plan before-, during-, and after-the-unit high-leverage team actions.

Mathematics Leadership Commitments for Well-Designed and Articulated Curriculum and Assessments

District's Role	Site-Level Leader's Role	Collaborative Team's Role
Provide opportunities for all stakeholders at every site to have a voice in the development of the guaranteed and viable curriculum (content and the Standards for Mathematical Practice).	Provide supportive conditions for teachers and collaborative teams to understand the intent of the guaranteed and viable curriculum, including time during the school day to learn from others.	Team leaders and course-based, grade-level leaders work with team members to ensure all team members understand the big ideas of the grade or course and define the guaranteed and viable curriculum.
Focus on developing the essential learning standards and provide a coherent unit-by-unit progression.	Demonstrate interest in the development of the unit plans and provide supportive conditions for teams to reflect on implementation.	Team leaders and grade-level leaders work with team members to develop a focused, coherent unit plan that develops procedural fluency through conceptual understanding and application.
Provide opportunities for collaborative teams and teacher leaders to validate and reflect on the alignment among the assessments, unit plans, and daily lesson design.	Engage site teams to reflect on the alignment among the assessments, unit plans, and daily lesson design.	Collaborative teams review assessment evidence to ensure that it aligns to the intent of each essential learning standard.
Create systems for vertical teacher leaders and teams to support the development of standards with an equal intensity of conceptual understanding, procedural fluency, and application (mathematical rigor).	Engage grade-level and course-alike teams in vertical articulation to ensure that they meet expected learning outcomes to support student matriculation through meaningful and connected mathematics.	Collaborative teams work with future and previous grade levels and courses to ensure that they connect essential learning standards for prior and future learning.

Mathematics Leadership Commitments to Monitor Consistent Expectations for Exemplary Instruction

District's Role	Site-Level Leader's Role	Collaborative Team's Role
Ensure the vision for high-quality mathematics instruction includes research-affirmed teaching practices.	Understand what the teaching practices look like in action from both the teacher and student perspectives.	Team leaders and grade-level leaders work with team members to identify research-affirmed teaching practices that best support student learning.
Provide learning opportunities for site leaders and collaborative teams in research-affirmed mathematics teaching practices and provide feedback on implementation of new strategies.	Provide supportive conditions (for example, time and opportunities to observe each other) for collaborative teams to grow their content and pedagogical knowledge.	Team leaders and grade-level leaders work with team members to collaboratively plan for specific teaching practices that focus on developing the mathematical habits of mind.
Develop a professional learning plan to train site-based administrators to: ◆ Collect evidence of student engagement in the Standards for Mathematical Practice ◆ Collect evidence of teacher engagement in NCTM's Mathematics Teaching Practices ◆ Engage in meaningful instructional conversations Improve the quality of formative feedback teachers receive after classroom visits.	As lifelong learners, site leaders engage in professional learning to improve their facility with effective classroom observation, with instructional conversations, and by providing formative feedback to teachers.	Team members invite site-based leaders into mathematics classrooms to contribute to their professional learning and to provide opportunities to receive instructional feedback.
Provide structures for instructional feedback and data dialogues with instructional data aligned to vision statements.	Review instructional trends and provide specific feedback to collaborative teams regarding instructional data aligned to the vision statements.	Collaborative teams review instructional feedback, provide peer feedback, and have conversations that foster instructional growth.

Mathematics Leadership Commitments to Activate the Student Voice to Check Alignment Between Vision and Reality

District's Role	Site-Level Leader's Role	Collaborative Team's Role
Collaborate with site-based staff to develop a state of readiness to receive feedback from students to inform instructional improvement.	Collaborate with teachers delivering mathematics instruction to address staff concerns about elevating student perspectives related to mathematics instruction.	Engage in discussions to identify the various ways that team members might use the student voice to improve their professional practice.
Develop structures for conducting student interviews to improve the classroom learning environment and the quality of mathematics instruction.	Collaborate with teachers delivering mathematics instruction to ascertain what information teachers wish to collect from students. After supporting the student interview process, facilitate the collaborative analysis and synthesis of student interview data. Develop strategic plans to address student concerns if necessary.	Collaboratively analyze and synthesize student interview data. Implement strategies to address student concerns if necessary.
Develop structures for engaging students as professional developers.	Empower students as equal partners in the mathematics teaching and learning community.	Empower students as equal partners in the classroom.
Develop structures for engaging students as curriculum developers.	Recruit students to be part of curriculum workshop teams.	Recruit students to be part of the school improvement planning team.
Provide students with the knowledge and resources to advocate for effective mathematics programming.	Listen carefully to student feedback and consider appropriate actions for growth.	Develop formative feedback tools to gather information about the student learning experience. Take action on student feedback that informs instructional practice.

Mathematics Leadership Commitments to Empower Families as Informed Advocates

District's Role	Site-Level Leader's Role	Collaborative Team's Role
Develop parent-training workshops to clearly communicate mathematics pathways, college readiness expectations, and strategies to advocate equity and access in mathematics programming.	Empower families as equal partners in the mathematics teaching and learning community.	Clearly communicate mathematics pathways, college readiness expectations, and strategies for advocating for equity and access in mathematics programming to students and families.
Develop resources to assist families with supporting mathematics learning at home.	Recruit families to be part of the school improvement planning team.	Invite parents into the classroom to observe mathematics teaching and learning.

Mathematics Leadership Commitments to Build and Engage a Strong Network of Partnerships

District's Role	Site-Level Leader's Role	Collaborative Team's Role
Enlist community leaders and business partners as active members of the mathematics community.	Engage community partners in school planning processes to ensure that students have access to community resources and enrichment experiences.	Design and teach lessons that focus on the applications of mathematics in the community to build student interest and engagement.
Work with community leaders and business partners to collaboratively design programs to engage students in internships and community enrichment experiences.	Select and manage community programs that provide students with opportunities to participate in internships and community enrichment experiences.	Actively recruit students to participate in community and business initiatives.

Appendix B

Cognitive–Demand–Level Task–Analysis Guide

Source: Smith & Stein, 1998. Copyright 1998, National Council of Teachers of Mathematics.

Table B.1: Cognitive-Demand Levels of Mathematical Tasks

Lower-Level Cognitive Demand	Higher-Level Cognitive Demand
Memorization Tasks <ul><li>These tasks involve reproducing previously learned facts, rules, formulae, or definitions to memory.</li><li>They cannot be solved using procedures because a procedure does not exist or because the time frame in which the task is being completed is too short to use the procedure.</li><li>They are not ambiguous; such tasks involve exact reproduction of previously seen material and what is to be reproduced is clearly and directly stated.</li><li>They have no connection to the concepts or meaning that underlie the facts, rules, formulae, or definitions being learned or reproduced.</li></ul>	**Procedures With Connections Tasks** <ul><li>These procedures focus students' attention on the use of procedures for the purpose of developing deeper levels of understanding of mathematical concepts and ideas.</li><li>They suggest pathways to follow (explicitly or implicitly) that are broad general procedures that have close connections to underlying conceptual ideas as opposed to narrow algorithms that are opaque with respect to underlying concepts.</li><li>They usually are represented in multiple ways (for example, visual diagrams, manipulatives, symbols, or problem situations). They require some degree of cognitive effort. Although general procedures may be followed, they cannot be followed mindlessly. Students need to engage with the conceptual ideas that underlie the procedures in order to successfully complete the task and develop understanding.</li></ul>

continued on next page ⇨

Lower-Level Cognitive Demand	Higher-Level Cognitive Demand
Procedures Without Connections Tasks ♦ These procedures are algorithmic. Use of the procedure is either specifically called for, or its use is evident based on prior instruction, experience, or placement of the task. ♦ They require limited cognitive demand for successful completion. There is little ambiguity about what needs to be done and how to do it. ♦ They have no connection to the concepts or meaning that underlie the procedure being used. ♦ They are focused on producing correct answers rather than developing mathematical understanding. ♦ They require no explanations or have explanations that focus solely on describing the procedure used.	**Doing Mathematics Tasks** ♦ Doing mathematics tasks requires complex and no algorithmic thinking (for example, the task, instructions, or examples do not explicitly suggest a predictable, well-rehearsed approach or pathway). ♦ It requires students to explore and understand the nature of mathematical concepts, processes, or relationships. ♦ It demands self-monitoring or self-regulation of one's own cognitive processes. ♦ It requires students to access relevant knowledge and experiences and make appropriate use of them in working through the task. ♦ It requires students to analyze the task and actively examine task constraints that may limit possible solution strategies and solutions. ♦ It requires considerable cognitive effort and may involve some level of anxiety for the student due to the unpredictable nature of the required solution process.

Appendix C

Mathematics Professional Development Plan for a School Year

Source: Phoenix Union High School District, 2013. Used with permission.

Effective mathematics leaders create intentional districtwide professional learning opportunities during a school year. The professional learning is aligned to the year's strategic goals and builds the capacity of individuals, collaborative teams, team leaders, and site-level leaders. The plan is articulated to all stakeholders before the opening of the school year to provide teams and site-level leaders choices to best support their learning needs. Appendix C is an example from Phoenix Union High School District during the final phase of implementing the new curriculum. See tables C.1 and C.2.

Strategic Goals of E² Math

The purpose of E² Math is to create equity and excellence for all mathematics students in Phoenix Union High School District. We will complete this by engaging in the following actions.

- Ensure that curriculum provides rigorous learning opportunities and prepares students to meet the demands of the Common Core State Standards (CCSS).

- Focus on the key instructional shifts (focus, coherence, and rigor) in the CCSS by providing instructional units and lessons that develop students' mathematical practices.

- Encourage reflection and active learning for all students, teachers, and leaders.

- Enrich students through accelerated programs to increase college and career readiness.

- Integrate advanced technology to make mathematics meaningful and relevant.

- Sustain a system of articulation with our partner districts to provide a seamless transition from eighth-grade to high school mathematics.

Table C.1: Mathematics Professional Development Opportunities to Meet Strategic Goals

Type of Team	Team	Description
Curriculum Team	Algebra 3–4 Training	All algebra 3–4 teachers will attend four half-day trainings throughout the school year to support Arizona College and Career Readiness (ACCR) curriculum implementation.
		<u>Friday, August 29, 2014</u>
		◆ 8:00–11:00 a.m.: Trevor, Chavez, Maryvale, Fairfax, Bostrom, Franklin, Carl Hayden at CES—Boardroom
		◆ 12:30–3:30 p.m.: Camelback, North, Central, Metro, South, Alhambra, Suns Dback at CES—Boardroom
		<u>Friday, September 26, 2014</u>
		◆ 8:00–11:00 a.m.: Camelback, North, Central, Metro, South, Alhambra, Suns Dback at Metro Tech—Banquet Room
		◆ 12:30–3:30 p.m.: Trevor, Chavez, Maryvale, Fairfax, Bostrom, Franklin, Carl Hayden at Trevor Browne—Community Room
		<u>Thursday, November 20, 2014</u>
		◆ 8:00–11:00 a.m.: Trevor, Chavez, Maryvale, Fairfax, Bostrom, Franklin, Carl Hayden at Trevor Browne—Community Room
		◆ 12:30–3:30 p.m.: Camelback, North, Central, Metro, South, Alhambra, Suns Dback at CES—Boardroom
		<u>Friday, February 13, 2015</u>
		◆ 8:00–11:00 a.m.: Camelback, North, Central, Metro, South, Alhambra, Suns Dback at CES—Boardroom
		◆ 12:30–3:30 p.m.: Trevor, Chavez, Maryvale, Fairfax, Bostrom, Franklin, Carl Hayden at Trevor Browne—Community Room
		Teams will sign up on Career Track.
	Algebra 3–4 District Team	Districtwide team application process
		8:00 a.m.–4:00 p.m., location: Alhambra High School—Mega Lab
		◆ Saturday, August 30, 2014
		◆ Saturday, September 27, 2014
		◆ Saturday, October 18, 2014
		◆ Saturday, November 22, 2014
		◆ Saturday, January 24, 2015
	Geometry	Districtwide team *application process
		8:00 a.m.–4:00 p.m., location: Alhambra High School—Mega Lab
		◆ Saturday, August 30, 2014
		◆ Saturday, October 18, 2014
		◆ Saturday, January 24, 2015

Type of Team	Team	Description
Instruction and Assessments Focus Professional Development	Mathematics Modeling	Dan Meyers will be our special guest as we look at three-act tasks. Watch for updates in November. *Invitations are required and registration is limited to seventy. Wednesday, January 15, 2014
	Assessments—What Should We Expect in 2015?	Coaching per site. We will schedule once state has announced the assessment.
	Math Gatherings	Teachers will have an opportunity to gather and discuss the new content in algebra 3–4, statistics and functions. The guest facilitators of the discussions are from Maricopa Community College. Teachers will have opportunities to explore the content and become deeply engaged in the Standards for Mathematical Practice tied to the content. Following are the dates and topics. Teachers can register on Career Track. Location: CES first-floor training room Wednesday, September 24: statistics Monday, October 20: functions Thursday, November 6: statistics Monday, December 1: functions Monday, January 26: statistics Monday, February 2: functions Wednesday, March 4: statistics Monday, April 6: functions
	Edgenuity	(Register on Career Track.) Dates to be determined.
	LaurusSoft	Contact LaurusSoft (trainer) to set up training at your site.

	Technology Tuesday (Spring 2015)	Topic	Date	Location
		Tablets	To be announced	To be announced
		Clickers	To be announced	To be announced
		TI-Nspire	To be announced	To be announced
		TI-84	To be announced	To be announced
		SMART Board/Promethean	To be announced	To be announced

Type of Team	Team	Description
District Collaboration	Intervention Team	Lab teachers will meet monthly for two hours at Metro Tech High School from 4:00 to 6:00 p.m. on the following dates. Thursday, September 4, 2014 Tuesday, October 21, 2014 Tuesday, November 18, 2014 Tuesday, December 2, 2014 Tuesday, January 13, 2015 Tuesday, February 10, 2015 Tuesday, March 31, 2015 Tuesday, April 14, 2015 Tuesday, May 5, 2015
	Team Leader Training	Mathematics instructional leaders and team leaders from algebra 1–2, geometry 1–2, and algebra 3–4 will meet on the following dates. 12:30–3:30 p.m., location: CES Boardroom Wednesday, September 10, 2014 Wednesday, November 5, 2014 Wednesday, February 4, 2015
	Districtwide PLC Collaborative Teams	Districtwide teams (AP statistics, AP calculus, discrete mathematics/modeling, mathematics technology, trigonometry, survey of mathematics) 8/20, 9/17, 10/15, 11/19, 1/21, 2/18, 3/25, 7:30–9:30 a.m. ♦ Metro Tech: Discrete Mathematics and Modeling (Room 9223) ♦ Metro Tech: Principles of Mathematics Technology (Room 9229) ♦ Metro Tech: AP calculus (Room 9225) ♦ Survey of mathematics: location and leader to be announced ♦ North: AP statistics (Room S-50) ♦ Trevor Browne: Trigonometry (Room 9006)
Assessment Team	Inclusion Teams and Algebra 3–4 Team	8:00–4:00 p.m., location to be announced *application process Saturday, August 30, 2014 Saturday, September 27, 2014 Saturday, October 18, 2014 Saturday, November 22, 2014 Saturday, January 24, 2015
Professional Growth Courses		These are the tentative mathematics professional growth courses offered this school year. Teachers can register on Career Track. Literacy in a mathematics class: dates to be announced Standard content 2: mathematics content knowledge ♦ 9/2, 9/9, 9/25, and 10/14 (twelve hours in class—three independent) Teams of four: dates to be announced Lesson design ♦ 1/12, 2/9, 3/2, and 3/9 (twelve hours in class—three independent)

Mathematics Professional Development Opportunities by Month

First Semester

August

- Districtwide PLC 8/20
- ACCR algebra 3–4 district CT 8/29
- ACCR algebra 3–4 curriculum 8/30
- ACCR geometry curriculum 8/30
- Assessment team 8/30

September

- Pro-Gro: standard 2 9/2
- Intervention team 9/4
- Team leader training 9/10
- Districtwide PLC 9/17
- Statistics math gathering 9/24
- ACCR algebra 3–4 district CT 9/26
- ACCR algebra 3–4 curriculum 9/27
- Assessment team 9/27

October

- Districtwide PLC 10/15
- ACCR algebra 3–4 curriculum 10/18
- ACCR geometry curriculum 10/18
- Assessment team 10/18
- Functions math gatherings 10/20
- Intervention team 10/21
- Assessment team 10/26

November

- Team leader training 11/5
- Statistics math gathering 11/13
- Intervention team 11/18
- Districtwide PLC 11/19
- ACCR algebra 3–4 district CT 11/20
- ACCR algebra 3–4 curriculum 11/22
- Assessment team 11/22

December

- Functions math gatherings 12/1
- Intervention team 12/2

Second Semester

January

- Pro-Gro: lesson design 1/12
- Intervention team 1/13
- CCSS modeling with Dan Meyer 1/15
- Districtwide PLC 1/21
- ACCR algebra 3–4 curriculum 1/24
- ACCR geometry curriculum 1/24
- Assessment team 1/24
- Statistics math gathering 1/26

February

- Functions math gatherings 2/2
- Team leader training 2/4
- Intervention team 2/10
- ACCR algebra 3–4 curriculum 2/13
- Districtwide PLC 2/18
- CCSS geometry curriculum team 2/22

March

- Statistics math gathering 3/4
- Districtwide PLC 3/25
- Intervention team 3/31

April

- Functions math gatherings 4/6
- Intervention team 4/14
- AP mock exam TBD

May

- Intervention team 5/5

Table C.2: Menu of Mathematics Job-Embedded Professional Development

Team Learning	Individual Learning
• Focused work on instructional shifts • Selecting, implementing, and supporting mathematical tasks • Lesson design • Educator toolkit to develop instructional strategies • Lesson study • Instructional rounds • PLC progression of learning • Before-, during-, and after-the-unit instruction artifacts • Looking at student work • Content discussions (math gatherings) • Curriculum training • Assessment development • Technology training • Vertical alignment (across grade levels) • Book clubs • Unit planning	• Lesson design and focused work on the instructional shifts • Building Standards for Mathematical Practice • Practice-forward mathematics tasks • Student-to-student discourse • Video self-reflection • Common Core look for observational feedback • Content discussions (math gatherings) • Curriculum training • Assessment development • Technology training • Instructional resource training • Model lessons • Coplanning • Collaborative coaching (preparing, planning, teaching the lesson, observing, and debriefing)

REFERENCES AND RESOURCES

Achieve the Core. (n.d.). *The Common Core State Standards shifts in mathematics.* Accessed at http://achievethecore.org/page/900/the-common-core-state-standards-shifts-in-mathematics on March 17, 2016.

Ambrose, D. (1987). *Managing complex change.* Pittsburgh: Enterprise Group.

Armstrong, A. (2014). Professional learning as a creative process: A new learning map for differentiation. *Tools for Learning Schools, 17*(3), 1–3.

Ball, D. L., & Cohen, D. K. (1996). Reform by the book: What is—or might be—the role of curriculum materials in teacher learning and instructional reform? *Educational Researcher, 25*(9), 6–8, 14.

Barber, M., & Mourshed, M. (2007, September). *How the world's best-performing school systems come out on top.* New York: McKinsey. Accessed at http://mckinseyonsociety.com/downloads/reports/Education/Worlds_School_Systems_Final.pdf on November 19, 2015.

Barnes, B. (2015, June 1 [Blog post]). *Math gatherings: Innovative professional learning for teachers and leaders.* Accessed at www.solution-tree.com/blog/math-gatherings on January 15, 2016.

Barnes, B., Wray, J. A., & Novak, J. (2012). [Student interviews]. Unpublished raw data.

Barnes, B., Wray, J. A., & Novak, J. (2015). [Summary of feedback and attendance for 2015 mathematics gatherings]. Unpublished raw data.

Black, P., & Wiliam, D. (1998). Inside the black box: Raising standards through classroom assessment. *Phi Delta Kappan, 80*(2), 139–148.

Briars, D. J., Asturias, H., Foster, D., & Gale, M. A. (2012). *Common Core mathematics in a PLC at Work, grades 6–8.* T. D. Kanold (Ed.). Bloomington, IN: Solution Tree Press.

California State Board of Education. (2015). *Kindergarten chapter of the mathematics framework for California Public Schools: Kindergarten through grade twelve.* Sacramento, CA: California Department of Education. Accessed at www.cde.ca.gov/ci/ma/cf/documents/mathfwkindergarten.pdf on November 18, 2015.

Conference Board of the Mathematical Sciences. (2013). *Common Core State Standards for mathematics statement by presidents of CBMS member professional societies.* Accessed at www.ams.org/news/Statement-for-CCSSMath7-24-13.pdf on April 1, 2016.

Conzemius, A. E., & O'Neill, J. (2014). *The handbook for SMART school teams: Revitalizing best practices for collaboration* (2nd ed.). Bloomington, IN: Solution Tree Press.

Covey, S. R. (2013). *The 7 habits of highly effective people: Powerful lessons in personal change* (25th anniversary ed.). New York: Simon & Schuster.

Csikszentmihalyi, M. (1996). *Creativity: Flow and the psychology of discovery and invention.* New York: HarperCollins.

Danielson, C. (2007). *Enhancing professional practice: A framework for teaching* (2nd ed.). Alexandria, VA: Association for Supervision and Curriculum Development.

Dixon, J. K. (2015, May). *Activating the Standards for Mathematical Practice.* Presented at Conference, Bowie, MD.

Dixon, J. K., Adams, T. L., & Nolan, C. E. (2015). *Beyond the Common Core: A handbook for mathematics in a PLC at Work, grades K–5.* T. D. Kanold (Ed.). Bloomington, IN: Solution Tree Press.

DuFour, R., DuFour, R., & Eaker, R. (2008). *Revisiting Professional Learning Communities at Work: New insights for improving schools.* Bloomington, IN: Solution Tree Press.

DuFour, R., DuFour, R., Eaker, R., Many, T. W., & Mattos, M. (2016). *Learning by doing: A handbook for Professional Learning Communities at Work* (3rd ed.). Bloomington, IN: Solution Tree Press.

DuFour, R., & Marzano, R. J. (2011). *Leaders of learning: How district, school, and classroom leaders improve student achievement.* Bloomington, IN: Solution Tree Press.

Dweck, C. S. (2006). *Mindset: The new psychology of success.* New York: Random House.

Eaker, R., & Keating, J. (2009, July 22). *Team leaders in a professional learning community* [Blog post]. Accessed at www.allthingsplc.info/blog/view/54/team-leaders-in-a-professional-learning-community on November 18, 2015.

Elmore, R. F. (2004). *School reform from the inside out: Policy, practice, and performance.* Boston: Harvard Education Press.

Every Student Succeeds Act, 1177 U.S.C. § 295 (2015). Accessed at www.gpo.gov/fdsys/pkg/BILLS -114s1177enr/pdf/BILLS-114s1177enr.pdf on April 27, 2016.

Fullan, M. (2011). *The moral imperative realized.* Thousand Oaks, CA: Corwin Press.

Graham, P., & Ferriter, B. (2008). One step at a time. *Journal of Staff Development, 29*(3), 38–42.

Grover, R. (Ed.). (1996). *Collaboration: Lessons learned series.* Chicago: American Association of School Librarians.

Guskey, T. R., & Bailey, J. M. (2001). *Developing grading and reporting systems for student learning.* Thousand Oaks, CA: Corwin Press.

Guskey, T. R., & Bailey, J. M. (2010). *Developing standards-based report cards.* Thousand Oaks, CA: Corwin Press.

Harrison, C., & Killion, J. (2007). Ten roles for teacher leaders. *Educational Leadership, 65*(1), 74–77.

Hattie, J. (2009). *Visible learning: A synthesis of over 800 meta-analyses relating to achievement.* New York: Routledge.

Haycock, K. (1998). Good teaching matters . . . a lot. *Thinking K–16, 3*(2), 1–14.

Heath, C., & Heath, D. (2010). *Switch: How to change things when change is hard.* New York: Broadway Books.

Hill, H. C., Ball, D. L., & Schilling, S. G. (2008). Unpacking pedagogical content knowledge: Conceptualizing and measuring teachers' topic-specific knowledge of students. *Journal for Research in Mathematics Education, 39*(4), 372–400.

Howard County Public Schools. (n.d.). *Secondary mathematics Common Core.* Accessed at https://secondary mathcommoncore.wikispaces.hcpss.org on March 17, 2016.

Howard County Public Schools Office of Secondary Mathematics. (2015/2016). *HCPSS Family Mathematics Support Center.* Accessed at http://hcpssfamilymath.weebly.com on March 17, 2016.

Illustrative Mathematics. (n.d.). *5.NF calculator trouble.* Accessed at www.illustrativemathematics.org/content -standards/tasks/151 on November 24, 2015.

Kanold, T. D. (2011). *The five disciplines of PLC leaders.* Bloomington, IN: Solution Tree Press.

Kanold, T. D., Briars, D. J., & Fennell, F. (2012). *What principals need to know about teaching and learning mathematics.* Bloomington, IN: Solution Tree Press.

Kanold, T. D., & Larson, M. R. (2012). *Common Core mathematics in a PLC at Work, leader's guide.* T. D. Kanold (Ed.). Bloomington, IN: Solution Tree Press.

Kanold, T. D., & Larson, M. R. (2015). *Beyond the Common Core: A handbook for mathematics in a PLC at Work, leader's guide.* T. D. Kanold (Ed.). Bloomington, IN: Solution Tree Press.

Kanold-McIntyre, J., Larson, M. R., & Briars, D. J. (2015). *Beyond the Common Core: A handbook for mathematics in a PLC at Work, grades 6–8.* T. D. Kanold (Ed.). Bloomington, IN: Solution Tree Press.

Kotter, J. P. (1996). *Leading change.* Boston: Harvard Business School Press.

Kouzes, J. M., & Posner, B. Z. (2003). Challenge is the opportunity for greatness. *Leader to Leader, 28,* 16–23.

Lambert, L. (1998). *Building leadership capacity in schools.* Alexandria, VA: Association for Supervision and Curriculum Development.

Larson, M. R., Fennell, F., Adams, T. L., Dixon, J. K., Kobett, B. M., & Wray, J. A. (2012a). *Common Core mathematics in a PLC at Work, grades K–2.* T. D. Kanold (Ed.). Bloomington, IN: Solution Tree Press.

Larson, M. R., Fennell, F., Adams, T. L., Dixon, J. K., Kobett, B. M., & Wray, J. A. (2012b). *Common Core mathematics in a PLC at Work, grades 3–5.* T. D. Kanold (Ed.). Bloomington, IN: Solution Tree Press.

Learning Forward. (2011). *Standards for professional learning.* Accessed at http://learningforward.org /standards#.VlSPinarTct on November 24, 2015.

Marzano, R. J. (2003). *What works in schools: Translating research into action.* Alexandria, VA: Association for Supervision and Curriculum Development.

Marzano, R. J., & Waters, T. (2009). *District leadership that works: Striking the right balance.* Bloomington, IN: Solution Tree Press.

National Council of Supervisors of Mathematics. (2007, September). *Improving student achievement by leading effective collaborative teams of mathematics teachers.* Denver: Author. Accessed at www.mathedleadership .org/resources/position.html#2 on July 15, 2015.

National Council of Supervisors of Mathematics. (2008). *The PRIME leadership framework: Principles and indicators for mathematics education leaders.* Bloomington, IN: Solution Tree Press.

National Council of Supervisors of Mathematics. (2014). *It's TIME: Themes and imperatives for mathematics education.* Bloomington, IN: Solution Tree Press.

National Council of Supervisors of Mathematics. (2016). *Position papers.* Accessed at www.mathedleadership .org/resources/position.html on March 17, 2016.

National Council of Teachers of Mathematics. (1989). *Curriculum and evaluation standards for school mathematics: Prepared by the Working Groups of the Commission on Standards for School Mathematics of the National Council of Teachers of Mathematics.* Reston, VA: Author.

National Council of Teachers of Mathematics. (2000). *Principles and standards for school mathematics.* Reston, VA: Author.

National Council of Teachers of Mathematics. (2009). *Focus in high school mathematics: Reasoning and sense making.* Reston, VA: Author.

National Council of Teachers of Mathematics. (2014). *Principles to actions: Ensuring mathematical success for all.* Reston, VA: Author.

National Council of Teachers of Mathematics. (2016). *NCTM position statements.* Accessed at www.nctm .org/Standards-and-Positions/NCTM-Position-Statements on March 17, 2016.

National Governors Association Center for Best Practices & Council of Chief State School Officers. (2010). *Common Core State Standards for mathematics.* Washington, DC: Authors. Accessed at www.corestandards .org/assets/CCSSI_Math%20Standards.pdf on November 19, 2015.

Next Generation Science Standards Lead States. (2013). *Next Generation Science Standards: For states, by states.* Washington, DC: National Academies Press. Accessed at www.nextgenscience.org/next-generation -science-standards on February 11, 2016.

Phoenix Union High School District. (2013). *E² Math: Equity and excellence in mathematics—Five year plan, 2013–2018.* Accessed at www.azed.gov/leadingchange/files/2013/06/th-211a.pdf on April 27, 2016.

Popham, W. J. (2009). Curriculum mistakes to avoid. *American School Board Journal, 196*(11), 36–38.

Porter, A. C., & Smithson, J. L. (2001). Are content standards being implemented in the classroom?: A methodology and some tentative answers. In S. H. Fuhrman (Ed.), *From the capitol to the classroom: Standards-based reform in the states* (pp. 60–80). Chicago: University of Chicago Press.

Reeves, D. (2006). *The learning leader: How to focus school improvement for better results.* Alexandria, VA: Association for Supervision and Curriculum Development.

Reeves, D. (2011). *Elements of grading: A guide to effective practice.* Bloomington, IN: Solution Tree Press.

Schilder, D. (1997). *Strategic planning process: Steps in developing strategic plans.* Accessed at www.hfrp.org /publications-resources/browse-our-publications/strategic-planning-process-steps-in-developing-strategic -plans on April 27, 2016.

Sergiovanni, T. J. (2005). *Strengthening the heartbeat: Leading and learning together in schools.* San Francisco: Jossey-Bass.

Sergiovanni, T. J. (2006). *The principalship: A reflective practice perspective* (5th ed.). Boston: Pearson.

Smith, M. S., & Stein, M. K. (1998). Selecting and creating mathematical tasks: From research to practice. *Mathematics Teaching in the Middle School, 3*(5), 344–350.

Stevenson, H. W., & Stigler, J. W. (1992). *The learning gap: Why our schools are failing and what we can learn from Japanese and Chinese education.* New York: Touchstone.

Teacher Leadership Exploratory Consortium. (2010, July). *Teacher leadership standards.* Accessed at www.ctl .vcu.edu/images/15138_TeacherModelStandards.pdf on June 26, 2015.

Toncheff, M., & Kanold, T. D. (2015). *Beyond the Common Core: A handbook for mathematics in a PLC at Work, high school.* T. D. Kanold (Ed.). Bloomington, IN: Solution Tree Press.

Toshalis, E., & Nakkula, M. J. (2012, April). *Motivation, engagement, and student voice: The students at the center series.* Boston: Jobs for the Future. Accessed at www.studentsatthecenter.org/sites/scl.dl-dev.com/ files/Motivation%20Engagement%20Student%20Voice_0.pdf on April 27, 2016.

Vagle, N. D. (2015). *Design in five: Essential phases to create engaging assessment practice.* Bloomington, IN: Solution Tree Press.

Webb, N. L. (1997, April). *Criteria for alignment of expectations and assessments in mathematics and science education* (Research monograph no. 6). Washington, DC: Council of Chief State School Officers.

West, L., & Staub, F. C. (2003). *Content-focused coaching: Transforming mathematics lessons.* Portsmouth, NH: Heinemann.

Wiggins, G., & McTighe, J. (2005). *Understanding by design* (Expanded 2nd ed.). Alexandria, VA: Association for Supervision and Curriculum Development.

Wiliam, D. (2011). *Embedded formative assessment.* Bloomington, IN: Solution Tree Press.

Wiliam, D. (2013, June). *How do we prepare students for a world we can't imagine?* Speech presented at the Minnetonka Assessment Institute, Minnetonka, MN.

Wormeli, R. (2006). *Fair isn't always equal: Assessing and grading in the differentiated classroom.* Portland, ME: Stenhouse.

Zikmund, W. G., & Babin, B. J. (2010). *Exploring marketing research.* South Melbourne, Victoria, Australia: Cengage Learning.

Zimmermann, G., Carter, J. A., Kanold, T. D., & Toncheff, M. (2012). *Common Core mathematics in a PLC at Work, high school.* T. D. Kanold (Ed.). Bloomington, IN: Solution Tree Press.

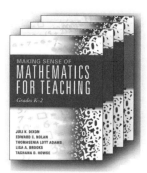

Making Sense of Mathematics for Teaching series
By Juli K. Dixon, Edward C. Nolan, Thomasenia Lott Adams, Janet B. Andreasen, Guy Barmoha, Lisa A. Brooks, Erhan Selcuk Haciomeroglu, Tashana D. Howse, George J. Roy, Farshid Safi, and Jennifer M. Tobias
Develop a deep understanding of mathematics. With this user-friendly series, K–12 educators will explore strategies and techniques to effectively learn and teach significant mathematics concepts and provide every student with the precise, accurate information he or she needs to achieve academic success.
BKF695, BKF696, BKF697, BKF698

Beyond the Common Core series
Edited by Timothy D. Kanold
By Thomasenia Lott Adams, Diane J. Briars, Juli K. Dixon, Jessica Kanold-McIntyre, Timothy D. Kanold, Matthew R. Larson, Edward C. Nolan, and Mona Toncheff
Designed to go well beyond the content of your state's standards, this series offers K–12 mathematics instructors and other educators in PLCs an action-oriented guide for focusing curriculum and assessments to positively impact student achievement.
BKF626, BKF627, BKF628, BKF634

It's TIME
By the National Council of Supervisors of Mathematics
Help all students become high-achieving mathematics learners. Gain a strong understanding of mathematics culture and learn necessary best practices to fully align curriculum and instruction with the CCSS for mathematics. You'll explore the factors that have traditionally limited mathematics achievement for students and discover practical strategies for creating an environment that supports mathematics learning and instruction.
BKF600

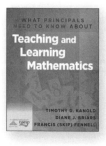

What Principals Need to Know About Teaching and Learning Mathematics
By Timothy D. Kanold, Diane J. Briars, and Francis (Skip) Fennell
Ensure a challenging mathematics experience for every learner, every day. This must-have resource offers support and encouragement for improved mathematics achievement across every grade level of your school. With an emphasis on the Principles and Standards for School Mathematics and Common Core State Standards, this book covers the importance of mathematics content, learning and instruction, and mathematics assessment.
BKF501

Leadership
By Lyle Kirtman and Michael Fullan
Develop a creative, productive school culture. Based on their decades-long work in leadership, the authors offer seven core leadership competencies for systemic change in schools, districts, and state education systems. Discover targeted strategies to move past failed initiatives and overcome initiative overload, explore how to cultivate effective work practices, and gain the know-how to create enjoyable, innovative learning environments.
BKF629

Solution Tree

Solution Tree's mission is to advance the work of our authors. By working with the best researchers and educators worldwide, we strive to be the premier provider of innovative publishing, in-demand events, and inspired professional development designed to transform education to ensure that all students learn.

The National Council of Teachers of Mathematics is a public voice of mathematics education, supporting teachers to ensure equitable mathematics learning of the highest quality for all students through vision, leadership, professional development, and research.